CASA NOSTRA

Views from a Tuscan Terrace

Roger Jupe

CASA NOSTRA

Hardback £25.00

Order direct from the author.

By e-mail: r_jupe@hotmail.com
By phone or text: 07770 966494

By post: 68 Salcott Road, London SW11 6DF

Please make cheques payable to RJ Jupe.
Price includes UK packaging and postage.

Why not send a book and a print as a gift to a friend?
Please indicate the message you would like to include when ordering.
Gift-wrapping available at no extra charge.

PUBLISHED BY PICI PUBLISHING

ISBN 978-0-9928932-0-0

CASA NOSTRA is about an Italy that other books simply don't know or care about. It is an essential read for anyone who loves Italian food and the Italian way of life. Part commentary, part travel book it looks at many of the things that make Italy a very different country.

Over a decade ago the author bought a property with his artist wife Val Archer on the Tuscan/Umbrian border, and started to experience and record Italian passions and the daily lives of their Italian friends and neighbours. His views on some of the things he discovered are the subject of this book.

From painters and paintings, partisans and politics to festivals and food; from fungi hunters to olive stuffers; from the church and the justice system to Italian godfathers and saying arrivederci to Berlusconi, CASA NOSTRA attempts to unravel why Italy is such a contradictory country populated by such contradictory people.

FREE LIMITED EDITION PRINT

A signed, limited edition giclee print by Val Archer of the painting featured on the cover of CASA NOSTRA will be sent with the first 100 orders received for the hardback edition.

The prints measure 140 mm x 195 mm.

'If you think you know a bit about Italy, if you want to know about Italy … here's someone who really knows and loves the place. Food, art, religion – a personal exploration which is perfectly simpatico.'

Sir Peter Bazalgette

'I have travelled the length and breadth of Italy with the author and always found his remarks on Italian art, food, society, politics or whatever, appropriate and shrewd. This book is a fascinating collection of anecdotes, comments, descriptions, legends and stories that guides you through the glories and the abominations of this beautiful country.'

I always find Roger so in tune with Italian life, so deeply Italian that I feel he should be given the Italian citizenship ad honorem.'

Anna del Conte

CASA NOSTRA

Roger Jupe was born in the UK but has been an Italophile all of his adult life. For 40 years he travelled widely in Italy and worked with Italian companies as a food and drink marketing and PR consultant. He has written extensively for business and has collaborated on many books with food writers and chefs.

Over a decade ago he bought a property with his artist wife Val Archer on the Tuscan/Umbrian border, and started to experience and record Italian passions and the daily lives of his Tuscan friends and neighbours.

His views on some of what he discovered are the subject of this book.

CASA NOSTRA

Views from a Tuscan Terrace

Roger Jupe

Roger Jupe (signature)

Pici Publishing

Casa Nostra

This edition first published in 2014 by Pici Publishing

Designed by Mike Nicholson

With special thanks to Carole Fries and Glynn Christian

A CIP catalogue record for this book is available from the British Library.

ISBN 978-0-9928932-0-0

Printed and bound in Great Britain by
TJ International Ltd, Padstow

Cover: Lettere by Val Archer
www.valarcher.co.uk

For Chloe and Eddie, Anna and May

CONTENTS

INTRODUCTION   1

1. PAINTERS & PAINTINGS   5

2. BUONA CUCINA   31

3. UNEARTHING THE PAST   53

4. POETRY OF THE AIR   77

5. TASTEFUL TOURING & GREAT ESCAPES   95

6. GODFATHERS   113

7. LA BELLA FIGURA   137

8. TRUTH, BELIEF & FAITH   153

9. ANYTHING FOR A PARTY   169

10. THE ITALIAN WAY OF JUSTICE   189

11. FORMAGGIO E VINO   209

12. LURKING IN THE UNDERGROWTH   225

13. WILL IT EVER CHANGE?   241

You may have the universe if I may have Italy.

Giuseppe Verdi

For 30 years the painter Val Archer, my ever-knowledgeable and talented wife, guided me on journeys of discovery in Italy from Venice to Naples, Milan to Mantua, to Florence, Ravenna, Perugia and Palermo and, inevitably, to Rome. Every year we planned an intricate journey that sought out the works of great Italian artists that could still be seen in the buildings for which they were created. We usually ended by spending New Year in Venice, Rome, Florence or Verona, and then returned to take to the road in spring or autumn.

We invariably focused on the work of a single artist – Piero della Francesca one year, Signorelli the next, Perugino another, then Lotto, Pontormo, the Crivelli brothers, Caravaggio and others. We tracked down rarely visited houses, chapels and *palazzi,* bribed custodians to open forgotten churches. It was nothing to drive miles to see a painting and then to find that it was *in restauro,* being restored elsewhere. We outstayed our welcome at more galleries, palaces and *duomi* than I care to mention.

We immersed ourselves in the lives and works of scores of artists, but we always seemed to end our travels to the south and south-east of Florence or further south in Umbria's Orvieto and Spoleto. Overall this is a relatively small area, but it's an amazingly fertile ground for Renaissance artists. Yet we had never taken a summer holiday in Italy and had never once dallied with the idea of buying a house there. Val loved her studio in London where she worked day and night preparing for exhibition after exhibition of her work. I was similarly focused, running a company that helped food and drink producers promote their wares.

A visit to Joe and Jos Tilson changed everything. Joe is a painter and Jos a sculptor. It was late summer and the great and the good of Siena were to honour them with an exhibition of their work in the city's Palazzo Pubblico. We were also invited and, as we sat on the terrace of their house under a starlit sky, I was seduced by the peace, smells and sounds of the Tuscan countryside. This is how life should be, I thought, how it could be if I dared. But there was another voice, too. The voice of reality kept pricking me, telling me I was just dreaming The Tuscan Dream, as millions of visitors probably do every summer.

Back in London, I was as surprised as anyone when I ditched the romantic vision and worked on how I could turn the dreaming impossibility into possible reality. I convinced myself with little effort that I needed a fresh challenge, something to take my mind off working so hard and something that would take me into uncharted waters.

Val was keen on Italy but not on another home to run; not least because, on top of her work and our house, she also had a very elderly father and his affairs to look after and that took her to the Midlands for two days most weeks. But I had become quite single-minded and arranged a house-hunting trip in our favourite areas of southern Tuscany and across the border into Umbria.

Eventually I settled on Casa Amari, in the hills to the east of the ancient Etruscan hill town of Cortona which sits high above the Val di Chiana, the famed Tuscan plain. Our first sight was of a group of dilapidated buildings on a hillside that skulked in a few hectares of a chestnut forest and overgrown, terraced land. Finding it had not been easy, but now each time we drive to or from Cortona we are entranced, beguiled and seduced all over again.

To get to us from the ancient walls of Cortona, you climb a narrow, winding road for 12km accompanied by spectacular views across the Val di Chiana. At about 900m above sea level, there's a small hamlet with a hotel and a separate bar/mini shop that's the hub of local life. The hotel has a vast restaurant that sadly never seems to get many customers. Yet the outlook to the plains from here is quite sublime and includes an eagle's eye view of the western end of Umbria's Lake Trasimeno.

Casa Amari is 4km further on from the hamlet. At first, you drive through pine woods and then cross a bridge over a mountain stream on a hairpin of the Cerventosa Pass. Just before the Pass, I'm always agog at an even more breathtaking view of Lake Trasimeno. The gullies and banks that hug the narrow road from the hamlet to Casa Amari are home to woodland strawberries, wild orchids and many other varieties of rare flowers. There are blackberry bushes galore and the occasional wild cherry tree and, in autumn particularly, our woods are home to some of the best fungi in the area.

The final part of the journey is an unmade track just wide enough for one car – for one ox-cart in the past, I suppose. This takes you through ancient chestnut woods to the head of a valley on a hillside. There seems never to have been a single name for the valley. There are over 100 different names covering the areas we see from the terraces of our house. Many take their name from a major building, like a convent or a farm, or a community that was once there . . . or is still there.

Further up our hillside, the nearest hamlet is a 30-minute sloping amble away. There are just four houses and an abandoned school next to an isolated church that is rarely used. Close by is the inevitable small, sad cemetery. The nearest town we can identify down the valley is Montone in Umbria. On a clear day we can see beyond it to Gubbio and then the mountain range that divides Umbria from Le Marche, part of the mighty Apennine chain.

Casa Amari is surrounded by chestnut woods that are home to wild boar, *cinghiale,* the *bastardi,* of which more later. Ancient woodcutters' tracks, thank the Lord no longer used, criss-cross our property. Every 20 years one of the few remaining local woodcutter families will still exercise their hoary rights to harvest another crop of chestnut timber, still the favourite Tuscan building material.

It's no secret that Val was not impressed when she first saw Casa Amari. It was essentially uninhabitable and its remoteness made the idea of renovation or rebuilding seem insurmountable. But I saw the potential and I pressed on, determined to prove I was right. Not just to me but to her.

Two years later we moved into a rebuilt farmhouse and were using another of the wrecked buildings as a terrace with a *deposito,* storeroom, below it. Two years further on another wreck was transformed into a studio for Val, with a separate floor that provides pleasant accommodation for guests. Casa Armari had been brought back to life.

My friends in television were probably disappointed that the project had not been suitable for one of those shock-horror property programmes. Everything was on budget and completed on time. Val and I agreed that this was because our builders, being true Italians, stopped for a proper lunch each day and we reckoned that's why they were such a joy to work with.

Even the shortest walk confirms that we live in the mountains, that we live in Tuscany and that wherever we look there is something to feed our souls. Soon we were walking six hours cross-country to the northern shores of Lake Trasimeno. There's another track that leads south-east to Mount Ginezzo for more unforgettable views. To our near-north is the highest point in our area, Alta di Sant'Egidio. From its 1,056m height there are 360-degree views of the landscape that we can never fully absorb or believe. We truly do pinch ourselves and need to remind one another that we are no longer tourists but this is our home, *casa nostra*, and that these are our views.

As we started to get our land in better shape, and lived and worked in the house and studio for longer periods of time each year, I wondered more and more about the things that make Italy a very different European country, about the history of the landscape that we could see from the terraces of Casa Amari.

Had partisans fought the Nazis on our land? What was the meaning of the M and F letters on the large gates up the road? Why was everyone so passionate about food and *feste*? Who were our local artists? Was the law respected? Were politics important? Why is Italy such a contradictory country populated by such contradictory people?

These are my views on some of the things I discovered.

Roger Jupe, Casa Armari, Cortona, June 2014

ONE

Painters & Paintings

The Lives of the Most Excellent Artists

I first became acquainted with the artist Piero della Francesca in my 20s. For this I will always thank the company that offered to educate me on the finer points of pasta making at their factory in Sansepolcro, a 1,000-year-old Tuscan town on the upper reaches of the River Tiber. There I first discovered the silence of paintings and how this prompts reflection and random reverie, making great art not only good for the soul but also the key to unlocking the past in most rewarding ways.

'No visit to our town would be complete without seeing at least one painting by our most famous son,' my pasta-making host insisted all those years ago. And so it was that I spent my first minutes gazing at the haunting fresco of *The Resurrection* by Piero della Francesca, still where he painted it 500 years earlier. The experience was profound.

After food it was Italy's paintings, sculpture and architecture that endeared me to this most cultured of countries, home to some of the greatest works of art in the world. It's no wonder her artists are so often seen as Gods.

Back in London I made the first of many visits to the National Gallery to study one of Piero's earliest works, *The Baptism of Christ.* I was captivated by its refinement and serenity, intrigued by his use of perspective which I was surprised to learn was something quite new at the time. The inclusion of an image of Sansepolcro in the painting made me want to return to the town and find out more about the man.

Piero della Francesca is now considered one of the most important artists of 15th-century Renaissance Italy, although his work was overlooked for hundreds of years. One of those who 'discovered' him in the mid-19th century was the first director of the National Gallery, artist Sir Charles Eastlake. When he was travelling in Italy with his wife and manservant Tucker, all three of them on the same passport, he purchased *The Baptism of Christ* with some of the gallery's annual budget of £10,000, enormous for the time.

From this masterpiece it is a few short steps in the gallery, and in knowledge, to appreciating the frescoes and oil paintings of Luca Signorelli, who was apprenticed to Piero della Francesca. Quickly I knew enough to recognise his master's use of perspective and foreshortening skills in the National Gallery's *The Adoration of the Shepherds,* commissioned from Signorelli for the cathedral of Città di Castello, a town close to Sansepolcro.

As my interest in these two painters grew, so did my fascination for the connections between painters and paintings: where they came from, who they worked for and where. In Italy it is often possible to trace these exactly, sometimes to stand in the same places they did as they painted and lived. The Piero Trail is followed by most art lovers who visit the area and dipped into by many of the ten million visitors to Tuscany each year, but this has created a conundrum in my mind. It's clearly a well-travelled road and yet Piero seems to be the least-known or talked-about artist outside the art world. How often do you see or hear him included in a list of such Italian masters as Raphael, da Vinci or Michelangelo?

During numerous visits over three decades to look at art in Italy, Val and I acquired a large collection of art books, exhibition catalogues, Blue Guides and maps. Most are still referred to but, early on, one man became, and remains, our favourite travelling companion, the Tuscan Giorgio Vasari.

Vasari's *Le vite de più eccellenti pittori, scultori e architettori,* translated as *Lives of the Most Excellent Painters, Sculptors and Architects,* was first published in 1550 and I profoundly believe it's the most important book on the history of art ever written.

Long before the age of bloggers, gossipy newspaper diaries and such magazines as *Heat* or *Hello!* Vasari was collecting anecdotes about the great artists of his generation and about earlier masters. He knew many of those he wrote about, so the gossipy stories he includes add a believable, human dimension to biographical details and scholarly analysis. After almost half a millennium, the book is still an essential read for anyone interested in Italy's artists and their art.

Vasari clearly favoured Tuscan artists, perhaps because he came from one of its main towns, Arezzo. We also felt at home among Tuscan people who seem to have a deep appreciation of the beauty and culture bequeathed by the artists of the past. Wherever we went, the splendour of the art was rivalled by the nobility of ancient towns and their serene, cypress-tree-studded countryside.

Giorgio Vasari, architect, painter and author, was born in Arezzo in 1511. In his late 20s he built himself a delightful and unpretentious two-storey town house at Number 55 in a quiet street now called Via XX Settembre. It remains much as it was when he lived there.

As we walk around its small, well-proportioned rooms, I always experience intriguing moments of oneness with Vasari's life and tastes. Many of the ceilings were painted by him and the walls are filled with 16th- and 17th-century canvases and panels by some of the best artists in his circle. Vasari was probably a better architect than he was a painter, which is why some say that the way he frescoed his house produced one of the brashest domestic interiors in Tuscany.

It seems that the moment Vasari closed his door on the rest of the world, he forgot all ideas of taste, harmony and discreet excess. There are far too many painted surfaces and frescoes on too many subjects. The ceilings and walls are also overloaded with decorative plaster decorations, hugely excessive for the size of the small rooms. You are assailed by assertive purples, brave oranges and challenging ochre in quite dreadful paintings by Vasari or his less famous chums, and there's gold everywhere and anywhere. If I'd been spirited into the place without knowing better, I'd have thought myself in the mad fairground of someone with religious connections.

Despite or because of this, I love immersing myself in the atmosphere of the place, imagining the daily life of the man who coined the term *Rinascimento*, or Renaissance, who knew Michelangelo and so many other great Italian artists. I imagine his cousin Luca Signorelli teaching Vasari how to paint or dining here perhaps discussing his own tutor, Piero della Francesca. It has the power to bring art history alive for me like few other buildings I know.

Unusually for a painter and architect, Vasari seems never to have been short of money. Apparently he was a likeable as well as a talented man and extremely conscientious. I feel he must have been easier to get on with than many other great men of the time who were invariably temperamental and dilatory.

He was the son of a potter, which may explain his name – *vaso* is Italian for a pot – and acquired the house when he was 29. He did not marry until he was 40 and it seems that he had a happy though childless marriage.

I always go via the *duomo,* cathedral, when I visit Vasari's house because it contains a small but beautiful fresco of *St Mary Magdalen* by Piero della Francesca. It is located in the north aisle in a cramped space by the Sacristy door. This awkward position in the church perhaps explains why it doesn't receive the attention it should. I particularly enjoy seeing again the exquisitely painted ointment jar I found in it because it's made from glass, something unusual at the time. Once you know about this you begin to look for other details.

The saint's handsome face is lowered in deep meditation and her calm pose has much in common with Piero's fresco of a pregnant Madonna in the village of Monterchi, an hour away to the east of Arezzo, although I am sure the model is a different woman.

It was three decades after I discovered Piero della Francesca that my wife and I bought our house less than 30km south-east of Arezzo, Vasari's home town. Its location means that Sansepolcro, Siena, Orvieto, Perugia, Assisi, Florence and at least 30 other art and architecturally rich towns are close-by, too. At last I could really immerse myself in the life and the legacy of Piero della Francesca and of his apprentice Luca Signorelli, the most famous son of our local town, Cortona.

Piero's Resurrection

I had already been introduced to the work of Piero della Francesca in Sansepolcro. So I returned again to his birthplace the day after we completed the purchase of our property on the eastern edge of Tuscany close to the Umbrian border, revelling in the simple pleasure of it now being just an hour's drive away.

Borgo Sansepolcro is always called Borgo rather than Sansepolcro by its inhabitants, an infuriating but common Tuscan habit. The town was named in honour of relics brought back from the Church of the Holy Sepulchre in Jerusalem by Arcanus and Egidius, two pilgrims who settled in the area. An abbey was built in the town in 1012 and became highly influential after it was granted privileges by popes and emperors.

As was often the case with city states throughout Italy in the 13th and 14th centuries, the town was constantly in dispute with powerful neighbours including Perugia, Città di Castello and, from further away, Rimini, the Papal States and Milan. Its fortunes were not helped by the devastation caused by earthquakes and the plague and then, in 1441, Sansepolcro came under Florentine domination.

Guidebooks to Tuscany invariably claim that Sansepolcro has changed very little since Piero della Francesca's time. This is not true since much of its Renaissance character dates from after his death. When Piero was born early in the 15th century the architecture of the town would have been dominated by a forest of towers, the sort you can still see in San Gimignano. They had been built by the nobility and the rich *borghese* of the Middle Ages as strong rooms, strongholds and status symbols. Although many were demolished in his lifetime, the towers he was familiar with shaped the skyline until the 18th century when most of them were toppled by earthquakes. The bases of a few still exist and the Torre di Berta managed to survive for over 700 years until it was blown up in the Second World War by the retreating German army.

There is no record of Piero's birth here, although it is believed to be between 1410 and 1420, more or less a century before Vasari lived. His father Benedetto was a tanner and bootmaker and a citizen of the town. His mother Romana came from nearby Monterchi. Vasari took pains to collect memories of Piero and writes that his father died before he was born, and it was his mother who 'helped him in the attainment of that learning to which his good fortune had destined him'. I puzzled over this and it only makes sense to me if you consider Piero's good fortune was the discovery of his skill as an artist.

With the increasing dominance of Florence, the town became a relatively peaceful place to grow up. Most days Piero would have been able to escape the intense confinement of a small community and walk in the freedom of the fields and vineyards outside the town walls. Here he was on the plains of the Upper Tiber Valley, rich with olives, vines and grain. White oxen, in use until the 1970s, would have been ploughing the land and transporting produce in heavy wooden carts at a leisurely pace.

It's known he went to Florence and was apprenticed to the painter Domenico Veneziano but by 1442, when he was in his 20s or early 30s, Piero had returned and was made a member of the town's council.

Today Sansepolcro is an attractive, restful Renaissance town built only of straight, flat streets lined with many fine houses, *palazzi* and churches. Spacious squares add to its charm and it is enclosed within ancient walls that were given a Renaissance facelift by the Florentine architect, engineer and sculptor Giuliano da Sangallo, builder of the double-spiral well in Orvieto.

Many of the town's surviving 14th-, 15th- and 16th-century palaces are strung along Via Matteotti and these include Palazzo Pretorio where Piero della Francesca painted one of the most haunting, poetic and mesmerising images ever produced at the service of Christian belief. The palazzo is now Sansepolcro's Civic Museum and this is where I headed as soon as we became homeowners in Tuscany.

I have long believed that Piero della Francesca's fresco of *The Resurrection* in Palazzo Pretorio must be the best picture in the world. I am not a religious person but I challenge anyone not to be captivated by its uncanny calm; not to feel that the artist seems to have been there and recorded the precise moment something extraordinary happened.

The town commissioned the work in about 1444, after the artist's return from Rome. Piero actually uses two points of vision, one in the lower part of the painting, the other level with the head of Christ which is exactly in the middle, his eyes alert, penetrating the viewer with all-seeing intent. One could say that this double perspective is a trick, but Piero was an exceptional mathematician and it adds to the image's compulsion.

The fresco is painted as though you are on the same level as the eyes, yet you have to look up to them as though somehow a penitent. The brilliance of Christ's ivory torso and rose-pink, toga-like robe are emphasised by the darker hues worn by the Roman soldiers lying asleep by the tomb. I often think Christ looks like an explorer of old, with his country's flag in hand, about to climb out of his ship onto a new land and claim it for his king.

Vasari says that it was Piero's custom to model figures in clay before he drew and then painted. This and his deep interest in mathematics and geometry go some way to explaining the perfection of the double perspective of the composition. To me, Piero had the power of creating images which immediately satisfy us through the genius of reconciling strict mathematical laws of proportion with the unbound vagaries of the stresses and tensions of human form and action.

The Resurrection is on a wall at the end of a plain room that was originally the main entrance to the palazzo. Directly opposite the building is Sansepolcro's duomo, which since the early 14th century has been home to a painting of *The Resurrection* by the Sienese artist Niccolò di Segna. It's a polyptych which means a work made of many hinged panels arranged around a large central panel of the subject image.

Surely Piero must have crossed the street to study this work, and perhaps it is in homage to this older masterpiece that he copied di Segna? In both images Christ rises in majesty from the tomb clothed in rose pink. But there's no mistaking who does it better.

Palazzo Pretorio also displays two fresco fragments by Piero della Francesca and the two panels that once hung either side of his *Baptism of Christ* which today is displayed in London's National Gallery. It also boasts his famous painting of the *Madonna della Misericordia,* or *Virgin of Mercy,* a traditional subject in Christian iconography which displays the Virgin Mary with a tent-like cloak outstretched to protect the faithful.

Piero's recorded life as an independent artist began in Sansepolcro in 1445 with a contract to paint this complex altarpiece for the *Campagnia della Misericordia,* Confraternity of the Misericordia, a charitable organisation devoted to assisting the needy that is still found in most Italian towns. Over 700 branches of the charity remain active and its volunteers provide essential care, medical aid and ambulance services (as part of the country's national fire/police/ ambulance emergency number 118, the Italian equivalent of Britain's 999).

The *Madonna della Misericordia* was painted against a traditional gold background where beaten pure gold has been applied micro-thin, leaf by leaf, onto a red, friable, earthy clay that is bound with egg white. The gold was then burnished with designs inscribed or punched onto it.

As was the tradition in medieval painting, the Madonna is portrayed larger in size than the figures she shields and, although I love her serene, detached countenance, I don't find this painting as moving as *The Resurrection*. But there is one striking detail I really admire: the brilliant way Piero resolves the problems of making people look real against his gold background. He places the kneeling members of a confraternity in the space created beneath the Madonna's heavy, fur-lined cloak, so it looks as though they are assembled in the apse of a church.

Records show that Piero was given three years to complete the commission but, because he was working on many other projects at the same time, it took 17 years. It was once a polyptych, but the hinged panels that surrounded the painting were dismantled in 1807 and what must have been an elaborate carved and gilded frame was also destroyed. None of that barbarism has diminished the beauty of the picture which seems perfect and complete without its framings.

THE PREGNANT MADONNA

To the west of Sansepolcro, past the place where Giovanni Battista Buitoni and Giulia Boninsegni established Italy's first pasta factory in 1827, road signs point to Monterchi. After spending time in Piero della Francesca's home town, it offers some of the pleasures of a pilgrimage to seek out his extraordinary fresco of the pregnant Madonna in this quiet, fortified village.

I first saw the *Madonna del Parto* in the 1980s after a journey involving much wandering and many missed turns before I reached a rustic cemetery on a hill close to Monterchi. Luckily the custodian understood the nature of my quest and unlocked the doors of a tiny graveyard chapel. Suddenly I was confronted by the splendid presence of a bigger than life-size Madonna only metres away from me. I am sure that the dramatic effect of this unexpected revelation was in Piero's mind when he composed the image, using two angels to pull back the flaps of an empty tent in which the Virgin, in the ninth month of pregnancy, stands weary and melancholy, one eyelid drooping, one hand on her hip, the other pointing to her swollen belly.

The classical calm and detached majesty of the pregnant Madonna – *parto* refers to childbirth in Italian – is unforgettable. The symmetry of the angels increases her hieratic quality and the Madonna's spell-binding gravity is further enhanced by the worn and faded blue dress that she wears. The fresco was painted around 1460 and how Piero came to paint it for such a remote location is not known. My guess is that because his mother came from Monterchi, she was laid to rest in its cemetery and her son lovingly painted the fresco in her memory. Piero della Francesca died in Sansepolcro in 1492 and is thought possibly to be buried in the Cappella del Monacato in the cloister of the town's cathedral.

After the fresco's restoration in 1993 it was moved to an old school building on the edge of the village where it is now displayed behind glass in a room where the light, temperature and humidity are carefully controlled. I return at least once a year to see this mesmerising image, but always yearn silently for that first revelation of its power so long ago in the churchyard.

Fresco painting was widely used in classical antiquity. Fascinating examples survive in the villas of Pompeii and are well known to the millions of people who visit the ruins each year. Excellent examples are also displayed in nearby Naples but the best, in my opinion, are in Rome.

These are the frescoes of an exotic garden in the *triclinium,* or dining room, from the House of Livia. Its overall blue-green effect is a luscious treasury of ancient Roman trees, flowers and shrubs, and the many birds include thrushes, a blackbird and a partridge. This wondrous survival of the personal life and taste of a Roman empress, wife of Augustus the first Roman emperor and mother of Tiberius, was frescoed sometime between 30 and 20 BC and is now conveniently displayed next to Rome's main railway station in a dedicated room in Palazzo Massimo, the National Museum of Rome.

The art of fresco was revived in 13th-century Rome and then became the most important art form in 14th- and 15th-century Italy.

Piero della Francesca and his pupil Luca Signorelli both used the *buon fresco,* or true fresco, technique, as well as *secco fresco,* dry fresco. My painter wife Val explained the difference to me. 'True fresco is when the paint is applied by brush onto freshly applied, wet lime plaster. Water is used as the vehicle so that the dissolved pigments in the paint penetrate the plaster. Then, as the plaster dries, the brushstrokes of colour are bound into the crystalline structure, becoming part of the wall as opposed to something applied to it.'

She was rather disparaging about *secco fresco.* 'The problem with this technique is that the paint lies on the surface and so later tends to fall off. It is applied to dry plaster using an organic medium such as an egg or size which acts as both vehicle and binder. Dry fresco was mandatory with certain pigments, such as deep blue made from ground-up azurite or lapis lazuli, which couldn't dissolve into the walls as *buon fresco.*'

Val's insights helped me to realise what an orderly, methodical process fresco painting was, requiring only a masterly single application of paint onto the plaster which was made of two layers. The *arriccio,* first layer, went on the bare brick and was a mix of coarse lime-and-sand plaster. The composition was drawn on this using red earth mixed with ochre, a stage called *sinopia.* Some painters also created preparatory cartoons or sketches on paper before drawing the composition onto that first layer of plaster. I cannot believe frescoes with such a complicated and unified design as those by Luca Signorelli in Orvieto were done without the aid of such well-considered drawings.

The overall fresco was divided into *giorni,* sections thought to be as much as the artist could paint in a day. The upper, fresh layer of finer plaster, the *intonaco,* was thin enough to be a little transparent but, even so, many artists rapidly redrew outlines of the composition into this wet plaster before they could start painting.

I asked Val how they made any alterations to the dried fresco. 'Not easily. The *secco fresco* technique could sometimes be used for minor alterations, but it must have been a nightmare to make design changes to big sections of *buon fresco.* For this, they would have had to lift out whole sections of painted plaster, throw that away and then start again with a fresh layer of wet plaster.'

Contrary to the popular belief perpetuated by the 1960s film *The Agony and the Ecstasy,* Michelangelo did not fresco the ceiling of the Sistine Chapel lying on his back. Just as Signorelli in Orvieto and della Francesca in Arezzo, Michelangelo constructed wooden scaffolding that supported steps and flooring before work commenced, and these were secured by roping them to metal brackets set into the walls.

Fresco paintings have to be finished while the plaster is still wet. This means fresco painters of the past needed a well-trained, rapid and resolute hand. Their brush strokes could not be altered by over painting and so colour graduation was achieved by hatching or by placing strokes of different tones side by side – and they certainly couldn't afford to splash or drop their jars of premixed colours.

These complexities were understood by the cognoscenti of the time, from Pope to painter's apprentice, and gave fresco painting a prestige little understood these days.

THE LEGEND OF THE TRUE CROSS

The joy of living at Casa Armari is that within the space of a day we can visit and revisit many of Piero della Francesca's finest works, still seen in the places where he painted them, in Sansepolcro particularly and in Monterchi and in Arezzo, our local provincial capital.

I like Arezzo and its two halves. It has a prosperous and well-ordered buzz about it, both in the older part around Piazza Grande at the top of its hill and in the more modern, business-like, shop-filled lower town near the station, which has a very handy car park. Long famous for its goldsmiths, Arezzo is still home to hundreds of artisan workshops that create gold jewellery, chains and medallions.

On the first weekend of each month, the historic part of the town is taken over by one of Italy's most famous antique and vintage markets. This covers an area of nearly a square kilometre around and down the hill from Piazza Grande, a delightful, idiosyncratic square which is neither symmetrical nor flat. Two sides are packed with handsome medieval houses and towers of differing heights. The whole of the north-east side is taken up by the graceful and extremely long portico of Palazzo delle Logge, designed by Vasari.

The lovely 12th-century Pieve di Santa Maria church seems to welcome you from one corner of the south-west side. But all is not what it should be, for this is actually the church's back where you'd expect its entrance. You are seeing the arcaded apse with the original *campanile* beside it and must walk around the building to Corso Italia, the town's main street, to find the superbly conceived façade. It's made of three tiers of colonnades and 68 diverse pillars that diminish in diameter towards the top, relentlessly pulling your eyes up into the sky and, perhaps, to thoughts of the Heaven believed to be there when it was built.

Even so, the greatest attraction for visitors to Arezzo is another of Piero della Francesca's acknowledged masterpieces, his frescoes of *The Legend of the True Cross* in a chapel in the Church of San Francesco.

When I first saw these frescoes in the early 1980s damp had damaged many areas of the chapel wall, but since then a 15-year restoration project has successfully returned the work to us. The scenes cover the whole of the sanctuary, and illustrate a theme of how relics of the True Cross form a link with the cycle of redemption that begins with humanity's original sin. The simple serenity and clarity, and the strong, beautiful colours of every scene are what first strikes me. It takes time to appreciate the magnificent clothing and varied head-dresses worn by the large number of figures represented.

The legend of the True Cross first became popular as a subject for painting in Franciscan churches at the end of the 14th century. This theme reflected a mania for relics and pictorially offered an opportunity for depicting pageant and anecdotes, something that Piero enthusiastically embraces in this fresco.

I often go to see his masterpiece and always start my visit by abandoning any analysis of form, colour or design, and then I simply follow the story from scene to scene, as Piero's patrons, the Bacci family, must have done.

The story opens on the west wall with the old age and death of Adam. Seth, the third son of Adam and Eve and brother of Cain and Abel, plants a fig tree on his father's grave; the tree from which Christ's Cross will be made. A splendid mature tree spreads out its branches to fill the top of the lunette.

From here I pass straight to the scene where the Queen of Sheba recognises the Sacred Wood. Two more majestic trees entrance me, and she has gorgeously dressed courtiers and two horses in attendance.

From there the legend continues on the lower panel to the right of the window with Constantine's dream, my favourite scene and the most dramatic. The emperor is asleep, tucked up in bed in his tent, dreaming of an angel presenting him with the Cross as if to say 'by this sign you shall conquer'. I am always mesmerised by the way Piero depicts this angel so realistically and with remarkable foreshortening.

The next panel depicts Constantine's victory over his rival Maxentius. The tiny Cross is held aloft and his soldiers' horses produce a sea of prancing hooves, while the sky is filled with colourful lances and banners as the army reaches the translucent blue of the Tiber River. From there the story continues with three episodes that show how, after the death of Constantine, the Empress Helena discovers the True Cross in Jerusalem and proves its authenticity.

Everything is geometrically perfect, reflecting Piero's deep interest in mathematics and his study of perspective; something he wrote about in his important treatise on artificial perspective when this was still a new science. After a while I begin to appreciate how many of the men and women in the frescoes exude calm and dignity. I feel an atmosphere of detached spirituality in the chapel that perfectly allows the revelation of events of universal significance to so many. There's never much touristic chattering or texting here, as very little in life can prepare you for its combination of energy and serenity. You have to be silent and allow the chapel's personal message to be absorbed by as much of your mind and body as you will.

No matter how many times I've tried, it's impossible to imagine the effect it must have had on 16th-century minds. Trying to understand this leads to a depth of astonishment in me that is as other-worldly as the experiences the religious must feel.

It takes about half an hour by car to return home from Arezzo. The main road follows an ancient route that both Signorelli and Piero della Francesca would have used. Like the traveller of today they would have passed through typical Tuscan landscape – land that's neither too flat nor mountainous, just green rolling hills, some of them quite steep, a few topped with little towns, each with its church and attendant campanile, at least one topped with a castle.

Unlike future generations of artists, the principal subject of Renaissance painters was never this landscape but it did help shape the backgrounds they fashioned for their paintings and, most importantly, instructed their palettes. Whenever I leave Arezzo after seeing Piero della Francesca's *Legend of the True Cross,* I feel myself travelling through his colours – the colours of Tuscan vineyards and those of grey-green olive groves, of brown earth, purple grapes and green vine leaves, often turned to blue by copper sulphate spray.

Where today people have the choice of dressing in the brightest clothes in whatever colour and pattern they might choose, Piero would have seen peasants only in blue cotton smocks that would fade to lavender, and white oxen dominating fields and tracks with their bulk and snowy splendour.

Then there is the sky. Summer days are big, brilliant and an intense ultramarine blue, a colour Piero reserved for objects of great dignity. And more often than not, all that I see will be peppered with the same stationary lenticular or lens-shaped clouds that are so Tuscan and that he featured repeatedly in his paintings.

The Gentle Charm of the Etruscans

The ancient Etruscan hill town of Cortona is just a 20-minute drive to the west of our house. It is here that we shop, meet friends in restaurants and bars, enjoy concerts in squares, streets and buildings that those 16th-century artists would recognise. It's built on the slope of a long hillside and, according to folklore, was founded by Dardanus who later established the city of Troy and gave his name to the Dardanelles.

Whatever its precise origins, Cortona was an Etruscan settlement in the 8th century BC. The Romans made it their own 400 years later, and in the 11th century it became a free commune constantly at loggerheads with nearby Arezzo and Perugia. During the 13th and 14th centuries the commune flourished independently, but from the 15th century onwards it became a dominion of the Florentine Republic.

Cortona's strategic position 500m above the Val di Chiana has always given it commercial importance, too. It is midway between Milan and Rome, and midway between the Mediterranean and Adriatic coasts. Both the Etruscans and the Romans made capital out of its location and both left their mark. The most fascinating are the Etruscan sections of the walls that enclose a large part of the town, and the Roman villas which archaeologists continue to unearth on the Val di Chiana plain below it.

Most visitors reach Cortona from this plain, passing ancient Etruscan burial sites before reaching the town's busy and friendly, modern outer suburb of Camucia. From here a 5km road climbs and winds up to Cortona through terraces of vines and olives and past the striking Renaissance church of Santa Maria del Calcinaio, built on the site of a former tannery and called *calcinaio* because tanners used *calcina,* lime.

During the Renaissance it was fashionable in Tuscany and Umbria to grace the outside of a town with a perfectly symmetrical church visible from all four sides. I think Cortona's early 16th-century masterpiece is the most graceful of all these ornamental set pieces. Luca Signorelli had a hand in commissioning the design, perhaps when he served as a town councillor, from the Sienese architect Francesco di Giorgio Martini, but Martini never saw the true majesty of his building because he died before it was completed.

Built on a Latin-cross plan, with an octagonal cupola and a serene white and light-grey interior, some say the stonework of Santa Maria del Calcinaio has been crumbling ever since worshippers were first welcomed inside, but I see only beauty in its disrepair and perfect proportions.

I tell visitors that the most rewarding way to appreciate Cortona is to walk through an arched *porta,* or gateway, in its ancient walls and then to head for the main piazza. Their prizes are cobbled, crooked and narrow streets, most of which are challengingly steep to all but the Cortonese, who stride confidently up and down with bulging shopping bags. Perhaps because many visitors are not as fit as the locals, most favour Via Nazionale, the town's only flat street, nicknamed *rugapiana* which means precisely that, a flat level place.

This is one of nine streets that lead into the most idiosyncratic main piazza in Tuscany, the town's irregularly shaped Piazza della Repubblica. Here the 13th-century Palazzo Comunale, home to the town council, is surrounded by a miscellany of arches, balconies, loggias, a few shops, benches, bars and buildings decorated with commemorative inscriptions.

Tall steps lead up to the palazzo and its adjoining clock tower which was added while Luca Signorelli was a town councillor. Little has changed in this grand building over the past 500 years', apart from it being recently voted one of Europe's most desirable town council offices in which to get married.

Piazza della Repubblica connects with a further misshapen square, Piazza Signorelli, which is dominated by Palazzo Casali, the impressive home of the town's ruling family in the 13th century who seemed to have spent most of the 100 years they were in power murdering one another. In 1727 a learned society dedicated to historical and archaeological research was established at Palazzo Casali, and it's now home to Cortona's museum of Etruscan and Roman antiquities plus an eclectic collection of precious works of art from all periods.

Subsequent governors of Cortona made sure they were remembered by having their coats of arms mounted onto the exterior of the palazzo. These are best appreciated over a glass of prosecco taken on the terrace of the adjoining 19th-century theatre, the intimate Teatro Signorelli.

Piazza Signorelli connects with Piazza del Duomo featuring the town's 16th-century cathedral and my favourite haven-of-peace in Cortona, the tiny Museo Diocesano, one of the most important art museums of its kind in Tuscany. The small but extremely choice collection, in what was once the church of Gesù, has superb works by Luca Signorelli, two exquisite pieces by Fra' Angelico painted for the church of San Domenico in Cortona, and a large painted crucifix by Pietro Lorenzetti, whose experiments with three-dimensional and spatial effects foreshadowed the art of the Renaissance.

CORTONA'S MOST FAMOUS SON

Luca Signorelli was born in Cortona in 1441 and was still actively painting at the age of 82 when he died in the town in 1523. His life is reasonably well documented, and much of his output still exists exactly where it was painted. Local tax receipts from 1427 describe his father, Egidio Signorelli, as a *sellaio di cavalli,* a harness maker, while other documents show the painter holding different official posts here from his late 30s up to the time of his death.

When Luca Signorelli was 11, his uncle Lazzaro de Taldi secured him an apprenticeship with Piero della Francesca. According to Vasari, 'Luca laboured to imitate the style of his master as a youth and with great success.'

Signorelli's solid figures and sensitive handling of light certainly echo his master's brush, but it is his often daring and terrible representation of action, reinforced by powerful and expressive use of anatomy, which makes him such a great painter. In much of his work he displays a mastery of the nude in poses that are only surpassed by the works of Michelangelo, whom Vasari says greatly admired him.

Exceptional paintings warrant viewing time and time again. Once I am in the Museo Diocesano, I never tire of looking at the scene of frozen drama in Signorelli's *The Lamentation of the Dead Christ* commissioned for the high altar of the ancient church of Santa Margherita. The power and energy of this painting, its size and shape, the liveliness of its colours and its strong and statuesque figures move me every time I stand before its silence.

The images include the Crucifixion, the Resurrection and an imaginary landscape with a surreal city by a lake that creates a fascinating background to the expressive and pained faces of the central characters gathered below the bloodied cross. Mary swoons over the head of the dead Christ nestling in her lap, while a saint unhurriedly pockets a crucifixion nail and the crown of thorns. Dominating the still scene is the beautiful physique of Christ's body whose face, according to Vasari, is that of one of Signorelli's sons, Antonio, who died in a plague in 1502, the year the painting was completed. Experts believe that this work is entirely by the artist's hand and, ghoulish though it might be, I can't help wondering if the body is also that of his dead son.

Below this wonderful painting, there are four *predella* (panels of related subjects at the bottom of the altarpiece). Of these, I'm always shocked by the physicality of Signorelli's *Flagellation*.

Amongst other impressive paintings from Signorelli's workshop, or the school that followed him, *Communion of the Apostles* is a further masterpiece signed by the artist in the Museo Diocesano.

It was completed in 1512 and I'm fascinated by the artist's use of perspective, only recently understood at the time. I always find myself drawn to the aesthetic design of large multi-coloured marble floor tiles in the foreground and the airy buildings of a revolutionary 16th-century school of architecture that frame the Apostles. Some of them stand around Christ, some are on their knees, all in sharp contrast to the traditional way Apostles are seated around a table in other painters' renditions of this scene. Judas is specially mesmerising, with an expression that clearly indicates shame at his imminent betrayal. And he always seems to look directly at me.

Church custodians are a special breed in Italy. They are nearly always old, stooped and uncommunicative, but have enormous power when it comes to who can enter the buildings in their charge, and when.

San Nicolò is not just a difficult church to find but can only be opened by the ultra-slow custodian if he has decided to be there, when it's not his lunchtime and if his deafness allows him to hear the doorbell.

Still, after seeing the Signorelli paintings in Museo Diocesano, it is well worth climbing the streets that lead to the highest point of Cortona where you'll find the large church of Santa Margherita and the nearby Medici fort. In a medieval neighbourhood below these two landmarks, the tiny church of San Nicolò hides, concealing two superb Signorelli artworks.

The building is unassuming and is fronted by an unwelcoming gravel forecourt. To summon the custodian you have to press the bell on the wall to the left of the wooden porch. If you hear a shuffling inside then you are in luck and the doors will slowly open. You are greeted by an intimate, low-ceilinged interior mainly of painted wood panels. On the north wall is an evocative fresco by Signorelli, reminiscent I think of his most famous frescoes in Orvieto, and above the altar there's a remarkable double-sided painting that doubles as a standard that could be carried in processions.

You must then hope the custodian can be persuaded to operate the neat hydraulic system that swivels these compositions away from the wall. On one side, is a perfectly preserved Signorelli of *The Deposition of Christ* surrounded by angels and saints. On the other, is an equally pristine and moving *Madonna and Child* enthroned with St Paul and St Peter. Any problems you've experienced to get here, because of the steep climb to the church, its hidden location and the unpredictable habits of its custodian, dissipate miraculously when you see this splendid work of art. The fact that it and the fresco have survived over 500 years in the place for which they were painted makes them all the more moving.

Via Berrettini is one of the many ways back to the centre of Cortona from San Nicolò. You pass the church of San Francesco where Signorelli is buried and there, amongst other less-likely relics, you may see St Francis of Assisi's 800-year-old cloak. It has recently been subjected to detailed scientific examination and the experts agree it was definitely worn by the saint. I find it so transfixing I have to believe them, and wonder why it's not the goal of many more admirers of the builder of the first Christmas Nativity scene.

By the time Signorelli was in his 40s, his reputation was high enough for him to be called by Pope Sixtus IV to work with Michelangelo, Botticelli, Ghirlandaio, Rosselli and Perugino on the frescoes in the Sistine Chapel. Well, that's what Vasari writes. Others say Signorelli was called to Rome only after the other artists walked off the job because the Pope hadn't paid them.

Whatever the circumstances, Signorelli completed the scheme with distinction, but it is generally acknowledged that his finest work is to be found in Orvieto's duomo, about an hour's drive south of Cortona.

Here he painted a magnificent series of six frescoes illustrating the *Last Judgement* and the end of the world. He laboured on these grand and dramatic scenes for five years, from 1499 to 1504, taking inspiration from Dante's epic poem *The Divine Comedy*.

I always enjoy visiting Orvieto. It's not just for the glorious duomo and Signorelli's frescoes in its Cappella di San Brizio, but also because beneath the town's magnificent position, atop a precipitous 315-metre high tufa crag, there's a labyrinth of over 1,000 man-made caves dug between Etruscan and medieval times.

Many of these can be visited, but I prefer another underground curiosity close to the funicular terminus and where the main approach road to Orvieto enters the town. Pozzo di San Patrizio is an extraordinary well, designed by Antonio da Sangallo the Younger. It's a remarkable 63m deep, 16th-century excavation with double-spiral staircases. Each spiral has 240 hand-hewn steps wide enough to accommodate a donkey undertaking water-carrying duties. For those who don't suffer from vertigo, as I do, I am told it is worth climbing down to the water level and back up again to fully appreciate Sangallo's design and engineering excellence.

Orvieto is one of the most visited towns in Umbria because of its closeness to the main north/south A1 motorway and its proximity to Rome. This is not the case with the monastery of Monte Oliveto Maggiore, a couple of hours' drive away in a beautiful, isolated position south of the broken, jumbled hills of Asciano.

Monte Oliveto Maggiore is one of the most important monasteries in Tuscany. It was founded in 1313 by Siena's merchant elite and sits aloof and dignified on a promontory in a dense wood of tall, black cypresses.

The great cloister has two storeys of loggias displaying 36 frescoes of scenes from the life of St Benedict. Most are by Sodoma, a little-remembered artist, but the first nine are by Signorelli who worked here before doing his better-known Orvieto frescoes. Both artists painted pilasters between the scenes, some of which are decorated by *grisaille,* a style of painting in greyish tints in imitation of bas-reliefs, and some of which are grotesques peopled with bizarre figures and objects.

Every Benedictine scene is a masterpiece of fresco painting. Each is in a picturesque, lively narrative style, and they also include the most charming and naturalistic detail. The use of colour and earthy imagery is impressive.

I particularly like the detailed landscapes, the rich costumes, the animals similar to those Sodoma was known to keep as pets, and the scantily clad boys he apparently preferred, explaining why he was called 'the Sodomist' and described by Vasari as 'a merry and licentious man…of scant chastity'. I'm also taken by the one where St Benedict is mending a broken tray, and another where he throws himself naked into brambles. Another features a self-portrait of Signorelli with Leonardo da Vinci and Raphael.

The inlaid choir stalls of the abbey church at Monte Oliveto Maggiore and the monastery's richly decorated Hall of Justice are also worth visiting, but best of all are the pharmacy, library and chapter house which are only open at the weekends. The pharmacy has an impressive collection of 18th- and 19th-century pharmaceutical storage jars and the library contains some 40,000 volumes, including important books of choral music and manuscripts from as early as when the monastery was established.

It is only a short distance from the abbey to Buonconvento, a pleasing fortified village with a tiny medieval centre and a fascinating museum of Tuscany's *mezzadria,* its crop-sharing system of agriculture. There are lots of these collections of what some would call 'old domestic junk' in our area, some claiming to be museums, others just road-side curiosities. This is much better than most and hefty white oxen, for centuries one of the most familiar sights in the countryside, loom large in most of the display panels.

A little further on is Montalcino, the lofty hill-top town that makes Brunello di Montalcino, one of Italy's best red wines. As you might imagine, this route makes an excellent day trip from Casa Armari and we send visitors off confident they will return with most of their senses truly gratified.

Unravelling a Mystery

Signorelli worked right up until his death. He was buried in Cortona, where he had been born and where he had spent most of his life, but there's intriguing speculation about how and where he died that I solved by wonderful chance.

We first met Lyndall Hopkinson at a friend's party in Cortona. She was introduced as the person 'who lives next door'. It turns out that 'next door' means the impressive 16th-century palace built for Cardinal Silvio Passerini, another of Cortona's famous sons.

Lyndall left England for Rome aged just 20. Within days she found herself living the life depicted in Federico Fellini's film *La Dolce Vita* and it never stopped. One day she was working for the UN, another day as a film extra, and then a script writer. Later, she met and married the pilot and explorer Count Lorenzo Passerini, and then moved to his family's ancestral home, Il Palazonne, that place next door.

We talked about the amazing city Rome was in the 1950s and 1960s, her mother, the brilliant, courageous yet tormented novelist Antonia White, and the day she first arrived at Il Palazonne. Eventually I managed to steer the conversation to where I wanted it to go. I had heard there was a Signorelli next door and in due course Lyndall showed me what turns out to be his last work. It's also the spot that is supposed to have hastened his death.

Il Palazzone was designed in 1521 for Silvio Passerini when he was appointed cardinal-bishop of Cortona, and at a time when he was already extremely rich and influential. His life was dominated by his relationship with the powerful Florentine Medici family and he was raised and educated at the court of Lorenzo de' Medici. He was very close to Lorenzo's son Giovanni who became Pope Leo X in 1513 and who then elevated Silvio Passerini to a cardinal's scarlet robes and biretta.

His Eminence Cardinal Passerini commissioned the design of Il Palazzone from the architect, painter and poet Giovanni Battista Caporali, a pupil of Perugino. It took six years from 1521 to build in Renaissance style on the site of a 12th-century palazzo, and from here he directed his diocese.

Il Palazzone is close to the top of Cortona's long hillside, just below the town walls, in a south-facing position with uninterrupted views across the Val di Chiana. It is impressive and princely, more like a small fortress than a villa, with double battlements on its distinctive tower. Although much is now comparatively modern, many walls and ceilings are still frescoed which gives richness to the interiors in spite of them being filled with utilitarian furniture by the university that uses many of the grand rooms. Only the private apartments of Lyndall and her late husband have the luscious antique furniture and rich fabrics that I expected. Lyndall's a willing expert on the building's history.

'Tommaso Bernabei, who was apparently Signorelli's best pupil and who studied with Giulio Romano in Rome, undertook most of the interior decoration', she explained. 'Like Luca he was born in Cortona and died here but was much younger and probably designed the palazzo in his early 20s.'

Luca Signorelli himself was commissioned to create a fresco of the *Baptism of Jesus* for the small family chapel. Even though the work is not in good condition, I commented to Lyndall how easy it was to spot which subjects he had painted and those he left to others. She surprised me by saying, 'But that was because he fell from the scaffolding and died as a result, either here in the palace or a few days later somewhere else in Cortona. The commission was finished by his studio.'

The circumstances surrounding his death have been passed down over the centuries from generation to generation of Passerinis. 'He died between 13th October and the beginning of December 1523. We know the former date from his last will, and the latter from a document which records an election of another works inspector to replace Signorelli in his duties at the church of Santa Margherita. He left the bulk of his property to son Pier Tommaso and to a grandson, Giulio, and requested that he be buried in the family tomb at the church of San Francesco.'

Piero della Francesca and Luca Signorelli are much less well known to the world than Da Vinci or Michelangelo. I think that's because they led less scandalous lives and perhaps that is why I like these men quite as much as their transcendental life works. They were both good men who worked hard but modestly, contributing to their communities without vanity or venery.

Vasari wrote of Signorelli: 'Luca was a person of excellent habits, sincere and affectionate with his friends, sweet and agreeable in his converse with everyone, specially courteous to those who had need of his help, and kindly in his instructions to pupils. He lived most splendidly, and delighted in dressing well.

29

For the which good qualities he was always, in his own country and elsewhere, held in the highest veneration.'

Every time I stand entranced before the silence of one of their masterpieces and think about the times so long ago in which they were painted, I'm sustained in my view that Vasari's summary of Luca Signorelli applies equally to his teacher, Piero della Francesca, the man who began my journey into 15th- and 16th-century Tuscany.

These were Excellent Artists indeed and both led Excellent Lives.

TWO

Buona Cucina

Pasta Comes First

Italians love to eat and much of Italian life revolves around the growing, buying, preparing and, above all, eating of food. Long before we moved to Italy it was Italian food that got to me.

The year was 1963 and the restaurant was the Amalfi in Soho's Old Compton Street. Using my first pay cheque, I had my first taste of an authentic spaghetti Bolognese eaten in a 'proper' Italian restaurant. The *ragù* was meaty and creamy; the long strands of pasta slightly chewy; the restaurant surroundings a kaleidoscope of multi-coloured tiles on the floor and the tables, tempered by roughly plastered white walls and soft lighting. This was a world apart from my only other experience of what I thought was Italian food – my mother's macaroni cheese which she said was made from 'that stuff that makes Italians fat'.

The influence of Italian restaurants on British food tastes started to take a hold in the 1960s. These were great times to be in your late teens and starting a career in London after growing up in a small country town in the south of England. London meant the opportunity for me to dine in restaurants, to discover foreign foods, and to savour wine rather than downing pints of bitter. My life-long love of most things Italian started then.

First it was the *ristorante* experience, closely followed by Italian coffee and clothes and then, later, Italian opera, Italian art, and the desire to live in *bella Italia.* As well as all that, pasta has been an important thread through how I've lived, personally and in business. I even spent years running a PR company tasked with getting Brits to eat more of it.

In Venice they say that Marco Polo brought back the idea of noodles from China, a story that has spread throughout the world. This is a pleasing romantic notion but does not square with the facts: a reference to macaroni can be seen in a 700-year-old document in the city archives in Genoa which is dated 16 years *before* Marco Polo arrived back in Venice from the east.

The Genoese cite this document as proof the Venetians are liars, then go on to claim that Genoese merchants saw a recipe from the nomadic peoples of

Mongolia and brought it back home. In Rome they claim that the senators and emperors of the empire ate pasta. In the far south the Sicilians insist that pasta arrived on the island with either the ancient Greeks or the medieval Arabs. In Naples, on the other hand, they will have nothing to do with this story, as Neapolitans think the original Greek and Arab pasta consisted of nothing more than rough pieces of dough, and it was their city's inventive macaroni cooks who made pasta what it is today.

Given that no-one can agree on the origins of pasta, it is perhaps not surprising that it hasn't always been called pasta. Early references to it include *itriyah,* the Arab word for string, which was in use in Palermo in Sicily in the 12th century. Then there is the will of a Genoese soldier in 1279 that mentions the bequest of a basketful of a *bariscella piena de macaroni,* a basket full of macaroni, plus Marco Polo's reference to *lasagne* a couple of decades later.

In the 15th century *fiedelini* was widely used, a word that originally came from Spain and is very similar to *fideos,* the name given today to pasta throughout the Spanish-speaking world.

John Florio, an Anglo-Italian language tutor at the court of James I, makes reference in his 1588 first English-Italian dictionary to *vermicelli,* calling it 'a kinde of paste meate like little worms'. This word for pasta was in common use throughout Italy up until the late 1700s. From then until the world settled upon the word pasta in the 20th century, the name macaroni stands out because it gave birth to so many meanings.

Most famous of these was as a slang name for English gentlemen of the 18th century who had been on the Grand Tour of Europe and wanted to indicate to others that they had travelled and were thus superior. To do this many of them became overdressed dandies with long, curly-haired wigs, affected Italian habits and spy glasses. They were mocked for their ways and nick-named *Maccaronis.*

Many of these *Maccaronis* were also witness to one of the most important developments in the history of the Italian diet: pasta's transformation into a food for everyone and what commentators at the time claimed was 'a good way to feed a large part of the populace'. Those who visited Naples to watch

Vesuvius erupt – as it did no fewer than eight times in the 1770s – also witnessed huge quantities of pasta being consumed by the locals, often in the streets. This was when Neapolitans were first called *mangiamaccheroni,* or macaroni eaters, and the city became Italy's pasta capital which it still is today.

As the quantity of pasta eaten by Neapolitans and other Italians increased, so did the number of different forms it came in. The last time I counted I found over 700 different shapes, of which less than 20 per cent are commercially available in Europe. To add confusion, many of today's most popular shapes are given different names by different manufacturers and often have different names in different regions of Italy. For instance the *tagliatelle* of Bologna becomes *fettuccine* in Rome, while *cavatelli,* a small pasta shell that looks like a tiny hot-dog bun, goes by over 20 other different names depending upon where you are in the country. We will probably never ever know the truth about pasta's origins, but what is certain is that there is a pleasing simplicity about how it is made.

Mills and grindstones have been a feature of civilisation since the beginning of time, certainly since man has eaten bread – and pasta. To make *pasta secca,* dried pasta, semolina, which is the middle part of durum or very hard wheat grains, is ground into flour and then mixed with water to make a paste. This paste is made into the required shape and then dried. In Italy it is never served as an accompaniment to other things (not even *polpette,* meatballs, always popular in Milan where they are called *mondeghili),* but usually after the antipasto as a *primo,* first course, and only rarely as the main or *secondo.*

Pasta secca made from durum semolina is rarely prepared at home and is always sold dried. This is by far the most-used pasta in Italy, for Italians love to point out that buying fresh pasta means you are paying over the odds for the weight of the water or egg in it. Fresh pasta, *pasta fresca,* is sold in specialty stores or made at home, *pasta fatta in casa.* The very high proportion of stretchy gluten in semolina dough really needs hefty machines to roll and shape it, so fresh and homemade pasta are made with a dough of softer wheat flour mixed up with egg and a little water.

Pasta secca has always been my main interest. It's a manufactured product with an impeccable tradition which elegantly overcomes the arguments for and against 'ready-made' foodstuffs. It can be split into two groups: *pasta lunga* and *pasta corta,* which translate to mean long shapes or short shapes. And as to which goes with what, the general understanding is that pasta with grooves in it or having twists, curls or caverns is meant for sauces that are lumpy in some way, perhaps with pieces of vegetable, meat or seafood. Smooth pasta is for smooth sauces but, as you might imagine, there are as many exceptions as there are rules.

Although pasta is invariably on Tuscan menus these days, it was never historically a part of the region's cuisine. 'A traditional Tuscan meal should start with soup, not pasta,' warned Signora Fossa, the mother of the daughters who run our favourite local restaurant in Cortona.

Val and I first met Signora Fossa soon after we moved into our partially renovated house, but still had no kitchen. Dinner in Cortona became the norm while we waited. Summer was long gone and the trattoria we chose, off Piazza della Repubblica in the centre of the town, was virtually empty. We were shown to a table next to a formally dressed, grey-haired woman of indeterminate age eating on her own. The smell of a hearty meat dish on her plate was impossible to ignore.

When we ordered, we asked what the signora was eating. Signora Fossa overheard us and said, 'It's delicious – no-one makes a better wild boar stew than my daughter Cinzia.'

We were treated to a running commentary about Tuscan food as our meal progressed to the wild boar stew via a first course of spicy tomato sauce on thick spaghetti, pici, that originated in Siena. Soon we had met both daughters, Cinzia and Lara, and knew much about the Fossa family.

The stew had obviously been cooked long and slow. We asked about the herbs that gave it such a delicious flavour. 'Fresh rosemary and sage and fennel seeds, all of which we grow. If you haven't already, you will soon discover herbs are ubiquitous in Tuscan cooking,' the signora explained.

Tuscan cooking is often referred to as the best Italian *cucina povera,* where the word *povera,* poor, in this context means lacking elaboration and based totally on the quality of the ingredients. I suppose it's because of my long association with pasta that both of my favourite Tuscan dishes are based on pasta. The one I enjoy most in winter is *pappardelle con la lepre,* a traditional Tuscan long, flat, wide pasta shape, like very large tagliatelle, with a rich hare stew. At other times of year I love a plate of Tuscan pici, that thicker than normal spaghetti, with *ragù alla Bolognese,* a rich, slow-cooked meat sauce made from lean braising steak.

Our conversation in the restaurant reminded me that Italy is not a country where there is a uniformity of taste, let alone culture, language or history. Every region is different and even within each region there are great variations. That is the appeal; and the basis of many, many discussions over many, many long meals as someone argues the superiority of their grandmother's method or father's secret ingredient over another.

HOME COOKING

Italians I know don't tend to eat out very often, but do relish eating whatever is in season. However, two meals a day is sufficient. *Colazione,* breakfast, is not considered a meal and is invariably taken on the run, limited to a coffee and maybe a small pastry.

Italians prefer home cooking and eating the produce they see growing around them. For this reason every piece of land surrounding a house, whatever its size, seems to be cultivated, and even garden-less apartments in towns fill their window boxes with herbs.

Signora Fossa's advice meant that growing our own herbs became a garden priority in those early days, together with dealing with the difficult soil. We quickly found that you didn't touch it when it was wet. Anything we planted in such conditions soon baked into a clay pot of our own making, airless in solidifying soil. It became vital to keep a constant watch on the ground and learn to gauge its state of friability before we attempted to dig, sow or plant.

When the conditions were right, we created a long, wide border just two paces over flagstones from the kitchen door. There we planted our first rosemary bushes, thyme, sage, basil and parsley. In due course we added cuttings from a tasty mint plant taken from my parents-in-law's house in England, and tarragon from a nursery in Tuscany's famous Montalcino wine-growing region where, according to legend, the herb was first cultivated in the 8th century.

The luxury of having herbs to hand just outside the kitchen door is not to be underestimated. Once our kitchen was completed, everything we cooked benefited from a handful of leaves of this and a few sprigs of that. Within a few short months, thyme became an essential ingredient for flavouring all manner of pork, lamb, rabbit and game dishes, the tarragon was for chicken and fish, and whenever we had a roast, grilled fish or sausages we always added a few sprigs of rosemary.

La ribollita, the Tuscan bean soup for which fresh sage, rosemary, parsley and thyme are essential ingredients; *fagioli all'uccelletto,* cannellini beans with garlic, oil and our own sage; or pasta served with fresh *pesto* made with copious quantities of our own basil, soon became firm favourites.

The rosemary loved our land and we loved its flavour and the way it looked. Soon many more bushes were purchased and planted alongside roses and shrubs in other parts of the garden. We also mixed rosemary and lavender to create a pungent, colourful blanket on what had been barren stony slopes above and below the house. Sage, like the rosemary, took a liking to our land and grew into large luminous bushes producing more healthy grey-green leaves than we could ever need for roasts, fish dishes and marinades for game.

Tuscany's favourite herbs dominated the conversation the first time we went for dinner with the Cipollas, our closest farmer neighbours. 'Sage omelette – and mint too – are very Tuscan though many people just roast sage leaves and eat them as a vegetable,' Silvio's wife Mara told us. 'Best of all is the centuries-old recipe for the egg and Parmesan custard we all make with young sage, leaves and eat as an antipasto.'

We were promised that recipe and others for sweet dishes that included rosemary. The tastiest turned out to be *castagnaccio,* a chestnut and rosemary tart that is a speciality of the wild and mysterious Maremma area around Grosseto on the Tuscan coast, a couple of hours' drive to the west of Casa Armari.

Mara Cipolla asked whether we had planted any tarragon. '*Dragoncello* is used very little in Italy except just around Siena here in Tuscany where it often replaces parsley in the traditional salsa accompaniment to boiled meats, *bollito misto.* I use it to flavour vinegars and occasionally when I am making batter I dip the leaves in it and fry them until the leaves are crispy – quite delicious.'

So many things were new to us that night, from our surprise at the large amount of bread our hosts ate, to the flavour combinations, especially fennel in different forms at the start and the end of the meal. Large coarse-grained slices of *finocchiona,* the pure pork Tuscan salami flavoured with wild fennel seeds, featured in the antipasti, while wedges of *finocchio,* raw fennel bulb, were served with apples and oranges at the end. Apparently it's been used as a *digestivo* for centuries, even in the Florentine palaces of the Medicis.

Our pasta course was pici with a chilli and anchovy sauce, *alla puttanesca,* which Mara dished out saying, 'We Tuscans love chillies but to confuse everyone we call them *zenzero,* the word for ginger elsewhere in Italy.'

Before we left, Silvio insisted we take a few of his chilli seeds and a cutting of his mint, the small-leafed peppermint *mentha requieni,* saying, 'You may find it grows better than your British mint.'

The next day I crossed my fingers and started germinating the seeds and planted the mint which later proved to be delicious in fruit salads and for sorbets and ice cream. Both this variety, which I was told came originally from the island of Corsica, and our own British mint, which we chop and sprinkle over grilled vegetables and use for fresh mint tea, grew equally well in our soil. I also found a couple of wild fennel plants beside the road and transplanted them, so I might eventually harvest their seeds. For someone who had never grown anything before I felt rather proud of myself.

If pasta is not a traditional staple in Tuscany, bread certainly is. Here, their traditional salt-free bread is eaten from breakfast time to dinner. Tuscans view it as a natural balance for the salted foods that make up so much of their *cucina povera* of cheese, meat dishes and sausages. References to plain Tuscan bread being compared unfavourably to 'the saltiness of other people's bread' can be found in documents from the Middle Ages.

The classic Tuscan unsalted loaf is the 450g *filone* which, along with crusty unsalted *classico integrale* made from semolina, are invariably found on the dining tables of most households. The enthusiasm for bread and bread specialities in the region is quite inexhaustible. Rustic loaves, whole wheat and fine wheat breads, corn bread from the Maremma, and many other local and seasonal specialities are baked using an extremely wide variety of flour blends. They come in numerous different shapes that vary from flat to long bread sticks and tall, round loaves, to ring-shaped bread and rolled-out lengths of dough that are twisted or braided into a serpent shape before baking.

Thanks to another neighbour, Signor Benelli, who had delivered the first example to our door just after we moved into our house, we were already familiar with *panina unta,* the saffron Easter bread from nearby Arezzo, but then we discovered another Tuscan Holy Week speciality, *pan di ramerino.* Sugar, raisins and chopped rosemary are added to the dough of this bread that has become so popular it is now on sale most of the year.

In Cortona artisan bakers are also creating new types of bread treats. Signora Gaetano and her inventive baker's hands produce the type of crackly, crusted, chewy loaves that still taste of the grains of the field. When figs are in season, she sells a delicious accompaniment to eat with them, *pane con l'uva,* a flat bread made from fine flour, yeast and olive oil, which she bakes topped with a generous layer of red grapes and a sprinkling of sugar.

In recent years *focaccia,* a speciality of Liguria, has become one of Italy's favourite breads. In Tuscany we have something similar which I think is better. *Schiacciata* is a squashed and flat yet light and fluffy bread made with flour, yeast, water and rendered pork fat, what we would call lard. A version made in Florence tastes slightly sweeter and another variation adds chopped walnuts and that favoured Tuscan herb, rosemary.

Of all the Tuscan dishes that use bread, whether it is croutons, *panzanella* salad, Arezzo's *acquacotta* vegetable soup ladled on to bread, or crostini, nothing is comparable to bruschetta.

Bruschetta's origins are in Lazio and Abruzzo, but today it's served all over Italy and the world. Yet, to us the best bruschetta by far is made from grilled Tuscan *filone* bread rubbed with Tuscan-grown garlic and topped with the best-quality Tuscan extra virgin olive oil, freshly ground sea salt and black pepper.

Other bruschetta toppings are many and varied. Like our neighbours the Cipollas, we always serve some with chopped wild fennel fronds, as well as the classic mix of small cubes of fresh tomato with freshly picked, coarsely chopped basil and a few spots of oil.

THE ESSENTIAL INGREDIENT

Tuscans claim their olive oil is the best in the world, and many people agree with them. They use it for everything from sautéing, frying, basting and simmering to dressings and giving a last-minute 'blessing' to vegetables, soups, grilled fish and meat. In fact they use it to dress any savoury dish you can think of, and even some sweet ones too.

Our local Cortona oil is well-balanced, full-bodied and fruity with green highlights and spiciness that has a hint of black pepper and artichokes. We use *olio extravergine di prima spremitura,* the best oil from the first pressing by local producers we know, to dress salads and vegetables, for bruschetta and for blessing our grilled meats and fish dishes just before serving. For cooking we use a basic *olio d'oliva* which we buy in bulk when it is on offer in our local supermarket.

As with all Italian olive oil, the extra virgin varies greatly from region to region and even area to area, especially in Tuscany. Whenever we travel through Chianti country, an hour or so to the north-west of our house, we always buy a bottle of the area's fruity and distinctly peppery oil to ring the changes.

Encouraged by herb-growing success, I turned my attention to olive trees and dreamt of producing my own oil. Neighbours told me that I should first talk to Giuseppe. 'He knows even better than anyone what does and doesn't grow on your hillside.'

Giuseppe used to live in a small house in the woods below the Cipollas. He, like them, had escaped city life and moved to the mountains in the 1960s, intent on a simple existence and living off the land. Growing things and becoming a self-sufficient vegetarian – a rarity in this big meat-eating region – gave him the best possible grounding for his future career as a gardener.

Giuseppe now lives in the Val di Chiana below Cortona. He doesn't do things on the spur of the moment. Rather than plant his own olive trees, he waited 22 years until an ancient grove on the town's prime southern hillside came up for sale. The price was important, he said, 'but the owners treasured it and were just as interested in the detail of how I would care for the land that had been in their family since the 19th century. I explained my thinking about the natural ways to combat diseases and attacks from pests, and about only picking the fruit by hand, and this seemed to clinch the deal.'

Our first meeting about planting the grove of my dreams was a disappointment. 'Olive trees will grow here of course,' he said, 'but I fear you are too high for them to produce enough fruit of the right quality.' I suspected he was being far too pessimistic, but agreed that it was probably best to plant a handful of mature trees initially, just enough for half-a-dozen bottles of oil at best, and see how they fared.

As the first Christmas on our hillside approached, I asked Giuseppe whether I could help with the picking of his 300 olive trees. Over two back-breaking days I learnt about the pros and cons of the main types of olive trees that flourish in Tuscany. These are Frantoio, much favoured for its fruity, aromatic oil; Leccino, which produces a pale, gentle, mellow and lightly fruity oil; Moraiolo which is viewed as a source of an ideal blending oil; and Pendolino, a popular cross-pollinator in the region. It is these varietals that help produce the distinctive, strong flavour of good Tuscan olive oil.

As soon as harvesting was finished, we took the fruit to the local press and watched as the very best-quality olive oil, *olio extravergine di prima spremitura,* was extracted from the first pressing. Then came the next level, *olio d'oliva vergine,* virgin olive oil from the second and a third pressing.

Extra virgin olive oil has to conform to a strict definition and has low acidity and a superior flavour; basic virgin olive oil has higher acidity and its taste is invariably described as good rather than anything special.

A further pressing produced *olio d'oliva,* what is called pure olive oil or simply olive oil in Britain, which Giuseppe told me would have an even higher acidity than the other types and be a blend of virgin and refined oils. And there was even one more, *olio di sansa d'oliva,* oil obtained exclusively from the pomace residues left after pressing which is extracted with the aid of solvents.

The reward for my labour was a decent quantity of *olio extravergine di prima spremitura* labelled, as all good olive oil should be, with the additional words *prodotto e imbottigliato* – produced and bottled – and the name and location of Giuseppe's grove.

Realising that this would not be enough to see us through the following year, I topped up our supplies with a couple of five-litre flagons from our friends, the Wilkinsons, whose house on a hillside above Lucca in the north of Tuscany is surrounded by olive groves.

The difference between the two oils was appreciable. The Cortona oil was well-balanced, full-bodied and fruity with green highlights and spicy with the typical Tuscan hints of black pepper and artichokes, while the oil from Lucca, although similar, had a slightly rounder flavour, a yellowish hue and was light and somehow more free-flowing than our local oil.

Tuscany's favourite sauce is a thread of extra virgin, vivid green olive oil. It wasn't long before we got into the habit of having a bottle of Giuseppe's, the Lucca or Chianti oil on the dining table to use as a condiment and as you would put butter on bread. Never do we use these for cooking since heat destroys all the finer flavours and savours of top olive oils.

As to my grand plan to surround the house with an olive grove and produce our own oil, after a few years the initial six trees had been joined by two others and most years they flowered and produced fruit. But the olives were simply not good enough for pressing, though with climate change who knows what the future may hold?

In the meantime I carry on playing the lottery every week and hope for a win. Then I could afford to produce my own wine as well as oil on the same bit of land. And it will have to be on our land, for you need more than a big win to buy a grape-growing property in the right spot. Even a small estate within sight of nearby Montepulciano's red-wine-producing slopes can cost over six million euros.

Home Grown

I have never coveted other people's talents but the more I saw of the rows of vegetables being grown below the largest house in the hamlet up the hill, the more I wanted my own orto, a vegetable garden. For someone who had managed to avoid any form of gardening for more than half a century, I now felt inspired by my herbs and wanted to move on to bigger things.

I introduced myself to the De Santis on a day when they were digging up potatoes from one of their long and wide cultivated terraces.

It is not unusual for Tuscans to have their main home in a town and a house in the country a short drive away. So it was with Giulio and Sophia De Santis who lived in Perugia close to their grown-up children, but had both been born and brought up locally – she in Umbertide and he in Vaglie, a hamlet the other side of our hill.

'Since Giulio has retired we have grown everything for all of our family,' Sophia said proudly, adding, 'He never liked having to work in an office and always wanted to be a *contadino* farmer.'

Up until then I had never thought of Italy as a potato country. '*Patate* came to Europe in the 16th century but we were one of the last countries to take to them,' Giulio told me. 'I like to think that is the reason why we don't just think of them as an accompaniment to meat and fish, but as the basis for dishes in their own right.'

The potato they were unearthing was typical of the Mugello variety, yellow, oval and medium-sized with a delicate flavour that has a hint of chestnut. 'These are the same as the ones you buy in the local shops. They are farmed on the high grounds of the Upper Mugello valley and around Firenzuola north of Florence, but we find they grow well here in the mountains too,' said Giulio. He pointed to the adjoining row. 'In there we have Spunta and Primura, along with some Agata, a very early potato.'

It took us a while to stop talking about 'potatoes' and to call them by their variety according to what we would use them for. Spunta, one of the most common potato varieties in the world, produces large, light-yellow, waxy spuds that are good for the roast and sauté potatoes that are so often served with Italian dishes and in salads. It's a second early variety, meaning it is ready 13 weeks after planting. Primura, one of Europe's most common general purpose varieties, has a protected status in the Bologna area. It's flattish, floury and very early. Agata is another early season variety, ready in ten weeks after planting and so available locally in quantity in June. It's mid-sized, often nearly round and soaks up other flavours well. It's quite moist after cooking and we found it especially good for an easy mash, made with olive oil rather than butter.

Sophia announced it was time for a break so we walked up to their house, each of us carrying a basket full of potatoes. Inside I only just avoided hitting my head on strings of garlic hanging from the beams and had to help move plastic washing-up bowls full of dried beans off a much-used and scrubbed kitchen table.

Giulio opened a bottle of unlabelled red wine, and took the remains of a cold pie and a small oval plate of dressed white beans out of the fridge. 'That is green bean and potato pie made to a recipe from friends in Liguria,' explained Sophia, 'but you will find local recipes for hot and cold potato pies in every region. The cannellini beans though are particularly Tuscan and the best you will ever taste, not least because we grew them ourselves.'

The beans had been stewed in a little stock and were simply finished with olive oil and pepper, and were very delicious. 'How else do you serve them?' I asked.

For the next half an hour I couldn't get a word in edgeways. Facts, tips and favourite recipes were revealed and I was cautioned never to use canned cannellini beans 'because they can take on the taste of the tin'. I knew this was an old wives' tale, especially these days, but didn't comment.

An earthenware pot was produced and I was introduced to the secrets of making Tuscany's *fagioli all'uccelletto.* Dried cannellini beans are first soaked and then boiled until tender with sage leaves, onion, garlic and a bay leaf in unsalted water before being drained. Then more sage and garlic are sautéd in olive oil, the beans added and simmered with tomatoes. The dish is always served from the pot hot, warm or cold but never, I was cautioned, never served chilled.

'It is perhaps for good reason that some unkind people refer to us Tuscans as *mangiafagioli,* bean eaters,' Giulio said, and went on to praise Sophia's soups. 'But they would be nothing without my cannellini beans and home-grown *cavolo nero,* our region's special cabbage which we prefer because it is slightly more bitter and less cabbage-tasting than ordinary varieties.'

When he finished Sophia lovingly squeezed his hand. 'He forgets that I also use *farro,* an ancient variety of durum wheat, in my soups. It is cultivated here in Tuscany in the Garfagnana region north of Lucca. Pearl *farro* is best I find, since the skins have been removed and it doesn't need soaking.'

I was amazed by their passion for food. We had nearly finished the bottle of wine between us and it was getting late.

Eventually I managed to change the subject to my plans for a vegetable garden. It turned out they had known the previous owners of our house and were familiar with the terrain. 'Badgers, porcupines and wild boar will be the main problem down there, as well as the quality of the soil,' Giulio warned me. 'If I were you I would first build a small walled orto, turn the soil with *concime,* manure, from Silvio's sheep and see how you get on.'

My First Orto

The hillside upon which our sloping land sits was once criss-crossed by tracks, and terraces supported by stone walls that have long since collapsed. In some places there are more substantial stones just below the surface, which were of a type and shape that made me think that they were once part of another building.

Sitting on my terrace I contemplated where to locate my first-ever vegetable garden, and read up on building battlements against any four-footed enemies. Over the following week, I found muscles I never knew I had and collected enough stones to make a six-metre long, half-a-metre high walled border around a small plot in front of a sunny south-facing wall close to the house. Still aching, it then took me another week to hand-mix 60 barrow loads of concrete, make the foundations, select the stones and build the wall. It was like trying to complete a complicated jigsaw puzzle in three-dimensions.

Val was very complimentary about my efforts, Silvio less so but he did offer much-needed help to dig-in his truckload of well-matured sheep manure from his flock of floppy-eared *pecora Appenninica*.

Living where we do in deep countryside, where families have grown their own products for centuries, most people have a good knowledge of agriculture. They love *cucina casalinga,* home cooking, and grow, buy and eat for flavour like all Italians. Most tend to purchase fresh fruit, vegetables, meat and fish in markets, local shops or the small family-run supermarkets to be found in every size of town. Although many ingredients are now available year-round, especially in the large supermarkets, food choices are still largely dictated by the seasons and what local farmers produce. The big national chains have undoubtedly changed Italian food shopping habits, but they don't have the same hold as they do in Northern Europe. In Italy supermarkets account for less than half of all food purchases, whilst in Britain 80 per cent are made from just four national supermarket groups. Furthermore, most Italian chains recognise the importance of buying from regional producers to give local people regional specialities and food with clear, traceable origins – a practice that many European and global supermarket groups say they favour but rarely implement.

Then came the enjoyable bit. The week before I went shopping for the orto, spring had officially sprung. The various plant and vegetable stalls in our weekly market in Camucia, Cortona's 'new town', are an inspiration to cooks and gardeners alike whatever the time of the year, but in spring they look fresher and more appetising than at any other time.

Carciofi, artichokes, have been a favourite vegetable in Italy since Roman times and are widely grown in Tuscany. Their beautiful heads vary from green to purple and, although enjoyed at various stages of maturity, it is the young, small ones that are particularly delicious. The market was full of them, along with artichoke hearts floating in acidulated water to stop them browning. We were surprised to learn these can be sliced thinly and eaten raw with a dressing, or stewed in olive oil with a sprinkling of finely chopped garlic and herbs.

The powerful and refreshing perfume of fresh mint filled the air and shoppers were eagerly buying the new season's calabrese, a mild-tasting broccoli, together with a profusion of wild salad leaves including dandelion, sorrel, sour thistle and wild rocket – plus vast quantities of superb spinach. We regularly filled two big bags with spinach, now our favourite vegetable, to lightly blanch and then serve at room temperature with the best olive oil, salt, pepper and a squeeze of lemon.

At the plant stall we selected four varieties of lettuce, yellow and green zucchini, and then got into a lengthy discussion about some of the 300 varieties of tomatoes that are grown in Italy and which ones I should plant. Eventually we decided on just two: *pomodoro di cerignola,* a sweetish cherry tomato, and *ramato* which gets its name from its strong branches, *rami,* upon which medium-sized tomatoes grow. That they would also produce a superb flavour was a given.

Like potatoes, tomatoes arrived in Europe in the 16th century but took until the mid-1700s to become accepted in Italy. They not only brought a new flavour and recipe possibilities to the Italian table, but added brilliance to what must have historically been a colourless cuisine. Today tomatoes are the most widely grown and consumed vegetable in the country, with annual consumption topping ten kilos per head.

I planted my purchases with loving care, hoped my stone walls were tall enough to stop wildlife eating the shoots, and crossed my fingers for a sunny, disease-free summer.

PLANNING FOR GROWTH

As spring turned to summer, we bought, cooked and tasted every type of vegetable as it came into season to find what we liked best and thus might plant the following year. At the end of May, we filled our shopping bags with fresh, young *fagiolini di Sant'Anna,* the French bean variety grown in Tuscany. We discovered carrots, onions anew and broad beans. Nothing is more delicious than new season's *fave* or broad beans, especially when eaten raw straight from their pods at the end of a meal with young pecorino Toscano, the creamy cheese made from the sheep milk of nearby Pienza.

Of course carrots and onions are available all year, but the sweet taste of the first spring carrots was a revelation. So, too, the flavour, size and texture of the new season's white and purple spring onions, most of which were the size of golf balls and kept their good looks when we cooked them whole with other vegetables. As always, our favourite vegetable stall had a story to tell about their origins. 'You've got purple Statina onions there,' the large and jolly *signore* told us as he took our money. 'We get them from around the little medieval town of Certaldo, west of Florence. Apparently they were first mentioned in that bawdy book the *Decameron* in the 14th century but why, I have no clue . . .'

Onions and peas are made for one another. In June freshly picked small young peas arrived in the market. Once again they came with advice. 'Always eat them straightaway and poach them in stock with an onion and prosciutto – and never, ever boil them.'

By mid-June my orto was indicating that I might, possibly, have green fingers. The tomato plants were climbing for the sky and sprouting little green fruits. For the first time we enjoyed lettuce that tasted of something, especially the curvaceous leaves of the Lollobrigida variety; the hale and hearty *lattuga romana,* Romaine or cos lettuce; and round and tender *lattuga a cappuccino,* cabbage lettuce.

Our zucchini plants seemed to be in seventh heaven and their big leaves and strong stalks just kept getting larger and larger. Every day there would be two or three new zucchini and we had to decide what to do apart from grilling them, experimenting with different zucchini and pasta dishes, making topping for bruschetta, and deep frying their flowers.

Our neighbours were useless. They were using them just like us and giving away and even composting what they didn't want. Two of our food writer friends, one British, the other Italian, were put on the case and came up with a handful of new ideas for soups and stuffing.

As summer strengthened, the market filled with large bright-red and luminous yellow peppers, with long, dark purple aubergines and their rounder ivory and purple-streaked cousins. Both varieties of *bietola,* Swiss chard, were on sale. The one colloquially called *erbette,* has a thin greenish stalk which we boil with herbs and serve with olive oil or use as a filling in ravioli. The other variety has thick white stalks. We cook its crinkly, slightly bitter leaves the same way as *erbette* but briefly cook the stalks separately before baking them with a cheese sauce finished with Parmesan or a local sheep-milk cheese.

In our new kitchen we over-indulged on plates of grilled or roasted zucchini, and on aubergines baked with sweet, thin-skinned peppers, all dressed with a sauce of pesto made from our own basil. After nearly three months of being in their prime, our zucchini plants then stopped fruiting and we gratefully turned our attention to a glut of tomatoes.

Nothing, but nothing, beats the flavour of home-grown tomatoes, especially those ripened under a Tuscan sun. We easily fell into the habit of snacking on the cherry ones straight from the vine and, unlike zucchini, we had no problem deciding what to do with our tomato harvest. Fresh tomato sauces became the base for much of what we cooked, from simple soups to a myriad of pasta, vegetable and meat dishes.

As the heat started to go out of the sun, boxes of summer squashes in different sizes, colours, shapes and textures appeared in the market, perfect for braising, roasting and making risotto, together with the last of our zucchini. By then I had shortlisted the vegetables to be planted the following year, and consulted Giuseppe the gardener on the practicalities.

As well as those I had grown successfully and the many others we had discovered in Camucia market, the list included good things to come in the months ahead. I wrote down such root vegetables as celeriac and fennel plus pumpkin, broccoli, celery, red-leaved, bitter radicchio and Tuscany's much-loved *cima di rapa,* turnip tops, also called *broccoletti,* which we parboil and then sauté with tomatoes. I even contemplated growing our very own cannellini or toscanelli beans. It was obvious that our single walled orto was already too small to meet my vegetable-growing plans.

Giuseppe had the answers. He suggested clearing the woodland in what would become a sunny, well-drained spot at the end of one of our grass terraces and so create a proper orto. Discussions about getting the acidity of the soil right, probable amounts of Silvio's sheep manure and other sources of goodness, hiring a mini-digger, the installation of a watering system, what to plant from seed or buy from a nursery took over my life, as did the question of pests and predators.

Until then we had seen few signs of the porcupines, badgers and wild boar supposed to share this land with us. Then, with the fruiting of our numerous fig, walnut and wild plum trees, six young boars appeared as dusk fell every evening, intent on eating the fruit and nuts before we did. Their appearance coincided with the hunting season and every conversation with our neighbours suddenly included mention of the 'bloody boar', the dreaded *cinghiale,* which in turn made me concentrate my urgent attention on walling and fencing matters.

Any pleasurable thoughts I had about vegetable gardening being relaxing were shattered. I had to accept that one day my efforts would come under attack.

THREE

Unearthing the Past

THE MEZZADRIA LEGACY

Franco Benelli was gathering moss when I first met him. It was a cold, damp and grey Christmas Eve, and he was on his hands and knees sliding an old kitchen knife under one of the deep-green cushions covering the rocks beside the road that runs above our house. I was on a late afternoon walk, breathing deeply of much-needed fresh air after spending most of the day inside dozing in front of a log fire.

With his eager eyes, slight stoop and long grey hair, Franco had a rather wild look. When he asked where I lived, I explained that Val and I had bought Casa Amari, the property on the slope directly below us, the one that was owned for years by the Cappello family. A raised eyebrow indicated that he knew more about our house than could or should be told over moss gathering. All he added was that many generations of his family had lived in the house up the hill from us.

The moss puzzled me. Franco explained that he was raised on what we already thought of as our hillside, and had always collected moss on December 24th for his family's *presepe,* a re-creation of the Nativity scene commonplace in homes, churches and public places throughout Italy at Christmas. We exchanged names and a few seasonal pleasantries then went our separate ways, leaving me wondering just what there was to know about the history of our house, and what we might be better off not knowing.

On Christmas morning Franco arrived unannounced, bringing seasonal gifts of *lonzino e fichi,* a fig dessert from Le Marche, and *panforte,* the peppery, spiced honey cake from Siena. I hoped a little alcohol would persuade him to spill some of the secrets behind his eyebrows.

'They were all *mezzadria,*' he said, relishing a glass of my best malt whisky, 'and they shaped everything you see from your terraces.'

Our ex-farmhouse sits towards the head of a wooded valley about 16km to the east of Cortona which, in turn, sits above the Val di Chiana. For a while, the land below us flattens out and becomes the favoured domain of tobacco farmers, but then it soon rises again to meet the mighty Apennine Mountains of Umbria and Le Marche on the horizon. Beyond them is the Adriatic. The house was probably built in the 19th century on the footings of a 14th-century tower using large, hard grey stones from ruins of this and other centuries-old buildings in the immediate area.

Occasionally the woods of mainly chestnut, oak, beech and pine trees that frame the view from our terraces clear to give sight of an old, grey stone or white stucco-covered house or *fattoria,* farmhouse.

These often-deserted houses and their land appear to have been there forever. Whatever the size of the dwelling, they have small windows and gently sloping terracotta-tiled roofs and are surrounded by man-made terraces still retained by the remains of what were once neat stone walls. Most of the terraces, which are the only practical way to tame our hill's slopes for cultivation and husbandry, are either a tangled wilderness or are grassed over. Only very few continue their traditional role as vegetable and fruit gardens.

Until as late as the 1980s, much of Tuscany was worked according to the *mezzadria* system, a sharecropping arrangement in use since the 13th century. It was these centuries of *mezzadria* farming that had shaped the look of every local hamlet, and that had dictated the appearance of every terraced domain in our view. Even the crooked access tracks and un-made roads that embroider the wooded hillside were servants of the system.

A *mezzadria* arrangement was between the landowner and the tenant farmers on his land. On our hillside, most of these reflected a *patti colonici,* a farm agreement, that changed little over six centuries. Just as unchanging, were many of the families who cultivated and farmed the same land generation after generation.

The landowner built and owned the farmhouse and kept it in repair. He bought half of what was needed to cultivate and improve the land and he paid for half the stock of cattle. When harvest time came, owner and farmer shared the crop equally.

Mezzadria farmers and their families lived a life of toil from dusk to dawn but, unlike many land workers in the south of Italy, Tuscan farmers rarely went hungry.

Signor Conti, 92-years-old and still driving a three-wheeled *ape* truck, brought reality to this life as we shared wine at our nearest bar. He had farmed in San Leo Bastia, further down the valley. 'As the male head of the family I was subordinate to the will of the landowner, but within my home I was invested with his authority in law. Most importantly,' he said, 'I decided what to grow and who did what and when.'

He was a proud man, yet grudgingly admitted that the women of the house probably toiled harder than the men. 'They reared the children, fetched the water, washed, made and repaired the clothes for all of us, as well as working on the land and tending the animals. And, of course, they also did the cooking.'

Signor Conti's large stomach indicated that he enjoyed his food and he gladly explained the poverty-based, farm-kitchen origins of *ribollita,* the Tuscan bean and vegetable soup now regarded as a gourmet speciality of the region.

'Soup from a cauldron over the fire was at the heart of most meals. But even though it was made from our own vegetables, it wasn't always tasty because it was constantly being topped-up and re-boiled,' he said, patting his girth. 'Soup has made me what I am. Along with the salt-free Tuscan bread my wife baked once a week in order to save time and fuel.'

Outside the bar I'd noticed a rusty, official-looking sign for *sale,* salt, and printed below the word was a series of numbers. The elderly signora running the bar explained that until 1975 she needed a licence to sell salt because the government had a monopoly on its manufacture and sale. 'Tuscan bread historically never had salt in it because it used to be so expensive,' she added.

When we were clearing some ruins close to our main house, that we planned to rebuild as a studio for my wife Val, we found the remains of a large, stone-built, wood-burning oven. The date 1930 was roughly carved into the main lintel over the oven's mouth. Our builder explained that a number of *mezzadria* families shared such an oven in which they baked bread just once a week. He gave a different reason for salt-free bread, saying he'd been told salt attracted moisture and thus could turn the bread mouldy and inedible before the end of the week.

The *mezzadria* system appears to have been very complicated and, at the same time, very elastic. There was always plenty of healthy grumbling on both sides, but it seemed to work because it suited the nature of the people and their land. More than one local family told me that this was because the interests of the landowner and the farmer were fundamentally the same. The *mezzadria* system was neither a landlord and tenant arrangement, as most Western countries know it today, nor that of employer and employee. It was more intimate than the former, more friendly than the latter. It was, I feel, a partnership with two winners.

Previous Generations

Our house is 750m above sea level and blessed with cooling breezes in the height of summer. That same elevation also means we can wake up to be floating on a lake of cloud that is waiting for the sun to hit the valleys before it burns away the mists and returns our view of the distant Apennines.

In winter the weather is not so kind. Rain, mists, cold winds and snow flurries are commonplace until May. As our first winter in Tuscany turned to spring and the sun made an occasional appearance, Franco appeared once again at our front door. It was Good Friday and I wondered if it was mountain manners only to visit neighbours on religious holidays.

His gift this time was a local Easter speciality from nearby Arezzo, *panina unta,* a saffron bread containing raisins and spices. I offered him a glass of malt whisky but he insisted Val and I go with him to meet his parents in their house in the nearest hamlet, closer up towards the mountain top.

Claudio Benelli and his wife Vera were elderly and reserved. She looked older than he did and both of them remembered the *mezzadria* family of 18 adults and children who lived in our house during the 1930s. Back then, they told us, what is now our closest terrace had been a two-storey building with cattle on the ground floor and sleeping accommodation on the first floor, where lack of space meant six children shared a single bed.

Facing this was the family's main house which then comprised a combined kitchen, eating and living room above cattle stalls. This is where we now live, having gutted the interior in the summer of 2001 with our builder neighbour and then, over the next year, rebuilt it on two floors with three bedrooms, two bathrooms, a living room and kitchen. Throughout we used such traditional Tuscan materials as chestnut beams for the ceilings and hand-made terracotta tiles for the floors.

Mixed farming, with vines, olives and wheat growing together, was common in Tuscany and the Benellis were sure that grapes and wheat were grown on our land until at least the 1950s.

Val and I began to walk with Franco as often as we could. Among the chestnut woods on the other side of the hill from his parents' house, he showed us the overgrown ruin of a farm he remembered visiting as a youngster. Here a family of 27 had lived and worked the land. He befriended them while taking his father's pigs to fatten on scavenged chestnut kernels and spent much of his early teens hunting wild rabbit and boar with one of their sons.

Today viper, wild boar and thick, tangled undergrowth have taken over where there was once mixed farming on neat terraces and where pigs, chickens, sheep, goats and fruit trees provided food for a family large enough to be thought a community. Access to the farm was down a steep, deeply rutted track that Franco remembered being just as bad 50 years ago. 'Those were the days when mules and white oxen pulling sleds were the only form of transport that could negotiate the terrain.'

The family who lived here pulled wood and chestnuts up this track each week to sell in nearby Cortona. The loads were transferred to a horse-drawn cart, which was permanently parked beside the Benellis house, for the slightly easier journey on established but unpaved roads into town.

Chestnut is used for all the main wood elements in a traditional Tuscan house, from doors, windows and beams to tables, chairs and cupboards. To this day, dried or fresh chestnuts and starchy chestnut flour find a ready market and chestnut bark is still used to tan leather.

Woods are one of the glories of Tuscany and account for nearly 50 per cent of the region, making it perhaps the most densely wooded region in Italy. Locally, ancient deciduous chestnut and oak trees are joined by more recently introduced evergreen pines, and by wild cherry and walnut trees that always provided an added bounty of fruit and nuts. So did the *frutteto,* family orchard, of apple, plum, fig and quince, so many of which now stand neglected and un-harvested.

For centuries Tuscan fruit trees provided sustenance for *mezzadria* families, but they gave much more, providing shade in summer, fuel in winter and wood for practicalities we hadn't expected. One day, in a local flea market, we discovered children's shoes made from fig-tree wood and this was one of the events that most made us aware that we knew so little about the realities of those who had lived here before us.

Near the abandoned farm buildings, Franco showed us the overgrown ruins of a large and once impressive house where the landowner had lived during the summer. It was disquieting to think that both parties to this ancient *mezzadria* partnership had now vanished and left the land to itself after centuries of mutual support, and that it had happened so comparatively recently, too.

I remembered to ask Franco's elderly parents about the remains of the bread oven we had found in the ruins on our terrace. They said that as recently as the 1950s there were still about 200 people living and working on our hillside. They baked bread in that oven and shared a communal washing sink for their clothes. Days later I found where this happened, too. Less than 50m from our house there was a large, shallow stone sink fed by a spring, both hidden by a jungle of wild vines and tangled brambles.

Suddenly the views from our terraces were peopled with the past. It wasn't difficult to smell the weekly bread baking or to overhear the slap of clothes on the sink. The tumbled remains of the ruin and of the age-smoothed sink conjured for us a privileged, personal insight into what it might have been like to share those long, conjoined centuries of common blood and toil, of the continuous traditions that were shared by each of those departed souls.

I was determined to know and understand more.

Fascism and the Second World War

Franco was nowhere to be seen during summer, but his father Claudio often greeted us on our walks along the woodcutters' tracks and old Roman roads that criss-cross the countryside. These invariably led to local hamlets that were once thriving villages. In most we found long lives remembered in cemeteries adorned with stern photographs of the dead, above inscriptions that demonstrated how frequently local families had married into other local families.

In time-honoured way, the approach to these small, walled graveyards, all built in Napoleonic times, was along a cypress-lined track. Surprisingly, we could never find memorials to those killed in the Second World War and when Val and I asked Signor Benelli what happened locally during the war he seemed not to hear me. I realised I was taking a risk by asking if he had been a soldier, but I knew that such recent history was much more relevant to our day-to-day life than the customs of *mezzadria* families. Eventually Claudio Benelli revealed how much he had hated being on the side of the Germans while Italy was first fighting on the German side.

When Italy changed sides, after the Armistice with the Allies was signed in September 1943, Claudio deserted his regiment to join one of the first local partisan groups to be formed. Its objective was to rid the country of the Germans who still occupied Northern and Central Italy, including Tuscany. A new Italian republic was created but it was still headed by their puppet Mussolini.

It seemed painful for Signor Benelli to have said even that much. It took only the briefest of glances from Val for me to drop the subject – for the moment, anyway.

Fascism dominated the political scene in Tuscany immediately prior to the Second World War. In fact, all Italy was dominated by Mussolini's obsession with fighting what he believed to be the decadent democracies of the West. These included Britain, which he dubbed 'the five-meals-a-day nation', and 'backward, incompetent Russia'.

Losing a war was inconceivable to Mussolini. Moreover, Britain, France, Russia and Germany had an empire and he wanted one too. He declared Italy's Empire in 1936 after conquering Ethiopia and adding it to Italy's North African possessions of Eritrea, Somalia and Libya, as well as extending Italy's European borders. He was a successful, conquering emperor in his mind and was thus ready to risk Italy's future in a bid for much greater power in the world.

Mussolini recognised Hitler as an equal champion of strong right-wing values and so, within months of the start of the Second World War in September 1939, he aligned Italy with Nazi Germany forming the core of the Axis enemy of the Allies.

After Germany's initial successes almost everywhere in 1940, there was a different story to tell at the end of 1942 and by then many Italians could see through the absurd exaggerations of Fascist propaganda. Lost battles at Stalingrad and El Alamein indicated that the tide was turning against the Axis forces, and gradually it became clear that, short of producing the secret weapons that Mussolini and Hitler kept boasting about, the Fascist powers had no chance of stopping the Allied advance in Russia or North Africa.

By January 1943 Mussolini had lost his African empire. The Americans were in Tunisia; and in Libya the Eighth Army of British and Commonwealth troops was moving towards Tripoli and ever closer to the Italian mainland. It was no wonder so many Italians thought their country might be invaded, and it was probably just as well so few knew Mussolini was ill at the time and had virtually ceased to function as *Il Duce,* The Leader, in sole charge of the country's future. In fact, the Italian war effort was largely directed from Germany.

One of the few physical reminders of the war locally is a roll of honour of 22 names at a road junction half-an-hour's walk away on the road to Cortona. This is also the location of our closest cafe, and here I first met our local priest Padre Latini who was relishing a larger-than-normal glass of red wine at 11 in the morning. He was old and short, but steady-eyed with an open if rather red face. The signora who runs the place had previously told me he was a mine of information about the history of our area, and was born in the nearby hamlet of Tornia just before the war. A refill got him talking.

'Before the war the problem for country people was that because they were so far from the main centres of power they didn't really comprehend the failings of Fascism – how cruel it was, how it oppressed minorities, how inefficient it was. Nor was it that easy to appreciate Mussolini's growing obsession with making war.'

He was ten years of age when the Second World War started. 'Apart from seeing a few German soldiers from time to time, nothing much happened here in the mountains for the first two years of the war. It was a bit of an anti-climax for all us youngsters.'

In June 1943 the Allies landed in the south of Italy, capturing the small island of Pantelleria. Next month, Sicily was faced with a full-scale invasion by 80,000 troops aboard 2,700 ships and landing craft. With this, Mussolini lost the support of other Fascist leaders. King Victor Emmanuel III, who reigned from 1900, had remained on the Italian throne and retained many powers; by the end of July 1943 he felt confident enough to order Mussolini's arrest. Field Marshal Pietro Badoglio was appointed the new head of government. In public Badoglio insisted the war would go on, but in secret he was busy negotiating armistice terms with the Allies.

'We heard the news on the radio that Mussolini had been arrested,' the padre remembered. 'Everyone in the village seemed to think it was a good thing but was worried about who or what would replace him.' He drained his glass. I took the hint and ordered another for him. 'A few days after, we went down to the main Arezzo to Chuisi road in the Val di Chiana to watch a huge convoy of German soldiers, their tanks, armoured cars and trucks heading south as fast as they could. That evening the radio reported that Allied planes from airfields in North Africa had started bombing Genoa.'

It took until September for the new government to make peace with the Allies. By this time Hitler had secured continuing Nazi occupation of Northern and Central Italy, including Tuscany. When Mussolini was freed from prison, he was appointed the puppet head of *Repubblica Sociale Italiana,* the new Italian Social Republic based in Salò on the banks of Lake Garda in Lombardy. Italy was divided again, only 80 years since Garibaldi had united the Kingdom of the House of Savoy, the Papal States and the Kingdom of the Two Sicilies.

The Allied Advance

On September 3rd, Montgomery's Eighth Army crossed the three and half miles of sea from Messina in Sicily to land on the beaches just north of Reggio di Calabria at the toe of the Italian mainland. The Italian Government had already signed an unconditional surrender in Sicily, but it wasn't until five days later, on the evening of 8th September 1943, that Italy's exodus from the Axis to the Allies was announced to the nation. In darkness, on the morning of 9th September, the second thrust of the Allied invasion of mainland Italy commenced with landings from the sea at Salerno, 40km south of Naples.

With sadness in his eyes, Padre Latini remembered that, once the Allies were on the Italian mainland, things changed for the worse. 'From then on until the end of the war, confusion reigned for Tuscany, and there were hardships and tragedy on a scale that no one could have envisaged.'

In the hours immediately after Italy's surrender was announced, there were mass breakouts from mainland prisoner-of-war camps by Allied soldiers who had been captured in Italy's ex-colonies during the battles for North Africa. More than 50,000 Allied soldiers held in the north made a break for it before the Germans could regain control of the camps. The situation was exacerbated by the Italian guards employed there, who deemed their responsibilities to be at an end and simply abandoned their duties. Some of the escapees made for the Swiss and French borders, but the majority headed south hoping to encounter the Allied forces advancing up the country.

For many of them, the remote mountain farms where we now lived became a temporary shelter and a vital source of food.

'Those on the move also included Italian troops who, after the 8th September announcement and with no guidance from Badoglio's new government, simply took off their uniforms and fled, intent on returning home.'

It took tact, persistence and great sensitivity, but over the coming weeks I found more local people who were prepared to remember the war years and to talk about them.

Signora Contini, a handsome, careworn woman whose family own and run one of the best hotels in Cortona, told me she had grown up believing King Vittorio Emmanuel was guilty of duplicity. 'My mother and father were profoundly shocked and humiliated by what they saw as the king's betrayal and that of Badoglio who replaced Mussolini. They felt that neither the Fascist misrule nor the Germans' behaviour justified this betrayal or retrieved the national honour. I sometimes wonder whether they actively supported the Germans in some small way. Of course there were others who held very different views from those of my parents and were openly anti-Fascist. Although they disapproved of the actions of the king and Badoglio, they waited with anticipation for the arrival of the Allies as friends, liberators and benefactors.'

The next time I saw Padre Latini I asked if these were commonly held views. He told me they were in the minority. 'At the time the king decided Italy should change sides, the vast majority of Tuscans were simply disillusioned, cynical and tired. They knew that more suffering lay ahead and felt they were part of a defeated nation where the only option was self-preservation. Those with sons of call-up age became preoccupied with hiding them so that they wouldn't have to fight alongside the Germans in the new Italian Social Republic.'

As autumn continued in 1943, it seemed everyone hid their treasured possessions and struggled to find the minimum of necessities to support them through the coming winter – food, fuel, light sources, clothes, boots and medicines. The change in the season also coincided with short supplies of accurate and up-to-date news. Not everyone had access to a radio, and although Radio Roma was an important source of information it was still German-controlled. Newspapers were hard to find and often arrived many days after publication. I slowly understood how confused and fearful these times must have been. Italy was now on the winning side but, even though Tuscany was Italian, it was still occupied by German forces and governed by the disgraced Mussolini as part of a newly created republic.

'The wise thing to do here was to keep a low profile,' the padre recalled. 'That meant keeping one's beliefs to oneself, never passing remarks about daily occurrences, and never getting caught up in trading rumours.'

This, of course, was easier said than done. Everyone had something to fear – or thought they had – and talking to others in similar circumstances helped share the burden of hardships. 'Soldiers and the police, all of them still Fascists in this region, found it much harder to enforce government regulations in the mountains and other country areas. They were less in evidence here than in Cortona and other local towns. But spies were everywhere,' he continued. 'To this day you will find some families still treated with suspicion because they were rumoured to have passed the names of anti-Fascists to the Germans. It was claimed others took bounty payments for information about Allied prisoners on the run, or about Italian deserters and young men avoiding conscription.'

In spite of these pervasive fears, everyone agreed that daily life in our mountains and other parts of the Tuscan countryside was much easier than in the region's towns and cities. For one thing there was more food, whereas people in urban areas were forced to resort to the black market – if they had the money.

Local *mezzadria* families remained largely self-supporting. They baked bread from their own flour, and most had chickens, turkeys, geese or rabbits, vegetable gardens and fruit trees. Pigs were invariably kept and provided hams and sausages; sheep gave milk and cheese. Nuts were always plentiful, fungi were collected and dried for later use, fruit was stored and bottled, and wild boar and birds were hunted. Many families made their own soap using olive oil residue or a mixture of kitchen fat, potato peel and soda.

The woods provided fuel including, in some cases, power for motor vehicles. I heard one story about a farmer from Teverina who mastered how to convert his truck and a friend's car to run on charcoal. When the Allied front came closer to Cortona, the truck was supposedly commandeered by a partisan group and used as a getaway vehicle. Presumably it must have been steam powered, but today there's no way of knowing if this is true or a fabrication. This little bit of local history is widely believed because it's accepted that the story perfectly illustrates how determined Tuscans were not to be defeated by what they largely saw as a war which was not theirs.

PARTISAN LIVES

After the Armistice in September 1943, Italian regiments unfortunate enough to be in the wrong place at the wrong time were deported to Germany by their former ally. These soldiers ended up in concentration camps or were made to work as forced labour in ammunition factories. But it wasn't only soldiers that the Germans vented their spite on after their defeat. Princess Mafalda of Savoy, the king's second daughter, was arrested on quite false charges at the German Embassy in Bulgaria, and ended up in Buchenwald concentration camp. She was seriously wounded during an Allied raid on a munitions factory on the site in September 1944, when 400 prisoners were killed. She died a few days later, shortly before her 42nd birthday, from injuries sustained when she was buried up to her neck in debris.

Other Italian units were quickly disbanded by their officers in the absence of any clear direction from Badoglio's new Italian government. The natural thing for these soldiers to do was to return home, and many who were originally from Cortona and the surrounding villages did just that. However, they risked being made to work for the Germans in the Todt, a military organisation responsible for the building and maintenance of roads and airports. Otherwise they might have to join the army of Mussolini's Italian Social Republic, and perhaps be expected to fight not only the Allies but other Italians.

Neither of these options was why these soldiers had managed to make it home to our mountains. Instead, many chose the secretive and perilous partisan life and created partisan groups to assist the advancing Allies.

After nearly a year of regularly meeting Signor Benelli on the road above our house, and taking him and his wife produce from our small vegetable garden in exchange for the cherries, apples, pears and peaches from their trees, he at last began to speak to me about his time as a partisan.

We sat opposite one another across his kitchen table. 'I was just old enough to be called up but, like all of my friends of a similar age, I didn't want to be conscripted into Mussolini's new army. Joining one of the local partisan groups seemed the right thing to do at the time. Many local men simply wanted to do something for their country and foreign prisoners of war who were on the run were joining them. I wanted to make a contribution, too.'

I asked him to tell me more about the types of local men who became partisans. 'Until the groups were properly organised many teenagers came from Cortona's aristocratic and wealthier families, not least because they saw the mountains as a safer place to be than in the town. The problem was that they really liked being free of their parents and, with a gun in their hands, they often frightened local people by making unwelcome visits to their homes where they were sure to find food and items of value. Perhaps not surprisingly, their unruly presence often caused resentment amongst families who had lived all their lives in the mountains.'

Signor Benelli went on to explain that, as well as different backgrounds, the local partisans also had differing politics and this made it very difficult to make a concerted, co-ordinated effort. By the end of 1943 there were two main groups, the Green Flames and the Garibaldi Brigades. The Green Flames were a broadly based, non-Communist group made up of Socialists, Republicans, Liberals and anyone else who wanted to get rid of Fascism and the Germans. The Garibaldi Brigades were explicitly Communist and political.

'There were also bandit groups with no interest in politics whatsoever. Two of these were notorious, no better than criminals, who stole at random and gave real partisans a bad name. La Teppa was a group of about 100 men in their late teens and early twenties. Bortoloni was led by a Frenchman and a mad Italian from the south. Its members included some extremely violent Russian and Algerian prisoners of war.

'I was with the 23rd Garibaldi Brigade, better known locally as the Pio Borri. We operated throughout Tuscany and there were two groups, one run by a local man called Spartaco Veltroni and mine, nicknamed the Poggioni, because our leader from Cortona was Bruno Valli, who'd been born in Poggioni a short distance from here. Whatever its makeup, a partisan brigade generally comprised battalions of 40 to 60 men made up of *squadre* of 10 to 20. Within each *squadra* was a nucleus of five or six men.'

Early in 1944, while the brigades were still being organised, the Green Flames and the Garibaldis formed a National Committee of Liberation in Milan. Its objective was to ensure a democracy in Italy where government workers, small farmers, artisans, all the trade unions and other organisations would share power.

This definition of democracy had little in common with the type of democracy known in Britain and the US, and it made the Allies, especially Britain, wary of putting too much power in the hands of the partisans.

That's all Signor Benelli was prepared to tell me this time, but some weeks later he surprised me by producing a faded, torn poster. It was an official notice signed by Albert Kesselring, who was Germany's Commander-in-Chief South and responsible for Hitler's war in both the Mediterranean and North Africa. There had been a partisan attack on Nazi/Fascist troops in Rome on 23rd March 1944. In retaliation, the poster announced that 'forthwith ten Italians will be executed for every German killed by a suspected partisan'. 'These posters were prominently displayed throughout Tuscany, and made it quite clear that our partisan activities would attract significant reprisals for innocent civilians,' he explained.

In the first few months of 1944 most partisans continued to hide with their families, but, as the summer approached and the Allied advance from the south came closer to Cortona, they went deeper undercover in our local mountainous countryside. Their targets were invariably the Panzer and Mountain Corps troops stationed locally and the Gestapo, whose numbers grew as the front got closer. 'We did anything that would disrupt the activities of the Germans and weaken their morale,' Signor Benelli said.

Val and I bought our house in 2000, and the previous owners told us that they had heard stories of it being used by partisans as a base for attacks on German convoys going over the bridge at the Cerventosa Pass, a short walk away on the main road. Signor Benelli confirmed this. 'We were always short of guns and ammunition and found one of the best ways of getting them was by holding up Nazi lorries as they drove onto the bridge at the pass. This always resulted in some form of reprisal by the Germans, from regularly plundering your house to the shooting of my boyhood pal, who lived next door to us.'

Ferdinando Ferri was minding a flock of sheep with a friend on the hillside close to the Benelli homestead when an armoured car suddenly appeared on the track by the church and started shooting at them. They ran for cover but a bullet hit 22-year-old Ferdinando in the head and killed him outright.

'He had done nothing and wasn't a partisan,' he continued. 'It was so sad. I think the Germans knew they had made a mistake, because when they caught up with his friend they let him go once he showed them his papers.

'After this troops went to what is now your house. They fired from one of the upper-floor windows on a member of the family living there who was working in the field below, hitting him in the chest but luckily not fatally. Then they took away the 15-year-old son of the Bruni family, who was in your house at the time. He was never seen alive again.'

The part played by Italian partisans in helping the Allied advance intrigued me. From what Claudio Benelli had told me, there appeared to be little co-ordination between the different groups about what to attack and when. Perhaps this was not surprising since some of them were principally political movements, and others were simply hooligans spoiling for a fight. Anyway, most of them were young men without combat experience or arms training.

Tuscany became a battlefield between the Nazis and the partisans. The districts across the Val di Chiana to the south-west and around Monte Amiata and the Val d'Orcia sheltered particularly strong partisan groups. But luckily our immediate area was never in the front line, and escaped the worst of the fighting and the bombing at Lake Trasimeno only 10km away.

THE PRIESTS' DIARIES

As usual Padre Latini was in the bar enjoying his morning glass of vino rosso, so I offered to pay for a refill and asked who he knew who would talk to me about their war experiences.

Uncharacteristically he refused the wine, but with a curious glint in his eyes. Instead of answering directly he mysteriously suggested we drive to the church at Tornia. 'There I will show you something that I am sure will satisfy your curiosity.'

Tornia is tucked into a pocket of the hillside on the edge of the chestnut forests that blanket the valley north of our house. We drove to the hamlet down an odd, steep, zigzag road, part dirt track and part highway. Eventually we arrived at a collection of run-down houses. Most were abandoned, a few were just ruins. The only signs of life were scrawny chickens pecking amongst the untended paths.

We walked up to the church that sat isolated some distance above the houses. Large trees cast gloomy shadows across the nondescript building. The land around was overgrown and incongruously contained a big, empty swimming pool down a bank in front of the main doors. Busy, buzzing insects swarmed around a puddle of stagnant green water at the deep end. 'We built it a few years after the war for everyone to use when there were many more people living here in the mountains,' the padre explained with a sigh for the past.

He took an ornate key from the folds of his cassock and opened the doors to reveal a gloomy interior. I followed him into the sparsely furnished vestry, which was dominated by a large padlocked cupboard along one wall. He put his hands down the back of his neck, pulled out a length of black ribbon and then used the key on the end of that to open the padlock. Inside were chalices, vestments, bottles of Communion wine, many musty hymn books, sundry bibles, and some large registers with a few school exercise books on top of them.

Padre Latini selected two of the books and placed them on the only table in the room. 'These are the diaries kept by two local priests during the time the Germans were here in these mountains.'

I flipped through one of them. The pages for 1944 covered the months from January to August. In the entry for the last weekend of April, spidery handwriting recorded the first killing by local partisans, 'of a Fascist and Nazi collaborator from Cortona in the woods below Teverina'. It named Signor Benelli's Poggioni *squadra* as the killers.

On Wednesday 21st June, there was commentary about partisans blowing up the bridge at Cerventosa, attacking a German lorry near our local bar and killing three German soldiers. A few pages later, mention of La Teppa partisans caught my eye.

The padre put his hand on mine. 'That entry records probably the most frightening thing to have ever happened in this community.' It took a little while before he could tell me the story.

'At the end of June 1944 La Teppa partisans made a number of attacks on German troops from the hills near where we met today. The Germans' instant reprisals included setting light to buildings on the road down to here. Then, here in Tornia, they took about 40 of the inhabitants hostage, searched and set light to more buildings, and demanded news of eight German soldiers who they said had been captured by the partisans.

'Tornia's priest, the author of one of the diaries, gathered all those of the village who had not been taken hostage. Peacefully and quietly, he led them in prayers and recited the *Atto di Dolore,* the Act of Contrition, from the Catholic catechism.

'God's presence had its desired effect. The German commander released the prisoners and then spoke to the priest and his kneeling congregation saying, "as a fellow Catholic it is my duty to release you despite the fact that you have all betrayed us and have given lodgings to those treacherous killers, the partisans, while my countrymen are fighting with your fellow Italians for freedom." But not everyone had the luck of facing a Catholic German.'

The second of the diaries was written by the priest of Ruffignano, another local hamlet. On the same day the Germans raided Tornia, he recorded hearing shots close to his church. The next day he discovered the corpses of three young men in the woods nearby, one of which he surmised was that of the Bruni boy abducted from what is now our house.

The danger the priests had put themselves in by keeping these diaries began to dawn on me. If the Germans had found them, they would certainly have been killed. As the padre locked the books back in the cupboard, he agreed.

'Of course it was stupid to keep these diaries, but the Bishop of Cortona insisted all his priests in the area do so. What he had in mind for them God only knows.'

With the help of the padre, I was able to read all of these extraordinary diaries over the next few months. What struck me was the relatively small number of recorded partisan attacks and that the Germans retaliated far less brutally than the 'ten dead Italians for one dead German' that Kesselring had commanded. Surprisingly, most incidents where partisans were killed involved the escaped prisoners of war, those thought to have most experience of warfare. Clearly, fighting in the deserts of North Africa and on the plains of Italy was no training for fighting in the mountains.

I thought the Germans had made only one local example of retribution, by hanging a former Russian soldier from a tree by the gates of the Villa Passerini in Pergo below Cortona, their local headquarters in one of the grandest villas in the area. Then I discovered the chilling entry about a massacre that took place five days before Cortona was liberated by the Allies.

Towards the end of June 1944, the Germans discovered the location of the headquarters of the Poggioni partisans in the hamlet of the same name, and attacked it with a large contingent of troops. Much to the frustration of the young Wehrmacht officer in charge, no partisans were to be found so he decided to take his revenge on innocent members of the local population. Yet, instead of doing this in Poggioni, the troops went to nearby Falzano, killing four people on the way. In Falzano, they destroyed the church, set fire to a number of dwellings and imprisoned 11 men in a barn before setting fire to it killing all but one of them.

The diary entry noted that those living in Poggioni and Falzano were so shocked by the massacre that they insisted the partisans cease their activities and hide their weapons.

The next time I saw Claudio Benelli, I asked him why he had not mentioned the Falzano massacre to me. 'It was one of the worst crimes to take place in Tuscany during the German occupation. I never talk about it, not least because for years and years after the war had ended many people said we Poggioni partisans had caused it.'

DIVIDED OPINIONS

The Eighth Army came triumphantly into Cortona at 11.45 a.m. on Wednesday 3rd July 1944, some four hours after the last column of German soldiers had left the area via a mountain footpath that goes along the ridge above our house. The partisan groups in the area had been active for less than three months.

Opinions still divide on the value of the partisans' activities in helping the Allied advance. I believe that, in our area anyway, it was overestimated and that they never really represented a threat to the Germans, or distracted and disrupted them as much as they could have done. The partisans' efforts were not helped by the attitude of many Allied soldiers who viewed them as Communists and shirkers avoiding military service, only interested in politics, and useless at fighting. Once Cortona was liberated, the first thing Allied troops did was to disarm the partisans, which bears out this view.

Yet, Italian partisans claimed that it was they, not the Allies, who liberated Italy. This can be explained in two ways. First, because they viewed Allied troops as Imperialists. And secondly, perhaps as a sort of payback for how the Allies lacked confidence in them and had refused to arm the majority of partisan groups.

Nazi German diaries reveal that the partisans were seen as an increasing threat by the German commander Kesselring. He recorded that, after his troops left Rome in June 1944, the partisans' war became a real danger to Germans and that elimination of partisans was of considerable importance.

Even if the efforts of the partisans did little to liberate North and Central Italy, the impact of their actions on innocent Italian civilians was significant. Most partisans still alive deny any link between their actions and reprisals by the Germans. It's certainly true that, as the Allies came closer to Cortona, the Germans made little distinction between partisans and ordinary farmers and families.

In the Arezzo province alone the Germans killed over 1,000 innocent civilians, many it is believed as acts of reprisal.

The words on the few memorial stones we found on our travels around Tuscany sum up the feelings of those local families that lived through the war, by referring to 'Nazi-Fascist barbarism', 'victims of Nazi-Fascist hate', 'fell during German reprisals' and 'a tragic massacre'.

They might not be celebrated as publically as Remembrance Sunday or Anzac Day, but private memories of the Falzano massacre and atrocities in other places throughout Tuscany live on all around us.

As Val and I enjoy today's uninterrupted natural rhythm of the seasons and the simplicity of life in the mountains, it is difficult to imagine the disruption, hardships, fear and pain the previous inhabitants of our area suffered during the war. 'My parents say 1944 was the worst,' Franco told us, 'and the uncertainties continued long after the Germans had left and we came under Allied protection.

'The war changed our way of life for ever. Young people like me no longer wanted to be beholden to the *mezzadria* way of life; we wanted proper jobs in towns and cities along with *gelato* shops, visits to the cinema, and Vespa motor scooters with the style and clothes that went with them. I moved away, but never lost the love of family. Christmas, Easter, local Saints' days and other celebratory fairs, feasts and festivals became more, rather than less, important as I got older. So did the trees, the wild flowers of spring, the heat and buzzing sounds of insects in summer, the sensuality of moss in winter.'

The longer Val and I live here, the more we, too, appreciate these cornerstones of the way of life in the mountains, cornerstones that sustained so many during so many sad days and frightened nights.

We also wonder if the increasing swarms of tourists ever give a thought for those men and women who fought and died within living memory for their freedom to wander in Tuscany's serene beauty.

FOUR

Poetry of the Air

RUBBING SHOULDERS WITH THE WORLD'S BEST

There's nothing that will change our mind. RAI Tre Radio is an Italian treasure. On balmy nights from the middle of July to early September, we sit on our terrace and listen to RAI Tre live broadcasts of the BBC Proms from London's Albert Hall. Programmes also include Wagner from Bayreuth, opera from the lakeside stage of Bregenz and concerts from Aix-en-Provence, Salzburg and Italy's many summer music festivals. We sometimes need to work hard to decipher knowledgeable Italian presenters' passionate analyses, and occasionally have to ignore unwelcome accompaniment from our farmer neighbour's son who has ambitions as a rock drummer.

RAI Tre Radio was founded in 1950 as the *Terzo Programma* and was loosely based on its British namesake of the time, the BBC's Third Programme, now Radio 3, which had made its début four years earlier. For me, as for millions of Italians, it is a beacon of sanity – a public broadcasting saviour on airways crowded with over 2,000 banal commercial radio stations. What poor homage these are to Signor Marconi, the Italian who discovered radio and made it all possible.

But this is Italy, home of many of the world's most beloved musicians, songs and singers, and Tuscany proudly claims an important role in the country's musical heritage. The violin and the pianoforte were invented and perfected here. Opera began here, too, when Jacopo Peri's *Dafne* was staged in Florence at Palazzo Corsi during carnival in 1597. This story of Apollo falling for the nymph Dafne used recitatives for the first time, setting speech to music as a link between arias.

A tidal wave of appreciation for the new art form spread through the rest of Italy to Europe. From the early days of the 17th century and on into the 18th century, first Monteverdi in Venice and then Scarlatti in Naples helped establish important centres of opera. In the 19th century, Vincenzo Bellini, Gioacchino Rossini and Gaetano Donizetti were the presiding geniuses of Italian opera. Verdi and Puccini continued Italian domination of the art form into the 20th century. While opera in other countries was something for the rich and noble, it has always been popular among all social classes in Italy, just as classical music is widely appreciated. In London, I have been privileged to see and hear some of the greatest artists in the world. Yet some of my most memorable musical experiences have been almost on the doorstep of our home near Cortona.

For years the annual Tuscan Sun Festival, or Festival del Sole, made me think I was under the wing of Apollo, the ancient god of sun and music. Frances Mayes, the American author of *Under the Tuscan Sun* which inspired the film of the same name, lives in Cortona. In 2003 she started the festival with the American artists' agent Barrett Wissman and cellist Nina Kotova.

For nine blissful years until the festival moved to Florence in 2012, Cortona played host for a week every August to the sort of internationally renowned musicians and singers that would pack out Carnegie Hall in New York, La Scala in Milan, or London's Wigmore Hall for months.

The festival had an intangible and intimate magic that I fear Florence may never ever recreate, a magic due in no small part to Carlo Gatteschi, the architect from nearby Arezzo, who rather cornered the market to design and build Tuscan and Umbrian theatres in the mid to late 19th century. In 1857 he constructed the small neo-classical Teatro Leopoldo for Cortona on a site once occupied by a church. The project came about because the town's music-loving bourgeoisie banded together to form the *Accademia degli Arditi,* an Academy of the Brave (or perhaps of Ardent Admirers). Whatever their name meant, each of the supporters sponsored a box in the new theatre and this funded the building works. A few years after it was opened, the theatre was renamed Teatro Signorelli in honour of Luca Signorelli, the Cortonese painter.

The exterior of the theatre is in the neo-classical style with a loggia made of seven arches. A small bar inside the foyer serves drinks and snacks on the terrace under the loggia, one of the best places in town to meet friends or simply sit on one's own and watch daily life in Cortona at your leisure. The mirrored foyer hasn't been touched for at least 50 years and still features its original ornate wood and brass ticket desk. The auditorium is like an elaborately decorated multi-tiered but inverted wedding cake, with three 'layers' of boxes each seating between three and eight people in comfort on well-upholstered gilt chairs. These boxes form a horseshoe shape around just 155 plush red seats in the stalls, creating an intimate and perfectly proportioned space within which the performers and audience are always in close proximity.

I boast to friends that I have seen and rubbed shoulders with the world's best, and all in my local town. One year it was acclaimed sopranos Cecilia Bartoli, Renée Fleming, Anna Netrebko and Angela Gheorghiu; another it was German superstar counter-tenor Andreas Scholl and the Argentinian tenor José Cura. It was a real privilege to hear the Takács String Quartet live and there were world-class violinists too, including the phenomenal Pinchas Zukerman and handsome young Joshua Bell, who played on the sensational 1713 Huberman Stradivarius, using a late 18th-century French bow by François Tourte.

The collaboration between the Austrian mezzo-soprano Angelika Kirchschlager and the French pianist Jean-Yves Thibaudet, in 2007, was a revelation. One particularly vivid performance was of the most perfect song composed by Brahms – *Von ewiger Liebe,* Of Eternal Love. This, and other songs by Grieg, Haydn and Liszt, pointed up several of Kirchschlager's greatest assets: responsiveness to the text, clarity of diction and a distinctive, flexible tone.

After this concert I found myself leaving Teatro Signorelli in the company of my restaurant-owner friend Signora Fossa. She told me that she played the piano and felt that Liszt's songs seemed to give a pianist more interesting material to work with than Brahms. We agreed with a previous reviewer who 'loved the graceful changes of colouration and the emphasis that Kirchschlager brought to each verse of *Die drei Zigeuner,* The Three Gypsies, and how these were mirrored in Thibaudet's account of the thoroughly Lisztian piano line'.

Today music is everywhere; it penetrates into every aspect of our lives, when we're shopping, in restaurants, in a lift. Such music is in the background and is not music that we've personally chosen. To speak with Signora Fossa about music – and with many other local people I met through the festival – it was reassuring to know that I lived amongst Italians who actively chose to listen to music, to engage with it, to focus their attention on it, and to listen attentively.

For all its star musicians, the Tuscan Sun Festival was never an exclusive event reserved for cognoscenti and the rich. Performers attended other performers' concerts, shared drinks or *gelato* with the audiences during the intervals, and generally enjoyed the relaxed and intimate atmosphere that makes Cortona a joy for locals and summer visitors alike.

Open-air concerts took place against the backdrop of handsome medieval buildings in the irregularly shaped and raked piazza in front of the theatre. In later years another venue – the square in front of the town's loftiest church, the Santuario di Santa Margherita – was also used so even more people could attend the most popular concerts.

We were also surprised with stars from other parts of show business. One year Sophia Loren arrived to open the proceedings, surrounded by fawning Carabinieri officers of a certain age. She talked with tears in her eyes about how she missed her husband Carlo Ponti, who had recently died, before introducing her handsome son, Carlo Ponti Junior, who proved to be an enthusiastic and workmanlike conductor of the Russian National Orchestra.

Robert Redford came, too, with his painter partner Sibylle Szaggars. He read American and Italian poetry at night, and she exhibited her work in a local church. Both were in the audience of every concert during the festival. Actor Sir Anthony Hopkins introduced his talents as a composer of classical scores as well as theme music for films at the Teatro Signorelli, and mounted an exhibition of his vivid paintings and drawings of landscape in the museum next door to the theatre. We'll miss them all now the festival has moved on to pastures new. Yet because this is Italy, there's not far to go for equal pleasures.

A FINE FIGURE OF OPERATIC PROPORTIONS

To the east of Cortona, some three hours' drive away, Pesaro on the Marche coast of the Adriatic has a theatre that has become a place of pilgrimage for opera lovers. Built as the Teatro Nuovo on the site of the 1637 Teatro del Sole, it was inaugurated on 10th June 1818 with a performance of Rossini's *La gazza ladra* (The Thieving Magpie), conducted by the composer who was born here.

The 860-seater theatre has an auditorium designed in the classic horseshoe shape with four tiers of boxes and a gallery. Recent restorations have brought to light some splendid 18th-century stucco decorations and brightly coloured floral frescoes. It changed its name to Teatro Rossini in 1854 and for the past 30 years has been the venue for the Rossini Opera Festival.

Gioachino Antonio Rossini was the most important, successful and influential Italian composer of the first half of the 19th century. His creative genius and efforts dragged the cumbersome and moribund forms of 18th-century opera into a new era. When only 24, he wrote *Il barbiere di Siviglia* (The Barber of Seville) in just three weeks, and it remains a masterpiece of comic opera. During the rest of his astonishingly short professional life, he created 38 stage works and superb sacred music compositions, chamber music scores, songs, and instrumental and piano pieces.

In spite of his early and wide success, Rossini retired from the theatrical world when he was only 37 and then devoted the remaining 39 years of his life to his other great passion – food. So much so that there are still dishes named after him. Val and I were lunching at an elegant, open-fronted fish restaurant on the Pesaro promenade when we heard about a local chef, Roberto Santini, who excelled at serving *Tournedos alla Rossini* and the lesser-known *Frittata alla Rossini,* an omelette studded with foie gras and white truffles. Suddenly food became as important as opera to us, and we justified our interest by telling one another that it would help deepen our understanding of Rossini if we ate the way he liked to do.

Roberto Santini trained in Paris and had cooked at London's prestigious Savoy Hotel. While he was in Paris he had become fascinated by the culinary creations associated with Rossini, who had lived there during the 1850s and 1860s. 'The recipe for *Tournedos alla Rossini* is one that he is supposed to have suggested to chef Adolphe Dugléré at the ultra-fashionable Café Anglais,' he told me. 'To say it is rich is an understatement. It's the best fillet steak pan-fried in butter, topped with a slice of whole foie gras, garnished with slices of black truffle, and then finished with a Madeira sauce. Not what you would call a light dish. Apparently the maître d'hôtel at the Café Anglais prepared the dish in front of the customer, but with his back to the other diners so that they would not witness its excess. In French the phrase "to turn one's back" is *tourner le dos,* and that's the derivation of *tournedos.'*

Rossini cut a figure of operatic proportions and eventually the consequences of his sybaritic existence caught up with him. Although he lived to be 76, he was plagued for years by medical problems, from chronic indigestion to gallstones and urinary infections. In 1840 his wife Olympe wrote to a friend complaining, 'We are unwell. It is from eating too much. The maestro and I live to eat.' She described herself as a 'fat woman who is occupied from morning to evening with digesting'.

Rossini's Saturday evening dinner parties were grist to the success of Parisian gossip columns, highly sought after in social and cultural circles. The table was always laden with an astonishing array of French and Italian dishes and delicacies. With these, the maestro conducted connoisseurship to extreme lengths. He would take cooked tubes of his favourite pasta, which had to come from Naples, and then use a silver syringe to stuff them with a paste of foie gras and truffles. He would pile these in a decorative pyramid on the table for guests to pick at and nibble. This was *Macaroni alla Rossini* and unsurprisingly this labour-intensive dish never really achieved the popularity of *Tournedos alla Rossini,* which today is more often topped with chicken liver pâté and served on toast.

Rossini was a leap-year baby, born in Pesaro on the 29th February 1792, and died in Paris on 13th November 1868. Until his retirement in 1829, he had been the most popular opera composer in history. His best-known operas include the Italian comedies *Il barbiere di Siviglia* (The Barber of Seville) and *La cenerentola* (Cinderella); and his best known French-language epics include *Le Comte Ory* and *Guillaume Tell* (William Tell). Their inspired melodies led to him being dubbed 'The Italian Mozart'.

We first went to Pesaro for its summer opera festival in 2011 expecting great music and great food. We weren't disappointed with either.

Geographically the Adriatic resort of Pesaro is practically perfect. Its beachfront location adds to the beauty of its ancient and traffic-free centre and backdrop of undulating hills. For five months of the year, tens of thousands of Italians come here to soak up the sun. They don bikinis and Speedos and pack themselves in neat lines on the sandy beaches under row upon row of brightly coloured sunshades.

These thousands of beach umbrellas are matched by as many bicycles, the preferred method of transport for young and old in Pesaro's flat streets, where high-rise concrete hotels sit cheek by jowl with 19th-century villas in the tree-lined beachside roads.

In the old town there's an imposing crenellated Ducal Palace. This was built at the end of the 15th century and still dominates the central piazza. Close by, the *duomo* features 6th-century mosaics that can be admired through glass panels set in a suspended modern floor. This vast work of art belongs to the same period as the magnificent Byzantine mosaics at Ravenna. In some places you can also glimpse an even earlier and deeper-set mosaic floor dating from as early as the 4th century.

The museum opposite is home to a fine collection of local majolica plates, pots and dishes, and excellent paintings including Bellini's immense 1474 altarpiece, *Pala di Pesaro,* the central panel of which depicts the Virgin being crowned on earth rather than heaven. She sits on a marble throne, except the back is a window through which you see a rocky landscape thus, unusually, creating a picture within a picture.

During the summer festival, extracts from Rossini operas are played over loudspeakers throughout the town – an unnecessary reminder that the composer was a local that possibly puts off as many as it amuses.

Proper opera performances are given in Teatro Rossini and at the Adriatic Arena, a vast and ugly, domed, out-of-town building constructed over 20 years ago. The quality of production at both venues can be world-class because, despite its many failings, the size of the Adriatic Arena encourages innovative productions. In 2011 Britain's Graham Vick directed Rossini's *Mosè in Egitto* (Moses in Egypt), an opera loosely based on the story of the exodus of the Israelites from Egypt led by Moses.

Ever controversial, Vick set the opera in a war-torn, modern-day city somewhere in the Middle East, complete with a wrecked palace and theatre, a makeshift synagogue and a terrorist hideaway. The orchestra was uncomfortably seated in the middle of this chaos.

In Act One bloodied chorus members wandered at random through the auditorium and later gun-toting terrorists ran up and down the aisles, for the Jews and their leader were presented as a terrorist group fighting Egypt's Pharaoh Rameses for their freedom. Both auditorium happenings seriously upset a lot of people. The man sitting on my left was one of these. At the end of the performance he stood and booed loudly, and then turned to me to say that for Vick to portray Moses as a Bin Laden-type leader was a mortal sin.

I thought it was superbly sung and an inspired production that perfectly reflected things we had seen during the previous year on trips to Israel and Libya. I smiled and got out as quickly as I could.

At the very least, Vick's production was a thought-provoking contrast to the traditional staging of Rossini's opera *Adelaide di Borgogna* (Adelaide of Burgundy) that we had seen the previous night at Teatro Rossini. And to me, the best of any type of art should make you think, rather than merely entertain.

THE TUSCAN GENIUS

Rossini remains one of Italy's favourite opera composers, but in the late 19th and early 20th centuries he was eclipsed by the extraordinary popularity of Giacomo Puccini. Living in our Tuscan farmhouse meant that, after years of enjoying Puccini's operas at the Coliseum and Covent Garden in London, we could at last make leisurely pilgrimages to Lucca where the composer was born, and to Torre del Lago where he made his bohemian home.

Lucca is a small, elegant Tuscan town with a self-contained historic centre and wealth based largely on its paper, marine, mechanical engineering, chemical and pharmaceutical industries, as well as the production of wonderful olive oil. It is quiet without being dull, and its appeal is further enhanced by the four kilometres of ancient, preserved ramparts that surround the town. These are surmounted by broad, tree-lined avenues that offer enjoyable walking and cycling.

On my first visit to the town, I checked into a small albergo near Puccini's birthplace and went straightaway to rent a bike, the most popular transport of those who live within the town's walls, *Lucca dentro.*

It is impossible to explore Lucca's flat streets and squares without encountering images of the hooded eyes, neat moustache and ever-present cigar of the town's most celebrated son. I rode over cobbled and paved streets, looked into the walled gardens of many *palazzi,* and browsed shops with fronts that hadn't changed since Puccini's youth. Café Simo was a favourite haunt of the composer. I downed a refreshing glass of beer there, regretting that Italy's whole-hearted ban on smoking in public places meant I couldn't light up one of Puccini's favourite treats – a cigar rolled from Tuscan-grown tobacco.

Giacomo Puccini was born in 1858 into a musical family in an apartment which can be reached from Corte San Lorenzo off Via di Poggio. Here it's easy to picture his early life studying and playing music with his uncle and friends. In its rooms you can view some of his early compositions, letters, family portraits and, if no-one is looking, you might touch the Steinway piano on which he composed *Turandot.* Just a stroll away is the church of San Michele, where Puccini played the organ from 14 years old.

It is a short drive from Lucca to the Mediterranean coast and Torre del Lago, the town on the edge of a lagoon that Puccini thought was paradise when he first saw it in 1891. Simonetta Puccini is the composer's granddaughter and lovingly runs Museo Villa Puccini, a museum in the waterside villa where her grandfather lived until 1921. He settled here in 1896 after he was made rich by the success of *Manon Lescaut* (1893) and *La bohème* (1896). The villa was originally a guard house on an archduke's estate, but Puccini completely rebuilt it and installed every modern convenience, including central heating and the telephone. With his ideal home complete, he could now afford to indulge his penchant for fast cars and motor boats. And to perfect his prowess as a hunter of wild fowl and attractive women.

Simonetta told me about her grandfather's stormy relationship with Elvira Gemignani, the most famous of his many outrageous romances. 'It was an extraordinary scandal at the time since she was a married woman who decided to elope with my grandfather. This really upset many of his fans and it seems the affair became a topic of conversation with just about everyone in Italy.

'Elvira bore him a son, my father Tonio, 18 years before she and Giacomo were married. There are many rumours about her being dull and passive, and that she may have limited grandfather intellectually and emotionally. Some say that, somehow, her influence discouraged him from making close friendships. I am not sure.'

Whatever his personal situation, I can't think it affected his talent for dramatising intense human-interest stories about doomed heroines with sweeping, memorable melody. These are years that supported the composition of *Tosca* (1900), *Madama Butterfly* (1904), and then *La fanciulla del west* (The Girl of the Golden West, 1910), *La rondine* (The Swallow, 1917) and the famed trio of one-act operas that includes *Gianni Schicchi,* which premiered at the Metropolitan New York in 1918. Not a bad output for a man said to be inhibited artistically by his wife.

Tosca is by far my favourite and was Puccini's first foray into *verismo*, the realistic depiction of everyday life in an opera. In 2009 I timed my first visit to Torre del Lago to coincide with a staging of *Tosca* at the 3,370-seat open-air theatre beside the lake that had been opened the previous year.

Sadly this unattractive structure appears to have been designed without giving thought to the setting or the acoustics, and by a committee more interested in making a statement with concrete and new wood. The stage masks any views of the lake and the sound is flat, actually fading away if you are more than 20 rows back in the raked auditorium, even on a still summer night. Simonetta Puccini told me she knows her grandfather never wanted his operas performed by the lake even though many others claim these performances are 'correct'.

The young daughter of a relative I took to see *Tosca* was a newcomer to opera, but came away feeling that Puccini really understood women. She was very taken with Floria Tosca's valiant struggle to save her revolutionary lover, and with her melodramatic leap to death from the top of the Castel Sant'Angelo in Rome.

When we left the theatre we walked back into town via Villa Puccini and talked about the scandals that surrounded the place at the beginning of the last century, and that still continue to this day.

Elvira Puccini was aware that her husband was often attracted to pretty women. She thought one of these was a young maid at Villa Puccini, whom she unmercifully hounded and accused of having an affair with her husband. The girl committed suicide and Elvira was jailed for five months for slander. Elvira and Giacomo separated and then reconciled, but their relationship was forever damaged.

In 1980 Simonetta proved in court that she was the illegitimate daughter of Antonio, the son of Giacomo and Elvira Puccini, who died in 1946 without a legitimate heir. She changed her surname to Puccini, took possession of the Torre del Lago villa and obtained a decree freezing the Puccini family's assets, so that no-one could siphon off, or illegally claim possession of, anything she now legally owned.

Many other stories exist about Puccini's affairs and more continue to surface. As recently as 2008 a local woman named Nadia Manfredi claimed that her grandmother had an affair with Giacomo, which produced an illegitimate son also called Antonio and that, as this Antonio was her father, she was the rightful heir to the composer's estate. Her grandmother was Giulia Manfredi, who worked in a bar opposite Villa Puccini and whom Elvira Puccini accused of being the go-between for Puccini and Doria, the maid driven to suicide but who was found after her death to be a virgin. What a subject for a Puccini opera . . .

Photos of Nadia's father were produced in court to show he bore a striking resemblance to Puccini and a request was made to compare his DNA with that of Puccini. In the event, a statute of limitation law covering paternity cases was cited and Nadia Manfredi's claim was dismissed. Rumours still circulate about other families waiting in the wings to claim some or all of Puccini's estate from Simonetta Puccini.

Critics have dismissed Puccini's work as overly impassioned, melodramatic and sentimental. Maybe it is, but is that a bad thing? Such critics are usually men and I think Puccini's genius lay in understanding feminine psychology, and converting their passions into music that perfectly illustrate these. I love his music being so emotional, so difficult to dislike or ignore. Yet, many critics seem to keep themselves in print by waspishly saying they are untouched by Puccini's great, hummable themes. I think they are frightened of facing true emotion, especially when accompanied and strengthened by music. As well as wilfully forbidding themselves to enjoy Puccini, I think they display their fear or misunderstanding of women in dramatic situations and its relevance to their lives.

Let those critics prefer Wagner with his gods and goddesses and Valkyries, I say, perhaps because they know they won't be confronted by the love problems of large women with horned helmets in everyday life.

What they don't realise is that all around them are real women and many men who understand that what happens in Puccini's operas could happen to them. Perhaps it already has. And the power of Puccini's music makes it as real as the real thing.

Jazz Legends and our Local Star

While the 1904 première of *Madama Butterfly* took place at La Scala in Milan, another audience at the nearby Eden Theatre was being introduced to jazz – a new music form from across the Atlantic performed by a group of Creole singers and dancers billed as the 'creators of the cakewalk'.

Italians currently view jazz with the same passionate seriousness they do their classical and operatic music heritage. The jazz being created here is among the most exciting and forward-thinking in the world. Although its roots were in the American jazz brought to Italy by the greatest 20th-century bands and soloists, Italian jazz has had a distinctive voice since about the 1960s, when it began to look into its own musical heritage for inspiration. There is no better place to appreciate this than at the Umbria Jazz Festival, which is held every summer in Perugia.

Perugia is the medieval capital of Umbria, our neighbouring region, and occupies a commanding hill high above the River Tiber. It's not just a magnificent *città d'arte* but one of the most vibrant, cosmopolitan university cities in Italy. And for nearly 40 years it has drawn thousands of music lovers of all ages and from all over the world, to hear and play all styles of jazz. Typically over 250 events take place in just ten days and much of the music is free.

The first time I drove to Perugia for its jazz festival, I parked in the Viale Pellini car park and then took the escalators and steep paths up to Corso Vannucci, the city's elegant main street. I had arrived in time for lunch and made for the Bottega del Vino, the suggestion of Aldo who teaches Italian to Val. I was greeted by the sounds of legendary Italian pianist Renato Sellani, then well into his 80s, soothing the audience into an early siesta with his original interpretations of jazz standards.

Instead of staying, I indulged myself in the visual treats of Perugino and Pinturicchio, whose ravishing paintings hang in the cool rooms of the ancient palace that houses the National Gallery of Umbria. By its door, a guitar and keyboard combo swung through the long, hot afternoon, drifting into the galleries and making a curious, uplifting accompaniment to the Renaissance paintings, especially the eight small panels of charming, imaginary town settings that the two painters worked on when young.

I spent longer than I thought in the gallery. A *custode* interrupted my concentration and in a whisper politely advised me that it was about to close. I went out into the warm air as the afternoon turned into early evening, that special Italian time when everyone interesting swaggers up and down streets during the ritual *passeggiata*. A couple of hippies were playing recorders opposite the palace, and further down the *corso* a Latin-American trio played salsa. Outside a shoe shop, a tattooed young man took out a clarinet from its case and asked if he could join in with a sax player and a Rasta playing bongos.

On Piazza IV Novembre, I joined an enthusiastic crowd listening to the rhythm and blues of King Pleasure & The Biscuit Boys from England. In the Giardini Carducci, I caught a Dixieland band with its Italian trumpet-playing leader, Guido Pistocchi, doing a credible impression of Louis Armstrong.

If I'd wanted to, I could have listened to free jazz day and night while mooching about Perugia's streets. But I was here to see my hero Stefano Bollani in person and hadn't minded how much I paid. I was introduced to Italian jazz through hearing Bollani on RAI Tre. I loved listening to his melodic creations and now I was going to see him live.

The 5,000-seater Santa Giuliana Arena was full to capacity that night, and I can rarely remember being so impatient and anxious for the music to begin. There was to be an extraordinary melding of jazz talents, with Stefano Bollani on one piano and the legendary American pianist Chick Corea on another. Both embrace the roots and traditions of jazz, yet refuse to be shackled. A love of Latin melodies is also common ground, but perhaps what binds them most are their boundless curiosity and an inherent desire to be at play. The concert was an extraordinary melding of crisp phrasing, elegant harmonies, and overall rhythmic ingenuity which made for compelling dialogues, some of which fused into lyrical monologues. The sensation throughout was of two kids, for the most part happy to share the same toy.

I stumbled out of the stadium drunk on jazz. It was way past midnight by the time I returned to the still-crowded streets around Corso Vannucci, where appreciative music fans continued to enjoy impromptu music while eating pizza and drinking beer. There I got into conversation with an alto sax player who had just been blowing his heart out at Rocca Paolina, the small Cannon Room of a half-ruined 16th-century fortress, one of the festival's many small and intimate venues. He advised me to check-out the performances the next night at the 18th-century opera house, Teatro Morlacchi, where I was sure to meet Carlo Pagnotta, the founder of the festival. I did, and I did.

Now in his 80s, tanned, fit, bright-eyed, with only a hint of too many late nights spent in smoky jazz clubs, Pagnotta told me about his life-long passion for jazz.

'My father was a famous restaurateur in the 1930s, with a place called Trasimeno, but as a young man my loves were jazz and clothes. I cut a dash by wearing classic British menswear at a time when such a thing was a rarity in Perugia,' Pagnotta recalled in his distinctive local accent peppered with Tuscan, Le Marche and Lazio elements. 'Perhaps not surprisingly I went into business running a high-end clothes shop specialising in well-tailored menswear in fine fabrics. I called it "Sir Charles" for reasons I have long forgotten, but I am pleased to say that it was a great success and provided me with the income I needed to indulge in my main passion – jazz.'

He told me that in the 1950s a small group would meet at Ceccherini's music shop on Piazza della Repubblica to discuss, but mainly argue about, traditional versus modern jazz, hot jazz against cool jazz, and their frustrations about there being no place to hear live jazz in Perugia.

'So it was that I started stopping friends and acquaintances on the streets, asking them for 1,000 lira and making them founder members of Hot Club Perugia. I did the same with customers at my father's restaurant, much to his annoyance. The club got itself a decent piano and then we set about finding sponsors for gigs. It wasn't easy, but in 1955 we somehow managed to persuade Louis Armstrong to come and play in Perugia, at Teatro Morlacchi. The next year we got Chet Baker. I still can't believe it.'

At the end of the 1950s Pagnotta spent time in London and Hot Club Perugia faltered, but upon his return to the city in 1960 he helped start Jazz Club Perugia. This soon had 300 members and the support of the town's *commune,* its council, which gave it the confidence to put on concerts again at Teatro Morlacchi. Soon Stan Getz, Dizzy Gillespie, Dexter Gordon and Teddy Wilson had all appeared.

In August 1973 the first Perugia Jazz Festival was held with Carlo Pagnotta as artistic director, a post he has held ever since.

Over 100,000 people attend the Umbrian Jazz Festival each year, but not everyone agrees that it is going in the right direction. In recent years jazz purists have been hyper-critical of the inclusion of such pop legends as Elton John and Simply Red, and I have every sympathy with that view.

Italy's pop music scene is something of a mystery to me. Our local MTV generation has tried to educate me about the delights of La Fossa, the Sardinian gangster rap crew. I've also listened carefully to such established rock bands as Litfiba from Florence and to chart-toppers like the Italian X-Factor winner Francesca Michielin. Yet I've discovered I don't even need to listen to this music to be admired and envied by its proponents.

Jovanotti is a widely popular singer, mixing elements of dance music with Italian pop and rap. The moment I say I come from Cortona, Jovanotti's home town, I have as many fans as he has.

Lorenzo Cherubini, to give him his real and rather fabulous name, was born in 1966. His early successes were based upon a mix of hip hop, rap and disco. He then departed into funk, world music, and even classical arrangements and Jamaican ska influences. As Jovanotti's musical influences changed so, too, did his lyrics and over time these have addressed more and more philosophical, religious and political issues in the tradition of the Italian *cantautore* singer and songwriter.

To the delight of the Cortonese, he married Francesca Valiani, the mother of his daughter, in the town's Church of Santa Maria Nuova in September 2008. Major and minor stars from the world of music, television and film turned up and provided good photo opportunities for the *paparazzi*. Next day, whilst national papers carried show-business wedding snaps, our local papers focused on what the guests ate.

This was of great importance to us. Jovanotti is a vegetarian and yet he was partying big time in the Val di Chiana, home to Italy's best beef from massive Chianina cattle. Direct descendants of the pale-skinned draft oxen that were once such a potent symbol of rural Tuscany, the best of them can put on 2kg of prime meat a day, and do this for many weeks.

The local press was polite and quizzical rather than critical, and obliged those of us who were not invited by printing every detail of every veggie dish, and publishing in-depth interviews with those entrusted with preparing the wedding banquet.

I realised yet again that, though Italians love their musicians and composers, there is no love more great than their love of food, especially here in Tuscany.

FIVE

Tasteful Touring
&
Great Escapes

A Food Lover's Paradise

Nothing prepared me for my first sight of one of the least known and most naturally beautiful landscapes in Europe. The Piana di Castelluccio is a lonely, upland plain surrounded by mountains, seemingly a world of its own, hiding close to where Umbria meets Le Marche on the Monti Sibillini.

This remarkable 16km square basin was once an ancient glacial lake. Its fullest beauty erupts in late spring when wild daffodils, violets, buttercups, cloves, shamrocks and dwarf gentians bloom into swathes of colour that reach their peak in June. I first discovered the plain in late summer when it was velvety green and criss-crossed by a handful of tiny streams. This lush carpet was thrown into sharp focus by the baldness of the mountains that surround it, and by the shadows of fast-moving clouds in late afternoon sun. On a small hill in the distance was the tiny village of Castelluccio, home to the world's finest lentils.

I took the one straight road that traverses the plain to reach the pale, greeny-blue fields of lentils that surround the village. Half-way across I drove past a rustic stable and corrals with horses to rent, and suddenly understood why Spaghetti Westerns might not be such a stretch of the imagination as I once thought.

Castelluccio was a town of 700 inhabitants in the 1950s, but today has a permanent population of just 40. Winters are so bad that the village is often cut off from the rest of the world for weeks on end. The lentils grown in summer become the staff of life in winter. They've always been grown here organically, using a system of crop rotation that eliminates the need for fertilisers. I had just missed the August harvest, but hoped I might see some of the hand-sorting of the pulses to remove any broken lentils.

Castelluccio lentils are notably fragrant and very small, about 2mm across, and are the seed of an equally small plant with a pale-blue flower. They are sweeter and more fully flavoured than others, need no pre-soaking, and keep their shape while cooking. Best of all to my mind, they do not have the papery skins of other continental lentils that stick so irritatingly between your teeth.

They make wonderful soups, and stewed Castelluccio lentils with pancetta, sage and onion are the ideal accompaniment to many different types of meat and sausages, especially the glutinous *cotechino* sausage eaten in Italy during winter and at New Year. There is an old wives' tale in these parts that says each lentil you eat on New Year's Eve represents a coin in your pocket and thus good fortune in the coming year, and so the challenge is to eat as many lentils as possible.

Still thinking of accompaniments to lentils, I headed down from the Piana de Castelluccio to Norcia.

Norcia sits in a fertile basin with hills on all sides. Unusually for this part of Italy, it is built on a single, straight and flat high street, Corso Sertorio, and none of its buildings is more than two-storeys high. This means that wherever you look you see sky and the surrounding hills. Once again I was somewhere that could have doubled as the set for a gritty cowboy Western.

Whereas Parma has just its ham and Parmesan cheese, Norcia embraces everything when it comes to food and all of it is very special, even by Italian standards.

This ancient walled town, mentioned by Virgil, is little known to outsiders but to the *buon gustaio,* or gourmet, it is a haven of everything delicious, rare and wonderful. The shoppers you see may have come from as far as Rome to stock their larders with truffles, lentils, cheese, olive oil and all manner of pork products. My first stop, before trying and buying, was the charming Piazza San Benedetto in the centre. Here two statues of friendly looking lions, with the biggest grins you have ever seen, flank the steps up to the 16th-century portal of the small but beautifully proportioned Palazzo Comunale town hall. Nestling next to it, is the fine 14th-century façade of the Basilica of San Benedetto, dedicated to Saint Benedict because the man who was to become the father of Western monasticism was born here in 480. To the right of this church and under a portico is a line of different-sized stone basins built into the wall at waist-height that were used in ancient times as measures for grain, something I had never seen before in Italy. On the opposite side of the square is a handsome fortified palace from the mid-1500s.

These architectural pleasures alone are worth a visit to Norcia, but the newer parts of the town are even more so if you are a location manager looking for a place to film romantic scenes for a Spaghetti Western – or perhaps more accurately a *Stringozzi* Western, honouring the local shoelace pasta.

The number of *salumerie,* delicatessens, in Norcia specialising in pork products is staggering, some smart and modern, others wonderfully antiquated. Most have a boar's head mounted above their doors. Many even have whole stuffed boars in front of their shops which made me aware of just how big, muscular and intimidating these potentially dangerous but delicious animals can be. Barrels of lentils and other pulses crowd the entrances, while inside you are engulfed by a huge array of salami, sausages and hams that hang from the ceilings exuding smoky, spicy, piggy aromas. Their counters groan with haunches of cured wild boar waiting to be carved, the skin often still covered in tufts of black hair.

Here, the craft of the *norcino,* pork butcher, is at its best. A traditional producer will use only the meat of Umbrian black pigs which are particularly tasty, a result of the way the animals live in the mountains, feeding on wild herbs and plants, perhaps even on truffles.

I could have spent a fortune with favourite products I knew from the Ansuini brothers' salumeria in Via Anicia and Norcineria Felici in the main corso, but decided to stick to local specialities and those that I had not tried before. I contemplated, but left to another time, *coppa di testa,* a type of pig's brawn flavoured with lemon and orange peel. I also passed on nuggets of salami known as *coglioni di mulo,* or mules' balls, on wild boar sausages and the 'hybrid' salami made from wild boar and domestic pig. I had particular trouble not buying *salame Toscano,* also called *finocchiona,* flavoured with garlic and lots of wild fennel. *Capocollo,* a cured meat made from the upper part of the pig's neck and part of the shoulder, was also difficult to ignore.

Instead of these favourites I took home some carefully cut slices of *prosciutto di Norcia,* an air-dried ham that is savoury but not salty in smell or taste and with a unique nutty flavour, that is specially delicious with summer's figs. I also bought *lonzo,* salted and air-dried salami made from the leg muscle of pigs unique to Umbria and Le Marche. I couldn't resist big, fat, fresh pork sausages because I knew we had the perfect potatoes for mash in our vegetable garden. I also succumbed to a very dense salami that was new to me which had been pressed between boards into what looked like a small, leather-covered flask. Then there was my first taste of *guanciale,* cured pigs' cheek, that gives another sort of bacon and what we Brits once knew as Bath Chaps. Once started, I couldn't stop and to my haul of pork products I added a selection of cheeses from Castelluccio – ah yes, the cheeses. In Norcia this largely means types and ages of pecorino sheep-milk cheeses. We've always liked those with black peppercorns, but today they even come flavoured with truffles which seems a very happy combination, even if the flavour isn't always from truffles but from man-made flavourings that emulate their aromas.

From Castelluccio come hand-made, cone-shaped mounds of salted and bran-dusted ricotta cheeses. Ricotta means re-cooked and it is properly made by boiling up the whey from cheese making. The remaining protein flocculates into clouds of ricotta that contain almost no fat, but which are naturally sweet. Well, that's how it should be, but these days whole milk is boiled up with the whey and so a traditional low-fat cheese has now joined the mainstream of cholesterol busters.

Norcia's knowledgeable shop assistants are always keen that you try the distinctive flavours and textures of their cheeses and of their cured pork meats in all their manifestations. But, sadly, they stay clear of offering shavings of truffle, the black diamonds that make Norcia and the region home to 60 per cent of the annual world harvest of black truffle, *tuber melanosporum,* which is identical to the better-known French black truffles from the Périgord.

The truffle season is mid-September to January for white truffles, December to early summer for black. Thus, for most of the year, every food shop has baskets brimming with aromatic whole truffles and wild mushrooms. Throughout the year, the shelves of every food shop are stacked with truffles in jars, truffle pastes, truffle oils, truffle-flavoured cheese, truffle-flavoured pasta and other unusual and often bizarre truffle-scented food and drink creations. Truffle honey is guaranteed to get the most difficult breakfast table chattering.

After a quick stop for a taste of the local chocolate at the factory of Vetusta Nursia just outside Norcia, I left this secret part of Italy with my mind fighting between enjoying breath-taking images of landscape and thoughts of exactly what Val and I would eat with what back at home in the kitchen of Casa Amari.

Meanwhile I headed through the Monti Sibillini National Park for Le Marche and the olive groves of its most beautiful town, Ascoli Piceno.

Stuffed Olives and an Excellent Agriturismo

Landscape can be both dramatic and magical at the same time, and it's both these on the Piano Grande above Norcia at the edge of Umbria. Across the border in Le Marche it still pleases but is more akin to a patchwork quilt thrown over a lumpy mattress. Mountains cover about a third of the region leaving the other two-thirds to lower, softer hills that are dotted with hundreds of small farms, tiny hilltop towns and woodland. These stop at the region's sandy, 180km-long shoreline and the waters of the Adriatic Sea, which sadly are often neither clean nor clear.

Ascoli Piceno is in the extreme south of Le Marche and it was here that I planned to see the town, stay with the Cicchi family, and to meet Signor Migliori, the best olive stuffer in the region.

The olive tree, *Olea europaea sativa,* came from Greece to Italy in c. 600BC and grows everywhere in the country, apart from in Lombardy and Piedmont where the temperatures are inclined to be too cold for successful cultivation. They are one of the glories of Italy, creating delicate green and silver tapestries throughout the landscape that shimmer and quiver at the slightest disturbance by wind. Benozzo Gozzoli reveals in his magnificent frescoes in Palazzo Medici-Riccardi in Florence that the ethereal silver-green of the undersides of their elegant oval leaves can make even the most distant olive trees appear to flicker with light.

The shapes and contours of the olive tree created much of Italy's landscapes, and have always given a sense of place and continuity to scenes of everyday life. But don't be fooled. These serene images belie the hard work and considerable skills involved in maintaining the land upon which they grow, and the pruning, harvesting and processing of their bounty. The results of all this effort are the fruit and oil that, along with bread and wine, are the bedrock of Italian cuisine, of life itself.

It was my increasing interest in the kinds and sizes of olives grown throughout Italy that brought me to Ascoli Piceno. This is where Italians say the largest, sweetest and brightest green olives are grown, and the flesh of the local variety represents nearly 90 per cent of the fruit.

Olive trees crowd the countryside around Ascoli Piceno, a small beguiling town of magical beauty. Piazza del Popolo, the traffic-free, travertine-paved main square, is a beautifully proportioned outdoor meeting place that must be the most elegant provincial square in all Italy. The harmonious arches of its arcades bustle with shoppers, while children ride bikes and play football on its shiny paving. The town people use the square the way we use our terrace, as an extension to their houses. To one side stands the Palazzo del Popolo, a splendid 13th-century building guarded by a monumental statue of the Farnese Pope Paul III. This was the pope who asked Michelangelo to relocate the ancient bronze of the Emperor Marcus Aurelius to Rome's Capitoline Hill, and who later appointed him to take over the supervision of the building of St Peter's Basilica.

Piazza Arringo is the town's other main square and is almost as impressive as its big sister. This was once the place to harangue officials at public meetings, hence the name *arringo,* and in Roman times it was the site of a forum. It is flanked by Ascoli's town hall and by its 15th-century, rectangular travertine-marble duomo, home to one of the best paintings by Carlo Crivelli, the 16th-century Venetian-born painter who lived in Le Marche and died in Ascoli Piceno.

Carlo Crivelli's paintings are unmistakable for their delicate colours and accurate design. They are particularly noted for their abundant use of fruit and vegetables, and for the obvious care with which he depicted his subjects. I challenge anyone not to marvel at the slender, tapering fingers of his saints and not to be astonished by the fruit and vegetables in his polyptych of St Emygdius in the duomo. Crivelli makes the peaches, pears, apples and cucumbers that feature so realistic, so modern, so ready for picking and eating that I always find myself considering how I'd use them, rather than reflecting upon their symbolic meanings as I am sure the artist intended I should do.

At the other end of Piazza Arringo from the duomo is Signor Migliori's food shop and restaurant where I had been promised a lesson in how to make *olive ascolana,* the town's speciality of deep-fried stuffed olives.

When I joined Signor Migliori at a table outside he was surrounded by bowls that contained large olives, minced pork and beef, grated parmigiano-reggiano, eggs, flour, dried breadcrumbs and a nutmeg.

'Le Marche is Italy's third largest olive-producing region,' he explained 'and the large size and sweetness of our olives cannot be equalled. Only the large, fragrant and crunchy fruit of the local Ascolana tenera variety can be used for proper stuffed olives.'

I watched carefully and silently as he took a small, sharp knife and deftly cut away the flesh of a fat olive in a spiral, and then removed a completely clean stone. I tried the same operation only to end up with a pile of useless olive mush.

Over the next five minutes, another dozen olives were deftly dismembered by Signor Migliori and then he wrapped each of the green spirals around a walnut-sized stuffing of pork and beef. Next he lightly coated the stuffed olive flesh with flour, rolled them quickly in beaten egg and then breadcrumbs before throwing the still green balls into a pan of boiling olive oil.

In the same time it took to open a bottle of prosecco and to pour out a couple of glasses, the hot *olive ascolona* were ready to eat, fresh tasting on the outside with a rich soft centre, crisp, succulent and exceptionally delicious.

'Apparently they first appeared on dinner plates some 200 years ago,' Signor Migliori told me, 'so we like to think of them as very Baroque. One theory is that they represent the union between the daughter of an olive grower and the son of a butcher, but who knows?'

I stayed the night in Ascoli with the Cicchi family at their charming *agriturismo*, Villa Cicchi. In Italy the word *agriturismo* is a legally recognised term for a farm that takes paying guests, and for many years it was one of the country's best-kept accommodation secrets. In a typical *agriturismo,* your room is invariably in the farmhouse and often the owners will serve meals based upon their home-grown and local produce. Despite the rural nature of the lodging, one might expect a rustic experience, yet many *agriturismi* feature rather luxurious accommodation as well as swimming pools.

The Cicchi family's house is a large, rambling affair with a chapel and considerable terraced gardens planted with vegetables, vines, olive trees of course, and here they also breed rabbits, chickens and pheasants for the table. The house was probably once a series of 18th-century buildings that had been knocked together over the centuries.

'It was in a poor state of repair until my late father started restoring some of the rooms, something me and my sister and our husbands are still doing with my mother,' Elena Cicchi told me.

The decoration in the rooms I saw was certainly stylish and emulated the late 18th century with frescoed ceilings, colour-washed walls in rich ochre and greens, much worn terracotta floors and antique farmhouse furniture. It created an atmosphere of faded glory, and the daughters, their mother and grandmother tackled the task of running the place and serving exceptional food with great gusto.

Before I sat down to dinner, Elena brought me a plate piled high with the villa's own large, bright-green olives and joined me in a glass of local, clear, straw-yellow-coloured Falerio dei Colli Ascolani wine. She needed little more than a sip or two and the certainty of my impatient ear to tell me what I wanted to know.

'Olives can be picked unripe, green in summer, or during the winter when they are ripe, black, and more oily. Some varieties are more suitable for one, some for the other. The challenge is to convert the hard, bitter fruit into something edible by curing then storing them in oil or various kinds of pickle, whole, stoned or stuffed. Different techniques are used for different olives. In Calabria they use simple soaking and mild salting. For these,' she said pointing at the olives on the table, 'we cure them for ten days in a light brine of water and sea salt, and sometimes add fennel that imparts a mild, delicate flavour.'

And then came dinner. Within a few minutes three different pasta dishes, one a penne with zucchini, another orecchiette with peppery *broccoletti,* the other fettuccine with *porcini* were brought to my table, not just by Elena but by her sister and grandmother, too. I was sternly told, 'You don't choose which one because we expect you to eat all three.' This was followed by succulent roast pork cooked in the kitchen's wood oven, accompanied by a selection of vegetables that minutes before were still in the soil of the garden. Fried in the villa's olive oil, they were served fresh and hot and melted in my mouth.

Even the dessert had its feet planted firmly in Villa Cecchi. *Ciambellone di mosto* is a cake made with must, the liquid from pressed grapes that are still in contact with the juice but before fermentation begins. And this was followed by a delicious, unexpected invitation to join the family upstairs to hear a local chamber music ensemble play one of Rossini's lesser-known compositions, an arrangement of his Sonata Number Four for flute, violin, viola and cello. 'My husband was a great supporter of classical music in the area,' Signora Cicchi told me, 'and we girls have carried on the tradition.'

Later, we talked about the Rossini Festival in Pesaro and the controversial production of *Mosè in Egitto* that I had seen there. 'Did you know that Rossini's favourite cellist was a Vitali, a son of one of our local noble families?' she asked. 'He remained a cherished friend all of his life and supplied Rossini with barrels of our local olives that the maestro claimed were the best in all of Europe.'

I went to bed very full and lay thinking about how much Rossini would have applauded the Villa Cicchi's generous sharing and enjoyment of food and music. And how the happy combination made me feel I had truly shared a little of life as lived by true Italians.

If all *agriturismi* experiences are as grounding and gratifying as this, Italy is in line for another Renaissance.

TOOTS AND SCARFACE

Drive a short distance south from Ascoli Piceno and you are soon in a land of mountains: the region of Abruzzo and its smaller neighbour Molise. The first time I was here was to meet 'Toots', a retired British army officer who was returning to its highest peaks for the first time in 65 years.

Toots Williams, Captain (subsequently Colonel) George Torquil Gage Williams of the Duke of Cornwall's Light Infantry, had been captured by the Italians in North Africa during the Second World War. Along with thousands of other Allied prisoners, he was herded from prison to prison on mainland Italy until he was finally settled in a 500-man prisoner-of-war camp at Fontanellato, between Parma and Piacenza.

That was the spring of 1943 when everything changed in Italy. Toots was one of the first British officers to escape from an Italian POW camp at the time of the Italian Armistice and to get safely back to Britain. He had done so by walking nearly 1,000km in 35 days from Parma in the north of Italy to Casacalenda, near the toe of the country.

Now aged 90 in 2010, Toots had returned to retrace parts of his escape route. And I had been invited to join him as he told me his extraordinary tale.

We met near L'Aquila, the capital of Abruzzo, the town that suffered the country's worst earthquake in nearly three decades in 2009. Over dinner he explained how he came to escape. 'At about eight in the evening on Wednesday 8th September 1943, the villagers in Fontanellato took to the streets celebrating the announcement made by King Victor Emmanuel on the radio that he had signed an armistice with the Allies. Italy had changed sides and Italians saw this as a sign the war was over. Nothing could have been further from the truth.

'Yet, by morning next day most of our Italian guards had disappeared, many heading home to fight the Nazis as partisans. We expected Jerry to arrive any minute to take over the camp, and so hundreds of us slipped out unchallenged and managed to get seven miles away by night, and then hid by an embankment in the countryside. The next day we decided to split up and make for home in different directions.

'I decided to set off south with two friends. We reckoned that part of the country was where the Allies would land and one of us had a compass. We walked close to hedges all day until we came across a hayloft near Fidenza sometime after midnight. We chanced our luck and slept there for the night.

'Next morning we were spotted by the French-speaking owner. He was obviously sympathetic, welcomed us into his home and gave us a very useful touring map of Italy. He let us listen to the BBC news on his radio, and we heard that troops had just landed at Salerno, south of Naples. We knew then that we were going in the right direction and perhaps stood a chance of meeting up with the advancing Allied armies.'

For the next 23 days the three soldiers walked through the countryside and by keeping landmarks such as the River Tiber in sight, scrambling through woods and keeping close to hedgerows, they managed to avoid the Germans. At night they usually bedded down in farm barns, always hopeful that the farmer would be friendly.

On the 26th day they started to climb the heights of the Gran Sasso, the highest mountain in the Apennines with a grand hotel high on its slopes. This mountain was to become the focal point of the short journey I was sharing with Toots.

The next morning we, too, headed for the Campo Imperatore, the Gran Sasso's skiing hotel built in the 1930s. From there we took one of the mountain roads up to where Toots and his colleagues walked on Tuesday, 5th October 1943. It was cold and desolate in the shadow of the Corno Grande. At nearly 3,000m above sea level, it's one of the highest points in the Apennines. But there the escapees had suddenly stumbled across a dozen mysteriously abandoned gliders.

Toots pointed to a piece of nearby flat land. 'That's where the gliders were and it was obvious that they had been forsaken only recently. We suspected they might be a sign of added danger for us and, as we were now desperately hungry, we hurried down a path to the little town of Assergi. Here we heard that we had just missed Mussolini being snatched from the hotel in what turned out to be one of the war's most daring and least-known great escapes.'

I had a vague memory of this story, but hearing it from a man who had been there at the time made it much more real and astonishing.

Towards the end of July 1943 Benito Mussolini, the Fascist dictator of Italy, was ousted and arrested by his own countrymen. Hitler could not retaliate by invading Italy to rescue Mussolini because the country was still his ally, and its new government had immediately assured him they were loyal to his cause. Despite this assurance, Hitler surmised that the new Italian government was looking to switch sides and would then deliver the arrested dictator to the Allies as a gesture.

Otto Skorzeny was summoned to Hitler's Wolf's Lair in East Prussia where the Führer entrusted him with the task of rescuing Mussolini.

Skorzeny came from a rich Viennese family and ever since he was 20 had been nicknamed 'Scarface', earning his 'scar of honour' during his first year as a member of a duelling society. He was a very active member of the Austrian Nazi Party as the outbreak of war approached, and then quickly rose through the ranks of the much-feared SS. By 1943 he headed an exceptionally skilled, brave and ruthless commando unit, able to undertake special missions behind enemy lines.

Skorzeny went to Italy, helping the German intelligence-gathering group there as best he could. He also set about recruiting a local crack raiding party and amassing equipment and disguises for them, from guns and explosives to priests' robes and hair dye. Yet they failed to find where Mussolini was being held, and so did the bizarre collection of astrologers and psychics Hitler consulted in Berlin. They didn't even discover that Mussolini was constantly being moved by his captors. His hideout was eventually picked up by the Italian police via a random message, just as the Allies were landing in Italy.

Scarface first flew over the peaks and slopes of the Gran Sasso in a Heinkel bomber and took photos of the Hotel Campo Imperatore with the German equivalent of a basic Kodak Box Brownie camera. And then this pre-James Bond character devised a simple plan.

Twelve assault gliders, each carrying nine troops and a pilot, would be released from their towing aircraft at the rate of one a minute and would attempt to land on a tiny patch of level soil adjacent to the ski hotel. The troops would then storm the hotel, grab Mussolini before his surprised guards realised what was happening, and then fly him off the Gran Sasso in a Stork light aircraft that would be waiting on the hotel's lawn. A secondary force would simultaneously secure the cable car that ran from the hotel to the bottom of the mountain in order to cut off this escape route for Mussolini. To help fool Il Duce's guards, Scarface also kidnapped a top general in the Italian Carabinieri and forced him to fly with the mission to the Gran Sasso.

The mission was a complete success but only just. Mussolini was bundled into the small aircraft and then, at the last minute, Scarface insisted that he flew with his captive. But Scarface was tall and heavily built. The plane was now overloaded and had insufficient power to take off from the incredibly short and rocky make-shift runway. Almost at once it dived down the side of a steep mountain slope. All the pilot could do was to pull back the joystick as much as he could. The aircraft only levelled out at tree-top height in the valley beneath, and then flew on to an airport near Rome. Within days the Germans installed Mussolini as head of the new *Repubblica Sociale Italiana,* a puppet government running North and Central Italy from Salò on Lake Garda.

After the war, Toots heard why Scarface had insisted on flying in the Stork. 'He was not willing to face Hitler if the plane had crashed after take-off and killed its prime prisoner. If Mussolini was to die, he said, I would rather have died with him.' Shortly after the rescue, the press named Scarface 'the most dangerous man in Europe'.

Scarface was imprisoned by the Allies, but managed to escape in summer 1948 and fled to Paris. From there, he went to Argentina and later established a successful engineering business in Madrid, but he was still overseeing undercover Nazi organisations. His name was linked, possibly apocryphally, with a plethora of causes and many famous names. These included aiding the CIA in Egypt, being the lover of Evita Perón, and helping with Britain's Great Train Robbery in 1963. He lived in County Kildare in Ireland during the 1960s where people still remember seeing him drive across the Curragh in a white Mercedes and popping into the local post office for groceries. He died in Madrid in 1975.

After we left the Gran Sasso, I surprised Toots by booking us into the monastery Fortezza di Santo Spirito, a few kilometres south-east of L'Aquila, where they were given sugared almonds, bread, cheese, wine and two packets of jam on the 28th day of their walk to freedom. It's now a hotel and, for all the changes this meant, we slept in the same monks' cells where he had slept on straw all those years ago.

This was as far as Toots' re-creation of his journey would go this time. Next day we drove back to Casa Amari and Toots clearly remembered many of the Tuscan hideaways where the three soldiers had rested on their journey south. When we drove past Assisi it was bathed in late afternoon sunlight. Toots smiled and said it looked exactly the same as it had done 65 years earlier. So did the River Tiber and the canal near Bevagna that they had walked along before taking to the hills to the east above Trevi.

At Umbertide we stopped for coffee and he recalled the welcome they had at a house where two members of the Brufani family, Perugia's most famous hoteliers, then lived. 'They served us an exceptional dinner of onion omelette, stuffed tomatoes, fried pimentos, copious quantities of bread, cheese, fruit and nuts, excellent wine, whisky, brandy, cigarettes, and we were able to enjoy a proper wash and shave and a real bed for the night.'

As we got near to Sansepolcro he said they were invited to join a family of 12 there for 'an excellent hot Sunday lunch' to be followed by an evening meal at a large farm near Città de Castello. 'It was a good dinner with plenty of wine but a damned cold night under a leaky roof.'

That night, Toots eulogised about how they owed their lives to the kindness and spirit of disinterested sacrifice shown by farming families for week after week of their journey. Most days they were at least given bread, cheese and wine, as well as being offered haylofts and cattle sheds to sleep in. Other days they enjoyed hot meals of chicken, rabbit or pasta and the comfort of mattresses on the floor. It wasn't just farmers who helped. Carabinieri, serving or retired, assisted and so did Fascists who were anti-German.

The major danger the escapees faced was from Fascist Blackshirts, who were promised an 1,800 lire reward from the Germans for every captured prisoner of war. But everywhere they went they also created danger for those who provided food and shelter. In the eyes of the Germans, their hosts and hostesses were guilty of collaborating with the enemy and punishments were severe.

Seven days after nearly coming face-to-face with Scarface and Mussolini, Toots and his colleagues met a Canadian scout car in Casacalenda, near the northern border of Puglia, and warmly embraced freedom. They had walked nearly 1,000km – 600km as the crow flies – in 35 days. Put like that it sounds brave but simple, yet I was particularly struck by the mountain heights they had scaled during their journey, and how difficult it must have been to keep up a brisk pace each day without being spotted. Toots then travelled by air and sea for nearly three weeks and arrived back in Glasgow aboard an ex-P & O passenger liner converted to a troop ship.

Toots' stories confirmed what I know from our time living in the Italian countryside. First, that Italy's farmers are invariably hospitable and welcoming to foreigners, especially the British. And second, it's astonishing what can be achieved if you have the simple pleasures of good bread, cheese, wine and olive oil.

SIX

Godfathers

Family Matters

'If we want things to stay as they are, things will have to change.' So wrote Giuseppe Tomasi di Lampedusa in his Italian classic, *Il Gattopardo (The Leopard)*, about the passing of an era and the impact on Sicilian society of the *Risorgimento*, the slow but determined revolution that finally united Italy into a single kingdom in 1861. It's a story of old nobility having to face up to the reality of the sudden power and influence of 'newly moneyed peasants' and 'shabby minor gentry'.

The Leopard is essentially about family matters. And, in spite of all that has changed in Italian society, family matters continue to dominate the way Italy works. For better or for worse, the family remains far and away the most important social, economic, organisational and political unit in Italy.

Think of a famous Italian brand name and you usually encounter a family rather than a disparate board of directors. Think of Fiat and the Agnelli family. Think of Prada, Benetton, Pirelli, Ferragamo, Barilla, Lavazza or Missoni. Below their surface success and glitter, these iconic families are not so different today from the nobility in Lampedusa's book, even though most have roots amongst 'newly moneyed peasants' and 'shabby minor gentry'.

Giovanni Agnelli was born to minor gentry in Turin in 1866. He originally pursued a military career and became a lieutenant in the cavalry. When he was 26 and stationed in Verona he resigned, married, and moved back to Turin. Soon he had a son and a daughter, Edoardo and Aniceta, and he began to look for ways to give security to his family in the approaching 20th century.

A chance meeting with an eccentric nobleman from Turin, who was keen to attract investors into a horseless carriage project, was just what Giovanni wanted. On 1st July 1899, four years before Henry Ford set up in America, *Fabbrica Italiana di Automobili Torino* – FIAT – was incorporated. Giovanni Agnelli was its managing director, aged just 30.

Within four years the company was making a modest profit from an annual production of 135 cars. Fiat became known for the skills and creativity of its engineering staff, and by 1906 was making over 1,000 cars a year for Italian and overseas customers.

Two years later Giovanni and his board were accused of inflating Fiat's share price and falsifying company accounts. Agnelli was cleared of all charges, but from then on he and the family took effective control of the company.

By 1911 Fiat was the largest of Turin's motor companies and by the start of the First World War was producing 4,000 vehicles a year, accounting for about half of Italy's cars and trucks. A year later, government orders for military vehicles and equipment meant Fiat was employing 10,000 workers. By the end of the war Fiat was Italy's third largest company.

Giovanni Agnelli liked power. In the 1920s, when motoring, ocean liners, electricity and jazz made the future seem ever more exciting, profitable and secure, he bought influence and diversification. Giovanni purchased *La Stampa*, an important newspaper, followed by a major share in Italy's largest circulation daily, *Corriere della Sera*. By the start of the 1930s, he was the senior member of a large family that included his son and heir Edoardo, Edoardo's seven children, plus the five children that his daughter Aniceta bore before she died giving birth in 1928.

It seems too tragic to be true but in 1935 Edoardo was also dead, killed in an air crash. The eldest of Edoardo's sons had the same name as his grandfather, which was soon shortened to Gianni. He was destined to inherit Fiat when his grandfather died.

During the Second World War the company once again reaped the benefits of big military contracts. Gianni followed in his grandfather's footsteps and became an army officer fighting, first, for Mussolini's army and then, after Italy changed sides, he fought for the Allies from the end of 1943.

Of his six brothers and sisters, the closest to Gianni was his sister Susanna, known as Suni, who was one year older. 'He was the perfect brother but that is not to say he was a flawless businessman or husband. We two always had the perfect rapport; we understood each other so well we didn't need to speak,' she said in an interview in 2003.

Both of them also felt the same about their father, mother and grandfather, which isn't saying much. '*Padre* was cold and difficult, our mother was impulsive, defiant and flighty. As soon as she became a widow she started such a flagrant affair that our grandfather felt it necessary to seize custody of us from her. We obviously had a fractured childhood and it wasn't helped by our grandfather who was haughty and domineering. Our mother, who didn't live with us, died when I was just 16. It was in a car accident and she was found with her chauffeur, trouser-less, beside her.'

A month later, just before Christmas 1945, the older Giovanni Agnelli died aged 79. Suni said, 'By then he was utterly friendless, embittered and roundly despised. His mercantile transactions with Mussolini were recollected with disgust upon his death. Only family attended the funeral, which so upset Gianni.'

Gianni was just 24 and felt to be too young to run the company, so it was put into the hands of Vittorio Valletta, a capable former professor of banking. Although he was now effectively head of Fiat, Gianni deftly avoided steady work from the age of 24 until he was 45, and during these 21 years led the fast and extravagant life of a playboy. Family friends say that he 'took a few years off and then a legend was born'. The press reported otherwise.

THE PLAYBOY LIFE

Gianni Agnelli moved to the south of France and bought a 28-roomed villa once owned by Belgium's King Leopold, where he gambled and found a liking for recreational drugs, including cocaine. A handsome, dark figure with the probing eyes of an eagle and an annual allowance of one million dollars a year, Gianni arrived in style with extraordinary-looking motor boats and cars, and cut a dash with his fastidious if quirky style. The collars on his crisp, white shirts were left unbuttoned; his gold Cartier watch was fastened over his shirt cuff. In the 1950s he pursued women galore, including the actress Hedy Lamarr, and was mixing with Aristotle Onassis and other Greek shipping magnates who had begun to settle in the south of France.

Among the women who set their sight on Gianni was Pamela Churchill, the ex-wife of Winston Churchill's son Randolph. She was almost exactly a year older than him and spent five years hoping to marry Gianni, meanwhile learning ever more about seduction and the ways of the super rich. To entice Gianni further, she even changed faiths from Church of England to Roman Catholic. Suni hated Pamela, describing her as 'a world expert on rich men's bedroom ceilings'.

Pamela introduced Gianni to her influential transatlantic friends, many of whom she had cultivated during her first affair with Averell Harriman, the American statesman whom she eventually married towards the end of her life. Among these friends was Franklin D. Roosevelt Jr, son of the man who was US President from 1933 to 1945. FDR Jr subsequently obtained the Fiat distributorship for North America and, after the Second World War, Fiat received a huge post-war loan from the US government but, as far as I can ascertain, no-one knows the exact connections.

When Gianni crashed his Fiat station wagon on the Corniche while apparently high on cocaine, his right leg was shattered in seven places. His convalescence was very long, and Suni and her sisters took the opportunity to introduce immobilised Gianni to the woman who would become his wife. Donna Marella Caracciolo di Castagneto was a former Vogue model with what the gossip columns described as 'a swan's neck and a melodic voice'. In his sisters' eyes, Marella Caracciolo was an ideal candidate to become Gianni's wife.

Marella's father, Filippo Caracciolo, was a diplomat with an impeccable Neapolitan lineage of nobility. Her mother, Margaret Clarke, was from the US Midwest and of considerable intellect.

Marella fell wildly in love with Gianni, but whether she was the great love of his life is unlikely. By then he had grown into a cynic and was not one to mistake any ardour on his behalf as enduring affection. Pamela was abandoned but with gifts including a Parisian apartment and a Bentley. She was also pregnant but Gianni insisted on an abortion in Switzerland.

Gianni married Marella in November 1953 when he was 31 and she was 27 and three-months pregnant. Marella had married one of the most difficult husbands in a nation renowned for difficult husbands. Gianni was still wild and still a womaniser.

Anita Ekberg came and went, the actress Silvia Monti was a friend, Jackie Kennedy went sailing with him and stayed interested for a long time. Some say Jack Kennedy's son, John, who died in 1999, looked more like Gianni than Jack.

Marella spent a fair proportion of their wedded life trying to undermine her husband's libidinous desires and to keep him in check. When he was present she appeared intimidated, nervous and edgy. For much of the marriage she seemed not to enjoy a moment of peace, yet the partnership endured, perhaps due to depths of their relationship kept secret from the rest of the world. Certainly her loyalty was something few others seemed to have understood. There could be a simple explanation. Gianni was a man of exquisite taste and Marella made a significant contribution to fabric design as a side-line. Perhaps they feared a life of lesser good taste if they separated and simply felt the risk wasn't worth the trouble.

Friends found that they had to choose between Marella or Gianni whenever she heard reports of him turning up at a party or their houses and introducing them to one of his 'tarts', as he insisted on calling all girls. Family was something Gianni seemed not to understand and he was awkward and remote to his children.

His first son Edoardo appeared to be neglected by his father and so grew up aimless. He took to drugs and spent his time searching religions and mysticism for something that would lead to a justification of his privileged life. The Italian press called Edoardo 'Crazy Eddie', and claimed that he had met Ayatollah Khomeini after leaving university and then converted to Islam. In 2000, when only 46, Edoardo committed suicide by jumping off a viaduct on the Turin/Savona road dressed in a brown corduroy suit with his pyjamas underneath.

A year afterwards an Iranian documentary film claimed that he was murdered, a victim of a Zionist plot to prevent a Muslim becoming head of Fiat. Marella believes that her son died accidently.

THE CRISIS YEARS

Fiat had been doing well without Gianni Agnelli at the helm. But that changed in 1966 when Vittorio Valetta, the iron-fisted head of the company, said he wanted to retire. The 82-year-old boss, only 5ft1in tall, whom rivals said 'produced little cars to match his height', clearly felt that with Fiat riding high it was the right time for 45-year-old Gianni Agnelli to take over.

Within a short while, Gianni opened Fiat factories in Eastern Europe, Brazil and Argentina. In 1969 he acquired Lancia and then added a controlling interest in Ferrari, followed by Alfa Romeo in 1986 and Maserati in 1993. But under his stewardship there would be a crisis every few years. The causes often stemmed from his desire for greater expansion, but he had neither enough old nor new capital and, as the years went by, the company had to face increasingly strong competition from German and Japanese car makers in European markets.

By the end of the 1990s, Gianni realised Fiat needed to establish a strategic alliance or it would probably collapse. At one point it nearly merged with Daimler-Chrysler, a deal which many of the 70 family members who hold shares in the company would have preferred. Instead, Gianni entered into a deal with General Motors. When Gianni died 20 per cent of his family company had been sold to GM and Fiat owned 6 per cent of GM. Unfortunately, Fiat's market share had slumped to just 8 per cent and the styles of its newer cars were not enchanting home-market consumers. Models sold in the all-important US market were proving to be temperamental in America's rough weather and on its salty roads.

Gianni had been diagnosed with prostate cancer eight years before he died at his home in Italy on 24 January, 2003, aged 81. By then his serious-minded older grandson, 27-year-old John Elkann, had been carefully groomed in engineering and international matters and was destined to head the company.

When Gianni Agnelli died the bulk of the company's investments were in Italy and France. By 2011 one-third of revenue came from North America, 38 per cent from Europe, and 29 per cent from the rest of the world. Today Fiat's biggest holding is a New York property company, and cars account for just 20 per cent of revenue.

The rich and the famous crowded into Turin Cathedral to pay their respects to Gianni Agnelli, this flamboyant, mercurial, charming, cunning and vastly wealthy man.

As well as the glamorous congregation inside the cathedral, Turin's streets were lined with those who had something to thank Gianni for … for their jobs, for their cars, for his perceived leadership and for his Godfatherliness. Gianni's tanned, craggy face symbolised the post-war Italian Miracle.

One mourner was a particularly notable beneficiary of the miracle, the billionaire Prime Minister Silvio Berlusconi. But unlike Gianni, who had a ruling aesthetic sense that never failed him, Berlusconi showed his innate crassness by arriving in a German car. He was roundly booed by the crowd of 100,000 mourners who lined the streets.

GODS AND FATHERS

In spite of their great riches and power, it seems to me the attitudes and values demonstrated by grandfather Giovanni, and to a certain extent by Gianni, are common in all ranks of Italian society.

Italians of all types have a Godfather figure at their head, a Mr Big. He can be a father, a grandfather, an uncle, an older brother, or even a godfather. These men demand respect, but often get it only through cunning and deceit. They hold enormous influence, even when it is plain for all to see that they are wrong in what they think, say or do.

Some call this tough love, but I've seen enough to know that inflexible, dominant toughness is not love at all but is arrogance, insensitivity and bullying, based as often on omission as on commission. Edoardo 'Crazy Eddie' Agnelli was one such victim.

I have an Italian friend who has spent his life switching between not speaking to his domineering father for months, and then both making up in floods of tears. But he is still left feeling he can do no right. Try as I might, I see nothing but selfish emotional bullying here, perhaps the only way the father can convince himself he is superior, or that he is a man at all.

Many nations applaud the way Italian families celebrate baptisms, birthdays and marriages *en masse,* and how there are always family parties on relevant Saints' days. This is especially so on August 15th, Assumption Day or *Ferragosto,* Italy's biggest national holiday. It's traditionally a day for all the family to get together but, after living here, I wonder how much of the attendance is real commitment and how much is blind obligation or fear.

How many at one of these apparent celebrations really love their families, and how many resent the burden and the insincerity of it? Many I suspect, but when you think about the political turmoil of the last 150 years perhaps family has been all Italians could rely on, regardless of individual gain or loss? I think it is for manageable security rather than familial love.

Family-owned businesses account for 93 per cent of all Italian companies. These firms intimately intertwine and manage the affairs of all with the same bloodline, profiting from the rest of the world from behind bastions built on demands of loyalty as strong as those of the Mafiosi's *omertà*.

In my experience of working with large and small Italian companies, family succession shapes every decision to do with education of children, and then to their choice of careers and life partners. Such decisions are invariably made by the titular head of the family, that particular Godfather. The impact of this is not helped by the apparent dichotomy of keeping business and home life very separate from one another.

Gianni Agnelli was not unusual in treating everyone he knew like keys to be put into the type of pigeonhole system you see in hotels. He had a keyhole for Fiat, a keyhole for his wife, others for each of his close family, a keyhole for girlfriends, and still others for friends.

I also have little doubt the majority of young Italians want independence from complicated love/hate relationships with their family. Yet moving out might not be an option when the comforts and conveniences of the family home are considered, especially in these difficult times and the economic realities of having a low wage or no job at all.

I've just as little doubt that respect remains the basis of relationships with older members of the family, no matter what their faults and no matter if that respect is earned or not. Young people I know believe they should 'give back' the affection that was given to them, not only by their parents and grandparents but also that from even older aunties and uncles who are not strictly blood relations. The problems arise when these dutiful sons and daughters leave it too late to move away from their elderly parents, and simply haven't the heart or the impetus to find a place of their own.

It happens to just as many men as it does to women, and is the main explanation for Italy harbouring a secret army of single, heterosexual men who are so attached to their mothers they can't form a relationship with other women.

It also explains why you so often hear Italy defined as a country of masturbators. This common thread of ungratified single men just might be what drives so many married men to excesses of Godfatherliness. On one hand, adherence to the family is admired, on the other, these unmarried men have not taken the place a man is expected to take in society. Blustery show is how family heads demonstrate their achievement in becoming married men, even when they have little understanding of their responsibility.

Taking the Field

One of the joys of living in deep countryside on a hillside in Tuscany is that it is extremely rare for conversation to turn to national politics. Whenever Silvio Berlusconi was mentioned, it seemed that he was of no relevance to our friends and neighbours or the way they lived. And certainly none of them would ever have admitted voting for him.

Silvio Berlusconi is known internationally as a politician with a huge fortune that might or might not have been built entirely honestly, and who seems to have been in court more times than a man of integrity might deserve. Yet, lift his tanned skin and you find much of the character of many Italian men in what makes him who he is. He is generous, yet inconsistent; he is an actor. He has stamina, yet suffers tactical lapses of memory and loyalty. He promises things he does not do, and does things that he prefers others not to know about. And he finds the English word 'accountability' difficult to translate into Italian.

Yet despite my neighbours' apparent lack of interest in the man who once described himself as 'the best political leader in Europe and the world', he stayed in power for the best part of 17 years and, whatever he did, Italians continued to vote for him.

I first became aware of Berlusconi when I worked in public relations in Britain which included getting more pasta, Italy's most famous gift to the world, onto the plates of British consumers. In planning pan-European marketing campaigns for clients, I was always surprised how often his name came up, not only as the owner of many Italian television stations but also as proprietor of *Il Giornale,* the leading daily newspaper and of Mondadori, Italy's largest publishing house.

It wasn't until 1994 that his political ambitions became obvious to me and to many millions of Italians. Val and I were in Venice for New Year and everyone we met seemed to be talking about the formation of a Christian-democratic, liberal and liberal-conservative political party by Berlusconi and others. It was called Forza Italia after the chant 'Go Italy' used by the fans of AC Milan, the football club he bought in 1986.

Back in the UK I seemed to read something new and positive every week about the party's progress in the Italian newspapers that came free with an espresso in Bar Italia in Soho's Frith Street. Then, friends in Italy sent me a copy of the nine-minute video Berlusconi had made at his Milanese *palazzo* about the new party and distributed to every Italian TV station. It was all about his new political party Forza Italia, and clearly showed a charismatic man cultivating his image as an outsider, as a different voice in Italian politics, but I doubted his taste and sincerity.

Silvio Berlusconi has always loved football and, in a country where soccer is almost a religion, he used football metaphors from his very first steps into politics. In the videotape, he promised to create a new Italian miracle based upon his skills as an entrepreneur and 'taking the field'. He said he was doing so because 'I've heard the game is getting dangerous and that it is being played in two penalty areas with the midfield being left desolately empty.'

Berlusconi carefully targeted what he saw as his core electorate: entrepreneurs, managers in private companies and housewives. Many of these watched his television stations and he took great care in controlling every detail of his on-screen appearances, right down to the colour of his tie and the use of make-up.

Forza Italia was an unusual beast in that it was a type of business association. It had no mass membership, no sections or branches but operated through clubs, just as the Mafia is a sort of club. You are invited to join and participate by scratching backs and having your back scratched. Networking was, and is, the thing but all had to agree Berlusconi's key role in helping individual members prosper, something he did do. The people who seemed really important were Berlusconi's business friends and contacts, and the networking opportunities they provided for his supporters.

Forza Italia had a national executive comprising mainly businessmen, but internal democracy was virtually unheard of, just as though it were a traditional Italian family. Berlusconi was simply a new sort of family head, the Godfather who could help you to better things, as long as you did it the way he said. So, unlike predecessors, Berlusconi made politics accessible and understandable by anyone with a family. Once he was Prime Minister, the electorate secretly hoped that he would allow them the same sort of latitudes he took. And so he did.

Berlusconi's football metaphors connected with a lot of people, millions of them. To my astonishment, he was elected Prime Minister only three months later in a coalition with the right-wing National Alliance and Northern League parties. This government lasted just nine months, its collapse caused by bitter rivalries between the leaders of the three parties. It wasn't helped by Berlusconi's indictment for tax fraud. In 1996 he stood for re-election but lost.

In 2001 Berlusconi won another election and was back running the country after forming a coalition with his former partners. Yet, being the man he was and is, allegations of embezzlement, attempting to bribe the judiciary, tax fraud and false accounting continued to dog him. Outraged, he claimed these stories alone undermined his position enough to cause his narrow 2006 defeat by Romano Prodi, an old political rival.

In January 2008 Prodi's government was defeated in the Senate and an election was called for April. Silvio Berlusconi, the maverick come-back kid, the former vacuum-cleaner salesman and cruise ship crooner, returned to power for a third term.

I began to see that a large percentage of Italians clearly thought of him 'as one of us', for Berlusconi was essentially saying it was OK to cheat the government, especially of taxes. This was an almost fiendishly clever plot that glorified everything that was wrong with Berlusconi on a massive scale, but chimed with that majority in small artisan companies.

In Berlusconi's third term, tax revenues dropped significantly. He had certainly helped the rich pay less tax, but suddenly a vast number of Italy's families of small butchers, bakers, greengrocers and restaurant owners declared annual incomes that were less, often much less, than a state pension.

In his way Berlusconi translated liberalism and the defence of liberty into a belief that tax was for 'little people', a quote also made by the Queen of Mean, Leona Helmsley in New York. She was sentenced to 16 years for tax evasion but served less than two years, which to many eyes made her more of a heroine. Italian surveys show this wilful attitude to not paying tax is still held by nearly half the population.

Put simply, I reckon Berlusconi worked on the principle that many Italians didn't care about his conflicts of interest because they had them, too. As to his problems with the law, it seems to me that he always relied on a fundamental belief that the public found defendants more *simpatico*, more likeable, than lawyers. He was simply a little man with the same problems as the little man, but bigger and better at it.

Some of my Tuscan friends still feel rather embarrassed by the way Berlusconi's antics and gaffes presented a poor picture of their country. Even so, life without Berlusconi running the country continues, with bills quickly scribbled on the back of cigarette packets and many transactions conducted in cash and without proper receipts.

Towards the end of 2011 he resigned due to lack of political support, but how had he continued to ride high for so long while the charges against him continued unabated? Why, as time went on, could he act more and more like a Roman emperor rather than as an elected Prime Minister? Some answers lie in Milan, his home town. Others lie in the bizarre impasse that brought him to power in the first place.

A Product of Italy's Economic Miracle

Berlusconi's rise as an entrepreneur took place against the background of Italy's so-called Economic Miracle during the 1950s and 1960s. The country moved from being largely dependent on agriculture to becoming one of the biggest exporters in the Western world. By the 1980s it overtook Britain as the fifth largest economy in the West and its relative wealth peaked. Much of the affluence was driven by the industries of Northern Italy, and this established Milan as the home of a new economic elite.

During the late 1970s and early 1980s, considerable changes had taken place in the Italian workplace and the way entrepreneurs operated. Mass production decreased in favour of industries built on the strong tradition of small artisan firms, while new high-tech retailing and design allowed these enterprises to flourish. This resulted in a new domination of the service sector, in tourism, the hotel industry and restaurants, transport and communications, financial services and public administration. By the start of the 1980s such services accounted for nearly half of Italy's jobs.

These changes, combined with major social and political shifts, created increasing individualism, hedonism and risk-taking, plus new forms of social division and power elites. Political allegiances built around the industrial working class were fragmenting, and the Catholic and Communist ideologies that had helped shape people's political leanings in the past were being seriously questioned. Even so, autocracy, paternalism, masculinity and a strong sense of hierarchy were still seen as the major characteristics of the successful Italian businessman, just as in Giovanni Agnelli's time.

Previously these traits had been associated, publically anyway, with honesty, integrity and the sort of family values preached by the Catholic Church – not any more.

Silvio Berlusconi was born in Milan in 1936, one of three children in a lower-middle-class family. Following strict schooling and attendance at the Università Statale in Milan, where he earned a degree in law, he entered the city's booming construction industry. In the early 1960s he persuaded the owner of the bank where his father worked as a clerk to lend him money. He used that to build apartment blocks that he sold with the aid of advertisements in the Agnellis' daily, *Corriere della Sera.* This was an early sign of Berlusconi's individual thinking, for property advertising was unusual at the time.

His big business breakthrough came in the 1970s when he built Milano 2 on the outskirts of Milan, an enclosed residential area for 10,000 people that featured artificial lakes, schools and a swimming pool.

To construct this development, he had to win over local bureaucracies, the unions and such authorities as those that ran nearby Linate Airport. Whatever the truth about the way he fought them, the battles he won helped shape his profile as a creative entrepreneur pursuing greater prosperity for ordinary people in the face of obstructive and politically motivated officials. Rumours still surface about where the money came from for Milano 2, or how he supposedly bribed air-traffic controllers to move the Milan flight path away from the complex and might also have compensated an over-keen member of the fiscal police by putting him on his payroll.

Berlusconi first got involved with television in 1974, by setting up the TeleMilano station for Milano 2 residents. This was, incidentally, the same year he bought Villa San Martino, his 147-room home in Arcore just 30km north-east of Milan. You'll still hear astonishment at the bargain price he apparently paid for this.

TeleMilano taught Berlusconi that owning television channels offered a populist way to bring his style and ethos into the public domain. In 1980 state-owned RAI had a monopoly on national broadcasting, and restricted the scheduling of popular TV programmes.

Berlusconi turned TeleMilano into Canale 5, a commercial network, and shortly afterwards he purchased two more private channels, Rete 4 and Italia 1. Their daily diet of quiz and variety shows, films, American soaps and cartoons quickly made television viewing an important part of life for ordinary Italians.

Even so there were protests, leading to court appearances and to his TV channels being taken off the air. Berlusconi persuaded Prime Minister Bettino Craxi, a close friend and political patron, of his best intentions and of the 'dryness' of RAI's programmes. Soon he was back broadcasting and building a loyal audience from targeted social groups, especially housewives, which he later cultivated as electoral supporters. All was set for the bigger game.

In the 1990s a series of judicial investigations revealed that corruption on a grand scale permeated the entire Italian political system. Overnight, often literally, the major political parties and their main figures vanished, and once famous names fled the country. Silvio Berlusconi stepped into the vacuum, even though his career to date was based on the system that had apparently just ended. He promised the earth, to sort out problems no one else could solve. These included the country's notorious bureaucracy and complex tax laws. He also talked about issues that had previously been taboo, like mass immigration from North Africa.

Italy had suffered a different government virtually every year for the previous six decades. When Berlusconi first came to power he had to allay fears of continuing chaos, so he moved decisively to end the judicial purge of politics and politicians. With the Italian Left in a mess and the Centre-Right seeming to be anaesthetised, his clear leadership began to represent a type of stability.

After losing the 1996 elections to Romano Prodi, Berlusconi fought his way back to win the 2001 elections. There were several reasons why he won. Not least was the failure of the Centre-Left government (1996–2001) to put through reforms that many hoped would create a new and 'normal' two-party system in Italy, built around Forza Italia and the Left Democrats. The government also failed to pass legislation to curtail Berlusconi's conflicts of interest, while he got on with rebuilding his relations with his former coalition partners, the Northern League and the National Alliance.

I have a piece of Berlusconi memorabilia that makes me cringe as much as his 1994 videotape – a copy of his glossy 2001 election brochure. It's stuffed with pictures of sun-tanned Silvio with his family, world leaders, television personalities, footballers and adoring crowds. The letter that accompanied it was from Club Forza Italia and promised lower taxes, more prosperity and greater efficiency; and refers to President Berlusconi rather than the more accurate Prime Minister, a title he clearly thought not grand enough.

I remain amazed that the conflicts of interest between Berlusconi's massive media business and his role as Prime Minister were not addressed at the time of the 2001 election. He also had, and continues to have, a huge stake in Italy's economy that supplemented his political power in a unique way. He came to power with a growing list of court cases being brought against him involving bribing judges, financial corruption and Mafia links. These were still around when the 2006 elections were called, but this time they contributed to him again losing narrowly to his old adversary Romano Prodi.

He was once more sworn in as Prime Minister on 8th May 2008, which lasted until he was hounded out of office in November 2011. After weeks of market turmoil that upended his defiant hold on power and threatened to tear apart the eurozone, Berlusconi stepped down amid jeers, cheers and heckles of *buffone,* buffoon, from the thousands who packed Rome to witness his government's downfall.

Handel's *Hallelujah Chorus* rang out in the streets of the capital to end his tumultuous 17 years in politics, which set in motion a transition aimed at bringing the country back from the brink of economic crisis.

Down But Not Out

Silvio Berlusconi left the country's top political job as one of Italy's richest men, owning a business empire that spans advertising, insurance, food, construction and the media. His wealth is estimated at over six billion euros. His influence as a media baron and as Prime Minister, with overall responsibility for state television as well as his own commercial networks, gave him a tool that none of his rivals possessed. He had a hold on the media that reached most of the voters but which his rivals could barely access. It's something that has created a call for press freedom in Italy.

Of course, Berlusconi's dominance of the media was not the only factor that determined the outcome of elections. Even today he is bright and quick, and ever since he entered politics he appealed quite openly to the millions of citizens who avoid paying tax. And, whatever any one said, his many facelifts, cosmetic surgery to his eyelids, injections of hyaluronic acid to get rid of wrinkles, hidden heel lifts in his shoes, and a perennial emphasis on physical prowess stood him in good stead with many sections of the electorate. And that was even though he never solved the problems of administrative red tape, of organised crime, of corruption, public debt, ageing infrastructure, or other long-term Italian problems.

Luckily, in spite of Berlusconi's clowning and the corruption scandals, Italy is not one country but thousands of municipalities all trying to do the right thing for their local communities. Most local politicians invariably demonstrate sound political and social sense, as is the case with those that run Tuscany, my local Province of Arezzo and the *commune* in Cortona.

Italians feel they belong more to a region than to a common state. This is because they see local governments usually working better, being far more approachable, and less corrupt and more respectful of the law than central government. Tuscany, like other regions, receives subsidies from the state, which it usually invests soundly in everything from the arts to education, to the roads and rubbish collection. It's easy for us all to see where the money goes. This doesn't alter the fact that Italy is a country where constantly shrinking budgets have had a major impact on schools and universities, hospitals and museums; where the impact of organised crime appears to continue unabated; where immigrants are feared and hated by many; and where many people struggle to make ends meet working in badly paid jobs that offer no security.

When Berlusconi stepped down the hope was that Mario Monti, the former European Commissioner and technocrat who replaced him, would be able to stop the Italian economy careering over a cliff. Where Berlusconi was colourful, controversial and out of favour with the markets when he finally went, Signor Monti came across as sober and honest. He is a well-respected economist, well connected to the upper ranks of the EU machine and has a reputation as a tough negotiator. The only problem is that he had no time to bring about cultural change – especially in the way rules are not observed and cheating is given a nod and a wink – before the general election of February 2013, an event that Berlusconi simply could not ignore.

Uniquely in politics, in his political heyday Berlusconi was the sort of figure millions of families recognised – a dominant, sometimes glittering figure who ruled right or wrong and has little thought for outside interests like international markets. You might or might not agree with what your particular Godfather decrees, cajoles or bullies, but if you want any sort of family life you have to comply. And at least he was taking charge and doing something.

Silvio Berlusconi was recognised by millions as the type of force that keeps families together in the face of adversity. Isn't this how they survived the perils of unification, the First and Second World Wars, the never-ending swirl of rising and falling political parties, and the whittling away of unions and the authority of priests and the Holy Father? Whatever else he is, Silvio Berlusconi is a man who lived, dealt and delivered on a huge scale to what happened in the smallest family. And that, of course, is also his weak point. Italian families with such powerful figureheads in command are not necessarily happy, cohesive or supportive.

Silvio Berlusconi is a man who is cocky, proud of what he has done, and convinced that he can say what he likes, whenever he likes and to whomever he likes. For a short while after his resignation he was notably absent from the front pages. But the court cases didn't stop. And nor did his belief that he could once again be voted into political power.

The End of an Era?

At the age of 77 Silvio Berlusconi is a divorced man with five grown-up children who, on the surface, seem to be very supportive and don't have a bad word to say about their father.

In 1965 he married Carla Elvira Dall'Oglio and they had two children. Maria Elvira, better known as Marina, was born in 1966 and his son Pier Silvio arrived three years later.

Marina is now one of the most influential businesswomen in the world thanks to her father. She heads up the family's investment arm, Fininvest, and is chairperson of Mondadori, Italy's largest magazine and book publisher. In 2001 she started living with Maurizio Vanadia, a ballet dancer at La Scala, by whom she has two children. In 2008 they married in great style. Naturally there was a big family party, attended in true Italian custom by Silvio with both his first and second wives.

Colleagues call Marina the Iron Lady, or the Czarina of Fininvest, and say she never minces her words. Certainly she has always defended her father by speaking out in the press whenever he has come under attack. The gossip columns, which comment upon her backcombed hairstyles, say 'she is not prone to sobriety' and that she has a penchant for plastic surgery. Like her father, she has been suspected of money-laundering and, although she has declared she is not interested in following him into politics, he may still persuade her otherwise.

Pier Silvio has also done very well for himself. He is top official of Mediaset, the Berlusconi media empire. When he was 20 he had a bad motorcycle accident and, once he was fully recovered a few years later, he chose not to go to college but went into the family business. In interviews when he turned 40, the young Berlusconi said that he grew up in a totally normal Italian family. 'A normal Italian family is one where certain values are always present. It is important to be there for one another, to respect your father and your elders. We did normal things: my father taught me how to swim, to play tennis. Most importantly he taught me to respect other people.' Pier Silvio was 25 when his father decided to go into politics and this was when he said 'papa totally disappeared and left me to get on by myself'.

Apparently his protestations of a normal upbringing do not ring true once you meet him. A British friend of mine, for years a major figure in television, had dealings in the recent past with Pier Silvio at Mediaset. He described him as more like an uncouth Italian thug than someone who naturally shows respect for others and readily accepts the country's tax laws. Like his father, he felt that business relationships could benefit from the company of a few, friendly young ladies.

By 1980 Silvio Berlusconi was deep in a relationship with the actress Veronica Lario, born Miriam Bartolini. He divorced Carla in 1985 and married Veronica in 1990, by which time they had two daughters and a son. This public flaunting of the sanctity of Catholic marriage is probably what millions of Italian men and women don't dare to do, so did nothing to damage his reputation.

In May 2009 Veronica Berlusconi filed for divorce, saying she could not stay with a man who sends emissaries for 'fresh stocks of virgins ready to sacrifice themselves to the dragon' and who 'consorts with minors'. Her anger was specially fuelled by her husband attending a glamorous blonde's 18th birthday party, where he gave her a diamond and gold necklace. He had failed to show up at any of their children's important parties.

Yet, all five children rushed to their father's defence when Dario Franceschini, Italy's Opposition Leader at the time, asked, 'Would you want your children to be brought up by this man?' Referring to Franceschini's children, Marina Berlusconi answered saying, 'They would be thrilled to have a father like mine.' Silvio's three children from his marriage to Veronica issued a further statement saying that they were brought up in a 'sensible, family environment rich with values'.

The divorce settlement between the Berlusconis was filed on Christmas Day 2012. Veronica Lario had initially asked for 42 million euros a year, her ex-husband had reportedly offered c. four million. In the event, he agreed to pay 36 million euros but, Berlusconi being Berlusconi, got this reduced to less than half this sum towards the end of 2013.

In November 2010 revelations emerged about Berlusconi's supposed relations with a 17-year-old Moroccan nightclub dancer, called Karima 'Ruby' El Mahroug. She was one of dozens of models and showgirls who performed striptease and pole dances at 'bunga bunga' parties at his palazzo near Milan. He was called upon to resign but, forever the survivor, Berlusconi scraped through a vote of no confidence in parliament. In April 2011 he was ordered to stand trial for paying for sex with Ruby, and was also charged with abuse of power in a related case where he had asked police to release her after she had been arrested for stealing jewellery.

In February 2012 new proceedings started with charges of molesting minors. His response to the allegations was that he had been the victim of a long-running campaign by left-wing judges, who must be 'reformed'. He also blamed the media, presumably those that he doesn't own, for defaming him by suggesting that his 'bunga bunga' dinner evenings, which prostitutes claim to have attended, featured anything other than dancing.

In June 2013 the case eventually came to court and Berlusconi was found guilty of paying Ruby for sex, as well as for abuse of power, and was given a seven-year sentence, which he is appealing against.

As well as this case, in March 2013 he was sentenced to one year in jail, subject to appeal, for involvement in the leaking of a police wiretap to a newspaper run by his brother. Then, eight months later, he was given four years for tax fraud and barred from office. This sentence was reduced to one year under a general amnesty and, although Berlusconi appealed against it, he lost.

Up until this point, Silvio Berlusconi had been proud to admit to over 2,500 court appearances at a legal cost to him that he claims exceeds 200 million euros. He has always denied wrong doing – and still does.

In my opinion, and those of many other people, he is a morally bankrupt figure. Yet, at his 18th-century villa near Milan, the man with the surgically assisted, wrinkle-free face, with a pacemaker, a year-round tan and a neat hair transplant that is regularly dyed, proudly shows visitors portraits of his five children. 'I have handed over my business reins to them and my companies are working well; they are all very good children.'

Is it possible that one day soon, Silvio Berlusconi will resign himself to living out his years simply loving his family, his soccer, the company of younger women and, of course, his money? I doubt it.

In mid-November 2013 he changed the name of his People of Freedom Party announcing that it would be henceforth called Forza Italia (Go Italy), the name it went under when he first came to power in 1994. But following a split in the centre-right movement, the event saw dissidents breaking away to form a new faction led by his former right-hand man, Angelino Alfano. Berlusconi's initial reaction was to brand him 'a traitor'.

A week later, judges in the case where he was found guilty of paying for sex with the under-age erotic dancer, Ruby 'the Heart Stealer', published a 331-page document naming Silvio Berlusconi as the 'director' of the 'bunga bunga' parties at his villa, and said he knowingly paid for sex with an under-age escort in a 'proven system of prostitution'.

A few days after this, the Italian Senate voted to expel him from parliament with immediate effect, a move that meant he lost his immunity from prosecution and left him at risk of arrest over other criminal cases. The vote also marked the end of a process which meant that Berlusconi cannot take part in any general election for the next six years. Silvio Berlusconi had finally earned the enmity of the Italian political establishment.

There is no doubt that his continued cheap behaviour over two decades made Italy and its politics into an international joke. Gianni Agnelli was always very stylish, whether up or down. Berlusconi is commonly thought by many Italians as little better than Don Calogero, the newly moneyed, 19th-century peasant in *The Leopard,* a type referred to in current parlance as *un uomo di piazza* or *scugnizzo,* a street urchin.

I wonder if the flashy, media-driven power of Berlusconi and today's 'newly moneyed peasants' will survive as long as the centuries of land-based stability that was the now-discredited power base of Italy's old system of nobility. How long will it be before the fashion for Berlusconi's Godfatherly methods of rule will, in turn, become out of date?

SEVEN

La Bella Figura

MADE IN ITALY

It's early evening in any town and city in Italy. The continuing tradition of walking in the main streets before dinner, the *passeggiata,* means putting on your best or most recent clothes, whether you are 9 or 90.

Clothes are never seen by Italians as a frivolity: they always mean something because of the importance of *la bella figura,* literally the beautiful figure – how one looks and how one comports oneself is an essential philosophy that rules the lives of *gli italiani.*

Tuscans equally adore dressing up for processions, competitions and parades, of which the *passeggiata* is just the most casual example. There's a regional obsession for recreating medieval contests and celebrations, typified by Siena's dangerous horse-racing *palio,* Sansepolcro's crossbow competition, and the 400 residents of Arezzo who parade in 17th-century dress twice a year to re-create an ancient jousting tournament.

The Meridiana building of the Pitti Palace in Florence is home to the largest state-owned costume museum in the country. And a towering force at the very centre of Europe's rag trade is Prato, Tuscany's second biggest city. Here the Museo del Tessuto traces the history of textile manufacturing in the area since the 12th century in a huge disused 19th-century textile factory. You discover how different textiles are made and dyed, examine and handle every type of cloth, and see examples of Italian clothing from the Renaissance up to the 20th century.

The story of textiles and clothing manufacture in Prato during the 20th century is something quite different and very un-Italian, largely because of a Chinese invention called *Pronto Moda.* San Pechino, or St Beijing, is what Prato's residents call the immigrant neighbourhood where at least 10,000 Chinese live, the largest concentration of Chinese in Europe, some legal, many more not, as well as great numbers of inhabitants from all parts of Asia and the Far East, from the Indian sub-continent and from Africa.

When the first Chinese came to lease factories here in the early 1990s, Italians laughed at them and wondered how they would make a living. Then these newcomers created *Pronto Moda,* perhaps best translated as Fast Fashion. Today they produce Made In Italy fashion at Made In China prices – inexpensive, off-the-rack fashion with which they flood the markets within days of the Milan and Paris fashion shows.

There are at least 500 *Pronto Moda* companies in Prato operating out of practical, faceless factories and under such innocuous names as *Nuove Tendenze,* New Tendency, and New Europe. Prato's residents say their cheaply made versions of Italian designs are ruining the reputation of Prato and of Italy for quality garments and is close to being unfair competition. And anyway, they add, *Pronto Moda* was their idea in the first place.

Francesco Pavese is one of Prato's textile-trade businessmen. He told me unsettling tales about the influx of illegal immigrants and of 'slave labour' which he claims is both the secret of the Chinese success and the Achilles' heel of legal Chinese immigrants. He might as well have been speaking as some Britons do about immigration, as he moaned about foreigners living in their own closed society, not speaking Italian, and of the high cost to Prato of interpreters in hospitals, schools and elsewhere. There are even courses in Chinese, operated by concerned Italians to encourage Chinese parents to keep their children in Italian schools instead of sending them to China for education.

Francesco explained further. 'In my father's time the Italian fashion industry learned the difficult lesson that it could no longer compete with China on price. So I, along with many other business people in the trade, decided that we would focus upon quality not quantity. But then the Chinese arrived turning Prato from the home of textile excellence into a low-end garment manufacturing capital.'

I sympathised with him but realised this was part of a wider Made in Italy problem. Italy's institutions are weak, on the whole, and Italians have a high tolerance for rule-bending; thus it is perhaps not surprising that the Chinese could blur the line between Made in China and Made in Italy, undermining Italy's cachet and ability to market its goods exclusively as high-end products.

Anyway, Italians' interest in good-looking clothes is matched equally by their passion for a bargain. These days, many thousands of the daily influxes of visitors to Florence are as likely to be heading for Outlet stores and villages. Factory outlets have become big business because so many of Italy's leading fashion brands are based in or near Florence. Gucci, Fendi, Armani, Dolce e Gabbana, Jil Sander, Helmut Lang and Prada all manufacture here, and attract dedicated followers of fashion and designer-label junkies looking for a bargain. 'Why pay more?' is more likely to be heard than any appreciation of Renaissance marvels. Florence, once the beating heart of the Renaissance, has become a base for out-of-town shopping sprees to places like The Mall at Leccio Reggello and to Prada at Montevarchi.

Montevarchi is a sleepy backwater about one hour south-east of Florence, where an anonymous-looking concrete warehouse in a small industrial estate is actually many people's idea of heaven. The few signs that exist are discreet, but the giveaway is rows of flashy Mercedes and BMWs in the car park and coach-loads of Japanese tourists.

Go to the Prada outlet at the busiest times, first thing or after lunch, and you will be directed to form an orderly queue by security guards at the entrance. Here you take a ticket from a machine, like the one at deli counters in supermarkets, and then wait for your number to be displayed on a board above the door before you can enter.

Once inside it is war without rules. The shopping experience is more akin to a supermarket at Christmas than a fashion boutique and, while prices are discounted by up to 60 per cent, the stock is mainly end-of-range and poor selling lines from previous seasons. Italians who can't get to such outlet stores have an easier solution – their local markets, where assiduous shopping can reap great rewards.

Italians spend on average 1,500 euros a head each year on clothes and shoes, and that's nearly twice as much per capita as any other European country. They seem to relish the fact that different seasons demand different outfits, and most women and many men appear to be avid followers of fashion. Above all else, they love shopping and getting something new and so much the better if it's also a bargain.

Nowhere is bargain hunting more obvious than in the markets that virtually every Tuscan town holds every week. Most are dominated by stalls selling the types of clothes and accessories that I wouldn't normally ever consider. Yes, that does mean that young Italians hanker for multi-coloured, man-made-fibre tops and track suit bottoms but that's just to please peer group pressure. Most have better stuff back home in their bedrooms, too.

There are especially good market finds for feet and hands. Italians make excellent socks, in every length and colour, as well as top-quality gloves. Just across the border from our adjoining region of Umbria, small Le Marche manufacturers make stylish, good-value leather and suede shoes that they sell in Tuscan markets. Their gloves are always worth seeking out, too, from slinky soft leather to thickly lined winter protection. Stall holders will always claim everything is *perfecto* even though much found on market stalls will be seconds, but with faults that are not easily spotted.

When it comes to trousers, gentlemen must be warned. Italian men can often be on the short side and, as they get older, are inclined to develop an expanded stomach. Trouser manufacturers and their market-stall cohorts are wise to the sartorial complications involved, and often cut them so they naturally hang below the paunch. This creates a problem for taller but equally full-figured Northern European types, of which I speak from experience. No matter how much you tighten your belt on these Italian-cut trousers, they head south and come to rest on your knees or, in extremis, around your ankles.

You'll enjoy finding your own bargains whenever you spot a market during your high-brow browsing of Tuscany's Renaissance treasures. But here's one special tip. On the shores of Lake Trasimeno are a couple of leading manufacturers of soft, light and superbly warm cashmere jumpers. No hordes of fashion victims here, just local people in the know buying colourful, comfortable and classic knitwear at bargain prices. A detour is recommended.

On every third Monday in September, the clothing section of our local supermarket stops selling summer cottons in favour of the latest designs in camouflage jackets and trousers, shirts and caps. Autumn and the hunting season are around the corner.

That same week Camucia market starts stocking cold weather and rainy day wear for country types. Short and long brown rubber boots and sturdy shoes replace summer sandals. Duvet coats, jersey dresses, thermal underwear, thick woolly socks, cord and moleskin trousers all take centre stage. Unlike the limited selection of camouflage wear in the supermarket, here every sort of garment, from underwear to combat jackets, is offered in what one market-stall trader told me was the traditional four-colour DPM – Disruptive Pattern Material – design. For the more adventurous, he showed me brighter versions of the same pattern, as 'genuinely worn by troops in the jungle,' he claimed, and tan and brown desert-wear patterned shirts and trousers that are apparently now all the rage.

HATS AND PLAITS

Until the 1960s most Italian men would no more have left the house without a hat than they would without trousers. Whatever the time of the day, or the day of the week, they would sport a trilby, a bowler or a cap during the winter and change to a Panama or a straw boater when the weather got warmer.

'I reckon it was the car that did it for the hat', explained my well-hatted friend Roberto Pedersoli, a stylish dresser now in his early 50s. 'As car ownership increased, fewer people took public transport, walked as much, or rode bikes to work. The hat was no longer needed to keep the rain and sun off your head. And Italian car makers started shrinking their cars, like Fiat and their *cinquecento,* 500, model which made wearing a hat while driving a physical impossibility.'

Roberto's view is that the type of hat a man wore up until the Second World War and during the immediate post-war period invariably reflected his place in society. Hats up until then had been big business. Then, from the 1970s until quite recently, they went out of fashion. 'But trust me, they are on their way back,' Roberto says with conviction.

Lorenzini's *cappelli e ombrelli,* hat and umbrella shop, in Piazza della Repubblica in the centre of Cortona is probably the most valuable retail site in the town. It can afford the cost because the shop is still doing brisk business in every type of man's hat, including superb straw boaters, from such leading Italian hat makers as Guerra and Borsalino.

They also sell the broad-brimmed straw boaters sported by Venice's gondoliers, but Roberto's is more like the one I used to wear to school in summer in England, much more rigid and with a shallower brim than the Venetian style. 'This is the most expensive straw hat you can buy,' he proudly boasted, 'it is made from the finest Tuscan plaits.'

The longer I live in Tuscany, the more surprised I am by the reputation it has for making so many world-class products and straw is another of these. Straw, the stalky residue of wheat, oats, rye and barley, is used for thatching roofs, making table mats, paper, mattresses, baskets, artificial flowers and much more. But these applications are insignificant in comparison to the place occupied by straw in the manufacture of hats.

Only certain areas produce wheaten straw suitable for hat-making plaits and it is agreed that Tuscany has grown the very, very best for at least 200 years. In pockets of the countryside, usually on comparatively elevated and arid land, they produce the ideal length of straw, with the right distance or 'pipe' between the knots, and straw that's not too brittle and has a clear, delicate golden colour.

The Casa di Monte wine estate in Montespertoli was once part of a larger farm owned by the Simoncini family, and they were one of the biggest straw producers of all. In the early 20th century the factory here had at least 60 women making Tuscan plaits for hat makers in Florence and for export to England.

The perfect Tuscan plait combines 11 lengths of straw, made from specially grown and harvested wheat. When the grain in the ear is about half developed, the plant is pulled up by the roots, dried in the sun, and then spread out for a few days to be bleached by both the sun and night-dews. Then only the straw from the upper joint is selected, made up into small bundles, and bleached in sulphur fumes in a closed container.

The very finest of all grades of Tuscan straw is *fontederas semone.* I was grateful to Roberto for that tip, and for telling me that in Tuscany those in the know call boaters *maggiostrina,* after the month of *maggio,* May, when gentlemen start to wear them. So Italian I thought. For those in the know, only the real thing and a rather secretive name known only to a select few.

Val says hats don't suit me but I did succumb to a near-perfect, lightweight grey *cappello di feltro* trilby made in Florence before the war. The purveyor was a persuasive stall-holder in Arezzo's antique market who said that because I had so little hair on top I was in *pericolo mortale,* mortal danger, of serious exposure from the summer sun.

After some years of wearing this antique curiosity, the constant draw of the display in Lorenzini's shop window and the appeal of owning a new Borsalino Panama became too much to resist. Incidentally, the Panama hat was invented in Ecuador in the early part of the 19th century, but initially most of the production was exported via Panama, hence the name that stuck.

When I was in my early twenties my favourite film was the French gangster movie *Borsalino,* starring Jean-Paul Belmondo and Alain Delon. Set in the 1930s and filmed in Marseilles, it was a kind of Gallic *Butch Cassidy and the Sundance Kid* with the outlaws wearing rakish trilby hats instead of cowboy hats. Their hats and the film's title were inspired by Giuseppe Borsalino, Italy's most famous hat-maker, who started business in Alessandria in the north of Italy in 1857. By the 1930s and 1940s his hand-made felt and straw hats were essential accessories for smartly dressed European men.

Today this family business continues to produce the finest felt hats from Belgian rabbit fur and straw hats from Tuscan plaits. Its range suits traditional hat wearers, like orthodox Jews, and also appeals to a new generation of fashion-conscious young men once they forsake ratty baseball caps and beanie hats.

Roberto joined me at Lorenzini's to select my new hat. First, I was measured with a tape measure across the forehead and around the head just above the ear line. 'Each centimetre equals an eighth of a head size,' he told me.

Of course, the hat I liked best was the most expensive, a staggering 750 euros, for a Borsalino Montecristi Superfino, unquestionably the finest Panama that money can buy. 'It's all in the weave and the blocking,' Lorenzini's owner explained. 'Poor quality means less than 40 weaves per square centimetre, this one is approaching 1,000.'

In the event, I went for something of 200 weaves but it was a genuine Borsalino and, most importantly, it got the thumbs up from Roberto – and from my wife Val.

THE LOOK IS EVERYTHING

The Italian fashion industry is a fairly recent phenomenon. Although Italy has produced luxury textiles, shoes and jewellery since the 12th century, it wasn't until after the 1950s that its clothing industry started to take off. New opportunities had come in the wake of the Second World War trauma. The Marshall Plan helped the garment trade create new factories that gave employment to skilled artisans from the hill towns of the north and from the impoverished villages of the south.

Such businesses were invariably run by entrepreneurial families who nurtured a new generation of Italian designers. Rather than ape French style, they discovered new designers and conceived a fashion identity that seemed singularly and idiosyncratically Italian. With modern factories, skilled workforces and a flair for design, the fledgling Italian fashion industry quickly developed an innate ability to market and establish differing brands, and realised the importance of a new type of fashion consumer – the post-war working woman.

Combined with shoe manufacturing and related services, the Italian fashion industry today employs close to a million people and has an annual turnover of more than 60 billion euros. From virtually nothing, it has become a major contributor to the Italian economy in little more than half a century.

Today Milan is the capital of the Italian fashion industry, but its first big push for recognition was given by a Tuscan in Tuscany. In 1951 G. B. Giorgini staged the first Italian Fashion Exhibition at his residence, Villa Torrigiani, in Florence. Without this event it is unlikely that the Italian fashion industry would have grown so quickly.

GB, or Bista as he was known to his friends, encouraged and promoted many gifted people who are today household names. These adroit and creative individuals realised the need for more accessible, comfortable, yet still refined and tailored clothes in the 1950s.

One of these talents was the three Fontana sisters who had all worked in their mother's dressmaking business, and had become apprentices as soon as they were old enough to handle needles and scissors. They were great pioneers, but hardly remembered today, being one of the first Italian fashion houses to branch out into accessories and ready-to-wear.

In the 1930s Zoe, the eldest of the three, left the family home in the countryside south of Parma to become an apprentice in Milan. She was soon joined by her sister Micol while Giovanna, the youngest of the three, continued to live with her parents. In 1934 Zoe moved with her husband to Paris where she continued her apprenticeship in an atelier. After returning to Italy in 1936, Zoe, excited by her experiences in Paris, moved to Rome and was soon joined by her two sisters. It was a major turning point in their lives. Initially Zoe went to work for the fashion house Zecca and Micol for another studio, Battilocchi, and Giovanna sewed garments at home. Based on their experiences in Milan and Paris, the sisters felt they were ready to go into business for themselves. Although French fashions were still dominant in the world of haute couture, the sisters opened their own workshop, Sorelle Fontana, in Rome in 1943. In the 1950s they were not only being patronised by leading members of the Italian aristocracy but were designing for many of the leading Hollywood stars of the day, from Ava Gardner to Elizabeth Taylor. In 1960, at the request of American customers, they introduced a line of ready-to-wear.

During the following decade, Gianfranco Ferré, Gianni Versace and Giorgio Armani each established labels that fused their creativity with Italian production prowess. Rather than make spin-offs from one-off couture, their factory-made collections were their main lines and these helped them become the starriest names in an explosion of Italian labels.

The Italian sense of entitlement to good design is just as strong in public servants and others who feel that what they do in the open-air deserves special fashions. This includes a range of officials as well as cyclists and hunters.

Cortona's local *vigili urbani* policewomen wear skin-tight, grey-blue trousers, high black boots, flattering short-sleeved blue shirts, full make-up, cute earrings and a jaunty officer's cap perched at a slight angle on perfectly coiffured hair. They work directly for the local town authority and their uniforms vary from town to town, but often have something in common with the other types of police you see on Italian streets.

The most famous of these is the *Carabinieri,* actually a special branch of the army that deals with serious crimes. Their everyday uniforms are black with a brilliant red stripe down the trouser legs and include a bright white bandolier worn across the chest, and an overlarge peaked cap very similar in design to a Nazi SS hat. Together with the gun they so obviously wear, the effect is extremely authoritarian and for ceremonial occasions they dramatically wear much fancier uniforms, with long cloaks and Napoleonic hats.

In a country where tax avoidance is rampant, it is perhaps not surprising that the tax man also dresses up in near-military style. The Italian finance police, the *Guardia di Finanza,* wear grey uniforms and drive around on motorcycles and in an assortment of grey vehicles marked with green and yellow stripes. They are equally authoritarian. Seeing a pack of jackbooted tax inspectors on large motorbikes suddenly appear to spot check the books of local retailers is rather unnerving.

One balmy August evening we were lingering over dinner at Trattoria Toscana in Cortona when two such uniformed tax officers walked slowly into the restaurant, and then cornered the owner to question him intently about his till receipts. Their overly polite yet authoritative manner made them particularly menacing.

After they had left, the still-perspiring owner explained that the law requires all shops, restaurants and bars to issue an official receipt for every transaction, even a coffee. He advised me never to throw away or destroy a receipt straightaway, in case a *Guardia di Finanza* policeman is watching the premises and asks to see it. This was, of course, for his benefit, not for ours.

If one of the aims of uniform is to dramatise authority, Italian cyclists go much further out of their way to impress, using fluorescent colours in stretchy fabrics that hug the body so tightly that every one of their physical assets features dramatically.

When we first settled in Tuscany, we were surprised to find our extremely hilly roads full every weekend with Lycra-clad men of every age moving at speeds I would never consider safe in a car, let alone on a bicycle. Yet they also had spare energy to talk loudly with each other, all the time.

More extraordinary than their stamina and bravado was the sleekness and colourfulness of their outfits. From the current season's 'must-have' designs of yellow, green or red studded cycling shoes, that were clearly unsuitable for walking, to skin-tight Lycra tops and buttock-padded shorts worn without underwear, the colours made me reach for dark glasses. And that's not all. Italian cyclists first make your eyes water with colour, and then also turn themselves into human billboards by emblazoning themselves with the names and logos of local cycling clubs, shops and race sponsors.

But they are not the first Tuscans to advertise their status through outrageous clothes. Nor are they the only modern ones, for the region's annual calendar of costumed parades and processions gives even the shyest a reason to be extreme.

CLOTHING SPECTACLES

Italian Renaissance paintings are an important source of inspiration for what to wear when taking part in these events, none more so than two by Bronzino and Gozzoli you can see in Florence.

Benozzo Gozzoli painted his masterpiece, the *Procession of the Magi,* in the Chapel of the Magi in Palazzo Medici-Riccardi, the Medici Palace in Florence, between 1459 and 1463. The walls of this intimate building are entirely covered with decorative frescoes in the most brilliant colours of the procession of the Magi to Bethlehem. Kings and princesses, knights and pages, horses, camels, leopards, apes and falcons wind in an endless cavalcade through a fabulous landscape, sauntering, gossiping and turning aside to hunt.

Coats and bridles of scarlet, blue and gold brocade, crowns and hats, velvets and furs glisten against the cool, dark green of trees and grass. The details with which the clothing and accessories are painted are exceptional and provide a unique record of Italian Renaissance dress.

You have to go to the Uffizi to see Bronzino's 1545 portrait of *Eleanor of Toledo.* She was the Spanish wife of Duke Cosimo de' Medici and she is painted with her son, Giovanni de' Medici. The remarkable dress she wears cost far more than was paid to Bronzino, and is an exceptional advertisement for the duke's revival of the silk industry that brought prosperity to Florence.

The dress has a white satin ground with large pomegranate motifs in gold-brocaded bouclé, one of which is emblazoned like a shield at the centre of the bodice. The sleeves, in the same material, are slashed and reveal the white silk of her chemise underneath. The square neck features a fine pearl and gold covering known as a partlet. At this time, pearls were sensationally expensive, far more so than diamonds, but Duchess Eleanor also wears pearl drop earrings plus two necklaces of large pearls and a striking gold-jewelled girdle with a seed-pearl tassel. The portrait provides the most detailed record of the grandest of Tuscan cloth and fashion of the Renaissance. No wonder Eleanor chose to be buried in this dress.

The textile museums in Florence and Prato and the insights provided by Bronzino and Gozzoli, together with the work of the Umbrian painter Pinturicchio, are major reference sources for those who create the costumes for Tuscany's many costumed events. It was by luck rather than design that I first became aware of the spectacular nature of one of these, Arezzo's *Giostra del Saracino,* Joust of the Saracen.

Val and I were still searching for furniture for our house in Arezzo's large, monthly outdoor antique market. We had parked by the station and then were walking up the hill into the town, only to be stopped by road blocks around Piazza Guido Monaco and Via Roma. A large crowd was waiting for something, or someone, important.

Shortly we heard the hypnotic rhythm of drums and the stirring call of trumpets in the distance. Over the next half an hour, the wide road was filled with a colourful cavalcade of women as beautiful in looks and dress as the Duchess Eleanor, each on the arm of noblemen escorts and accompanied by valets, infantrymen, knights and jousters on horseback, musicians and flag throwers, all in Renaissance finery. The young family waving yellow and crimson flags next to us explained that this was the cast of 400 going to take part in Arezzo's twice-yearly joust between the four main districts of the town. The colours of their flags showed the family lived in the Porto del Foro section of the town, and they said that tickets to the actual joust always sold out weeks in advance.

Two years later I secured seats for Arezzo's Joust of the Saracen the day they went on sale. As late afternoon shadows cast their coolness across the town, we entered Piazza Grande and settled in the grandstand just in front of the larger-than-life figure of a Saracen holding a target that the jousters would have to hit.

The 100 or so lords and ladies, soldiers, bands, servants, flag throwers and contestants from each of the four districts of the town entered the square in turn, walking slowly and majestically to the stirring sound of trumpets and drums. All of them knew exactly where to stand so that the last rays of sun highlighted the colours and tailoring of their gorgeous Renaissance finery to maximum visual effect.

After displays of flag-throwing prowess, and of musical and marching excellence, the rival supporters retreated to their own fenced-off area with police standing by, and started throwing insults as well as the occasional firecracker at one another. It was time for the contest proper to get under way.

Eight exceptional horsemen, two each from Arezzo's Crucifera, del Foro, Sant'Andrea and San Spirito quarters, rode full tilt with their long lances at the target held by the Saracen. It was rather like a highly athletic and mobile game of giant darts, accompanied by overly theatrical deliberations by the judges as to where the lances struck and the scores they were prepared to award.

Eventually, Sant'Andrea was declared the winner and what had been an ordered occasion descended into chaotic celebration. Barriers were broken and police ran for cover as hundreds of jubilant Sant' Andrea fans stormed the square and grabbed the victors' prize of a golden lance from a surprised-looking group of suited VIPs. Then they noisily made off to celebrate in their part of town.

The memories of that day stay with me, not so much for the competition itself but rather for the impact that the clothes had on the personas of the participants.

Clothes are never seen by Italians as a frivolity or mere covering. They always mean something, not least because of the demands of *far bella figura,* of making a good impression. On that day, every man and woman in costume was quite different from the person who had woken that morning.

Until I lived in Italy, I didn't really understand that clothes can suggest, persuade, insinuate, apply subtle pressure, or indeed lie. Clothes give clues about whether the wearer is speaking sincerely or telling you utter rubbish, is trying to be authoritative or hoping to charm you.

Giorgio Armani says the right clothes give people a better image of themselves and can increase their feelings of confidence and happiness. Does that mean our minds need window dressing with the right clothes quite as much as our bodies do? I think it does and perhaps that's something that has never changed.

EIGHT

Truth, Belief & Faith

From Cradle to Grave

Modern science is showing that the body parts of this or that saint, worshipped in reliquaries throughout Italy and Europe, are often not what they seem to be. One church claimed to have an arm bone of St Anthony of Padua, but it turned out to be a stag's penis.

Ninety-five per cent of Italians claim they are Roman Catholic, and the Catholic Church is still highly respected and its religious values are part of many millions of people's lives. Church weddings and first communions are still big events, while civil marriages remain a rarity and are regarded as slightly odd. As a reference point to morality, Christianity is as good as any other lifestyle choice, but many Italians aren't aware of choice and do not even know there is Christianity beyond Roman Catholicism. A recent survey in *La Repubblica* newspaper indicated that a significant proportion of Italians think Queen Elizabeth is a Catholic and that Protestants don't eat pork, don't believe in Jesus and don't celebrate Christmas.

From the 1960s until very recently, Italy claimed the highest church attendance figures in Western Europe, saying that half of its population went to church regularly and also that the number of churchgoers was stable. Early in 2007 the Patriarchate of Venice stepped out of line and undertook its own research amongst worshippers in over 600 churches. The results halved government estimates and showed that only 23 per cent of the population actually went to church regularly.

Roman Catholicism is a cradle-to-grave religion that is not just devotional but also political, social and aesthetic. Whether you are a believer or not, to be Italian means assimilating much of its customs, manners and morality. My friend Aldo says, 'It is part of our ears, our eyes, our imagination and our taste.'

The first time I was asked to state my religion on an official document in Italy, I wrote Church of England – the denomination of the Sussex church where I had been baptised. The homely woman behind the post office counter asked, 'Does that mean you are Christian?' I answered 'yes', only to be asked why I hadn't written down Catholic.

I find such ignorance and intolerance of anything outside Catholicism extremely irritating. The words Christian and Christianity are rarely used in Italy, just Catholic and Catholicism. Often the phrase 'The Church' replaces Catholicism in everyday language, as if Roman Catholicism is the only faith.

Like Italy itself, the Roman Catholic Church is extremely hierarchical. It is also extraordinarily conservative and domineering. It seems to me that the priests, the hosts of saints and every Madonna continuously conspire to get in the way of an Italian having a direct relationship with God – a stumbling point that was one of the major reasons for the Reformation and the Protestant movement. Here the congregation seems to be submissive, a recipient rather than a participant, and joyful singing is the exception rather than the rule. But this doesn't mean that what is preached to them is practised.

In countless towns and villages throughout Italy, people crowd pavements to weep with adoration when a statue of the Madonna is paraded through the streets, but back home they use contraception, pop a morning-after pill and discreetly sanction abortion. Even though contraception is not allowed here, Italy has one of the lowest birth rates in Europe.

How can so many marriages be annulled, when the Catholic Church teaches a sacramental marriage cannot be dissolved, thus making divorce or annulment impossible? The answer is that the sacrament of marriage means what the Catholic Church wants it to mean, and that there are just as many ways to claim an annulment, too. Such direct contradictions make a joke of what is, or is not, required of Catholics and make a miserable life for those not brave enough to question.

And who in the 21st century can believe that only Catholics will be 'saved'? This was a notion put together by men who didn't know the world was round, or the size of the rest of the world, or that many thousands, perhaps millions, of human beings lived in perfectly developed civilisations in the Americas, Australasia, the Pacific, and those huge parts of Asia of which none had the foggiest idea.

The way many Italians express their religious life may have changed during the 20th and 21st centuries, but I believe the Catholic Church's underlying principles are still at the heart of Italian society – generosity towards others, friendship and solidarity, charity and a good sense of togetherness.

I know this because I often talk to believers about what Catholicism means to them and I'm surprised how often it is regarded as something rather beautiful and noble. Confessing to a priest doesn't mean punishment, but is rather a private dialogue that results in a kindness, forgiveness and the taking away of guilt. Sharing the rite of communion is 'having a holy dinner', which makes a powerful connection to the family table and eating at it, both integral to the Italian way of life.

Who would argue with this? For almost 2,000 years the answer was that no-one would argue, even though accepting these beautiful and noble acts also meant believing a great deal of mysticism and myth. Today's science and modern media pose different questions and get different answers, and that gives even greater rein for charlatans to take advantage of the confused, the naive and the needy.

Our Mission of Faith

From our terrace we can see the roof of our local church, a short walk up the hill behind us. To the right of it are the tops of what now appear to be a number of farm buildings but were once the domain of a blind nun who apparently performed miracles. This was in the 1970s and her fame spread so far and wide that supplicants for her services came by the coach load.

She called herself the Mother of the Providence and, on that basis, established a so-called Mission of Faith. She told anyone who would listen that she had a vision when she lost her eyesight, allegedly in an accident at her school in Bolzano in Northern Italy.

To affect her 'miracle cures' she removed the leather eye-patches she wore and placed them on the sick person's body. The faithful and hopeful flocked to her, not least because she was backed by powerful people in the Catholic Church. These included the archbishop of our local diocese and a cardinal from Northern Italy who was close to the Pope of the time, Paul V1.

In the flesh she was a rather large, ruddy-faced woman in a white nun's hood over a black habit and always wore a flashy wristwatch, although quite why a blind woman should need such an accoutrement has never been explained to me. On most occasions she was accompanied by two male minders in black wearing sunglasses, which she also took to wearing when conducting business, presumably not to lessen the effects of ultra-violet rays but to protect others from the sight of her supposedly sightless eyes.

In the early 1980s our Mother of Providence attracted some serious funding and with it built, without planning permission, a place of pilgrimage for her mission. One of its attractions was its 'seven fountains of miracles', a feature that, unbeknown to the faithful, was achieved by tapping into a neighbour's water supply.

For a few years the place attracted hundreds of pilgrims, usually on a couple of days each month but sometimes over a full week. Much to the annoyance of everyone locally, these visits took place to the accompaniment of extremely loud music blasted all day long with the aid of two large speakers that bounced the sound around our quiet valley.

The Church explained the fact that no authenticated miracles were recorded by repeating that it must not have been the intent of God, Jesus, Mary, or some other saint to grant the desired relief. You might win or might lose, but the Church always had an explanation that was to its advantage.

A neighbour with a 12-bore shotgun finally silenced the blaring speakers and, after apparently taking this as a warning or as a sign from her God, the nun welcomed fewer and fewer pilgrims. Instead, the Mother of Providence ran a seminary or school of divinity for young men on the site. Parents, sponsors and home churches paid good money for men from mainly Third World countries to live like prisoners, work like slaves, and exist on a diet of pasta, rice and potatoes.

This venture ended upon the death of the nun's two chief ecclesiastical supporters, who coincidently died within a week of one another. Tellingly, the police moved in almost at once and arrested our local miracle worker and her cronies. They were charged with personal violence, theft, fraud, extortion and confining people against their wishes, and were set to be imprisoned. As is the way with such things in Italy, they appealed and got off a prison sentence by promising to pay back taxes. All the time the Mission of Faith was presenting itself as a tax-exempt religious organisation, it was actually being run by the nun and her henchmen as a nice-little-earner for themselves. And who knows what the reward was for the archbishop and the cardinal while they lived?

Today the hefty entrance gates to the property still carry a rather chilling MF logo. Occasionally we see low-key comings and goings, especially of young men from south-east Asia, but no-one really knows what goes on there.

This episode in the life of our local community confirms what I had always suspected. Italian Catholicism has evolved into a ragbag mixture of sacred, mythical, magical and humbug, from which anyone may easily find what they think they need. This can be seen throughout Tuscany in events such as the blessing of the horses that run in the *palio* at nearby Castiglione Fiorentina and the explosion of a cart – *Scoppio del Carro* – in Florence at Easter, where a rocket is sent from inside the cathedral to ignite the cart. No, I can't figure out any possible meaningful message.

But although local churches are now largely deserted, congregations dwindling and the Catholic Church more and more questioned, there is little diminishment in the love for St Francis or of his influence. This was amply demonstrated in 2013 when the new pontiff, former Cardinal Jorge Mario Bergoglio of Buenos Aires, decided that he should be called Pope Francis.

St Francis of Assisi

Casa Amari was previously owned by the Cappello family. The first time Val and I met them, they proudly showed us around depressing interiors, pointing out debatable features like a weird chandelier made from an old ox yolk and the stark concrete roof beams that had replaced the chestnut originals. Outside we walked down an overgrown path to the field below the house where Signor Cappello proudly told me 'St Francis walked across this land.'

I stopped myself from replying. He was a proud man who may not have reacted kindly to close questioning. But the longer we live here, the more we understand why it might still be important to today's Tuscans that the sandals of the most famous of saints may indeed have crossed our land. Francis is one of the few saints with a lifetime mission proven to be real – an honourable man who made a significant difference to the world and who can still change lives.

St Francis was born and is buried in Assisi, which nestles enticingly below the distinctive slopes of Mount Subasio, just 50km to the south-west of our house. Much authenticated material written while St Francis of Assisi was alive still exists. But it was a film from 1950 and an earthquake that set me off on a journey of discovery about the bald-pated, bird-preaching friar whose universal appeal is ecumenical.

One Saturday morning in London in late 1995, a few years before we moved to Tuscany, the arts pages of my morning newspaper listed the Vatican's Top Ten Films. It was the centenary of the cinema industry and Pope John Paul II had decided to create 'a reference point for Catholics of what the church considered worthwhile productions about religion, values and art'.

The list was something of a surprise because it included films like *The Lavender Hill Mob* and *Nosferatu,* as well as more obvious choices like Pier Paolo Pasolini's *The Gospel According to Matthew.* Of course Fellini's *La Strada* was there but I noted that he was co-writer with Roberto Rossellini of a film I had never heard about. Originally called *Francesco, Giullare di Dio,* or Francesco, God's Jester, it's now better known as *The Flowers of St Francis* and Pier Paulo Pasolini called it 'one of the most beautiful films in Italian cinema'. I soon tracked down a DVD of this 1950 film that was inspired by *I fioretti,* a collection of stories about St Francis called *The Little Flowers,* which was written at the end of the 14th century.

Rossellini made the film using real Franciscan monks and other non-professional actors that gracefully tell the story of a group of men for whom existence is a never-ending struggle to be good and to stay true to the Word of God. He avoids syrupy reverence – the central problem of all other films that have been made about saints. It was amazing and heartening to see a film in which a saint is treated with so little solemnity and I began to see quite how a man like this could have such an enduring legacy, and why paintings that feature him and his life are regarded so highly.

Two years later the greatest paintings in the world about the life of St Francis of Assisi were destroyed by an earthquake. The tremor occurred during the night of 26th September 1997 in the Apennine hills close to Assisi. People were tragically killed and properly mourned but the greatest calamity was agreed to be that Giotto's frescoes about the *Life of St Francis* lay in thousands of shattered fragments on the floor of the upper church of the Basilica of St Francis in Assisi.

Work on the basilica was started in 1228, the year Francis was canonised, and constructed slowly over the next 300 years. Sometime around the end of the 13th century, Giotto di Bondone, a young Florentine painter and architect, completed 28 frescoes in the nave of the upper part of the church. His scenes from the *Life of St Francis* depicted physical and spiritual essentials with simplicity and drama, and revealed a profound sympathy for the gentle spirit of the saint. They were full of the natural beauty that moved St Francis to such profound joy. The figures were mobile and expressive and contained a wealth of every-day detail – elements that had made the story of St Francis accessible to ordinary people for centuries. Now it seemed Giotto's frescoes, thought by many to be amongst the finest works of art in Italy, were lost forever.

Francis was born in Assisi around 1181 to Pietro Bernardone, a merchant, and his French wife Pica Bourlemont. He was christened Giovanni but his parents always called him Francesco, Francis to us. During a dissipated youth, he joined Assisi's cavalry and was captured in one of the towns many battles with nearby Perugia and put in prison for a year. He suffered periods of serious illness in his early 20s, and it was following one of these that he spent time alone in the countryside around Assisi and decided to change his life and live like Christ, in humility and poverty. Francis ditched the trappings of his privileged upbringing and made his faith in heaven his only faith.

He soon attracted a group of followers who, like him, were looking for something beyond the stick and carrot offerings of the medieval church. In 1210 the Pope authorised Francis and his followers to spread a message of the virtues of simplicity and poverty, and this marked the foundation of the Franciscan Order. In his travels and preaching during the next 20 years, Francis' extraordinary character and sanctity inspired a movement of spiritual renewal that spread across Italy and beyond. He died in Assisi in 1226 and is buried in the lower church of the Basilica di San Francesco.

Once the dust had settled after the earthquake, as soon as they could get safe access to the damaged basilica, a team of professionals, students and volunteers set about sifting through the tens of thousands of puzzle-like pieces that were mixed in with general debris. In less than five years they completed the restoration under the direction of Professor Giuseppe Basile of Rome's Central Restoration Institute. Much to my delight, they finished their work on the day Val and I moved into Casa Amari, our home in the Tuscan hills.

Our first visit to see the restored frescoes was a revelation. Each of the 28 panels depicting scenes from the *Life of St Francis* creates a small stage set on which Giotto has arranged the players, like a theatre director might do. The contents, compositions and colours he used, the way his love of all living creatures, especially birds and animals, are depicted are exquisite in every scene. Many are also extremely touching and I felt Giotto's genius lay in the way he had dramatised each event and given his figures a heroic stillness – a superhuman quality that nonetheless speaks to ordinary humans.

Over five million tourists a year visit Assisi, and many of them will be profoundly moved by the beauty and the message of the St Francis frescoes. Then most go on to La Verna where Francis received the stigmata, the wounds Christ endured at the crucifixion. It is not a place I warm to, for it has little of the simple Franciscan message about it.

The Franciscan monastery of La Verna sits high on a bizarre rocky outcrop about 120km north-west of Assisi. The land was given to St Francis in 1213 and, according to one of his visions, it was blasted into its wild shape at the moment of the crucifixion. Its churches, chapels and convent are simple, although the main church is decorated with some of the finest enamelled terracotta sculptures that Andrea della Robbia ever made. A few steps away from one of the chapels, there's a stomach-churning view of the sheer rock face upon which La Verna was built. There are also signposts galore that point to holy spots built into the rock and under huge boulders.

Coaches queue in the main car park to off-load thousands of fit and not-so-fit tourists of all ages and nationalities. On the cobbled access path to the monastery, bizarrely dressed pilgrims and hikers with sturdy staves and the types of sandal their saint may have worn must dodge priests and nuns who delight in driving their cars at speed, presumably relying on St Francis to keep both them and the tourists safe.

I much prefer to head a short distance south to the little hill town of Montefalco, the 'balcony of Umbria'. Here there's a completely different depiction of the *Life of St Francis* by Benozzo Gozzoli, who has become one of my favourite artists of the 15th century. His frescoes are in the main apse of the church that is part of the Museo Civico di San Francesco. The first time we saw them, Val said she believes their obvious element of joy is because Gozzoli relished colour and narrative for their own sake and truly loved painting detail. Certainly the colours he uses in his enchanting paintings are bright and festive, and he exhibits a sense of what is rich, lively and joyful in people and objects. Nineteen episodes from the life and work of the saint are condensed into 12 celebratory pictures of landscapes crowded with lovingly observed men, women, birds and animals.

Over a glass of Montefalco's superb *secco* wine opposite the Museo Civico, the bar tender told me his town was a 'factory for saints' and that the celestial world included eight sanctified former citizens. This made me wonder aloud. If eight had come from this tiny town of just over 5,000 souls how many Catholic saints must there be in total? '10,000', said my host, 'and the Popes keep them coming.'

The Relics Debate

After the death of St Francis of Assisi in 1226, Cortona was chosen as the site of the first Franciscan church to be built outside Assisi. The architect of the Chiesa di San Francesco was Brother Elias, a native of Cortona and the saint's closest friend and disciple, who combined this task with raising the basilica in Assisi in honour of St Francis. He died in the friary and was buried in the church.

Amongst San Francesco's possessions is a fragment of the True Cross, a piece of wood supposedly from the cross on which Jesus was crucified. Many other claims to have parts of the True Cross have been refuted, but Cortona's credentials have yet to be challenged by spoilsports because our local relic is said to have been brought back from Constantinople by Brother Elias. It's a provenance that is firmly rooted in the miasma of fiction and might-have-been that is a mainstay of the Catholic Church.

St Helen was the mother of Constantine the Great, the first Roman Emperor to become a Christian and who founded Constantinople. She lived from about 250 to 330 AD and is said to have dug a deep hole on the outskirts of Jerusalem and there discovered the remains of the Cross, identified the Tomb of the Resurrection, and much else that is vital to the Christian legend.

As this was about three centuries after the Crucifixion, St Helen's miraculous discoveries are rather like one of us discovering the block of wood on which Mary Queen of Scots lost her head (after several blows), or that which helped the despatch of Charles I or the French King Louis XVI and his Queen Marie Antoinette. Oh yes, and doing so on the very site where it was used so many hundreds of years before . . .

The reputed piece of the True Cross certainly looks old, and is encased in an equally ancient looking Byzantine ivory reliquary inscribed in Greek. Whatever else it does, it makes you think and that's no bad thing.

More impressive in size at least, is a cloak that St Francis allegedly wore some 800 years ago. When we first moved to Casa Amari the rough, brown garment just lay there on the floor of the chapel to the left of the altar of the Chiesa di San Francesco. It was unprotected and forlorn, but a water-stained, handwritten card claimed it was the real thing and most people believed this, or said they did.

In 2007 everything changed for this supposed miracle of survival, when someone in the church asked Italian nuclear scientists to verify the age of the cloak. The result of their tests was first presented in Florence at the unappealingly named European Conference on Accelerators in Applied Research and Technology, and showed that the cloak dated from between 1155 AD and 1225 AD, roughly contemporary with the saint. It was indeed a miracle of survival.

Today the cloak is displayed in a heavily alarmed glass display cabinet, together with a mortuary pillow and a gospel book, which are also associated with St Francis. Carbon dating of the pillow has shown that it is contemporary with the saint's life. And palaeographic experts at the University of Siena say the handwriting in the gospel book is in the style used at the same time.

Naturally the Franciscan order say with confidence that Brother Elias brought these relics to Cortona following the saint's death, so they might be housed in the church he was building in his memory. There's really no reason to doubt this and, to me, the three objects are all the more miraculous because they are not presumed or supposed to have mystical powers of healing or foresight.

Mystery, awe and faith are rather more put to the test in the case of the Shroud of Turin, believed to have wrapped the body of Christ between the Crucifixion and the Resurrection.

The shroud's great claim on the faithful's reverence is the image it shows of a bearded man who has been crucified. To this day neither science nor art has been able to say how the image was made on the linen of the shroud. It was heroic of the Catholic Church to allow a tiny shred of the cloth to be radio carbon dated in 1988. The result sparked particularly hostile debates between scientists and men of faith because the test dated the fabric from only 1260 AD. Could this be because the sample taken was from a medieval repair to the shroud, rather than from the original cloth? We may never know the answer because the Catholic Church has more or less closed its doors to investigation by science on the shroud and other relics.

Both clerics and scientists agree there are too many religious and political implications in proving or disproving holy relics, which shows only that each deeply suspects and resents the other's existence in the modern world.

Yet none of this seems to matter to the man and woman in the *strada*. Tell them about someone or something that claims a special relationship with a saint, with Heaven or with God him/herself and they still flock, and pay good money to do so.

Le Celle

Not far from our house, a windy, narrow lane takes us to the lower slopes of Monte Egido and to one of the most beautifully situated monasteries in Italy, the Convento delle Celle.

In 1211 St Francis and a few of his followers built a small hermitage here and the place has taken the name of Le Celle, meaning the cells, ever since. This is believed to be the place he rested on one of his last journeys before his death. To this day you can still see his small cell carved out of rock and the stone platform he slept upon as a bed.

St Francis had a knack of choosing geographically significant locations to meditate and for his sanctuaries. While La Verna is high above the surrounding landscape on top of a rocky crag, Le Celle is close to the floor of a valley amongst boulders shaped by water that rushes down from the mountains, becoming a torrent in winter.

The monastery is a collection of simple, rustic buildings with terraced fruit and vegetable gardens. These cling to one side of a huge rocky escarpment split by the river. Hidden from view until you are close to the steep path that leads down to the monastery buildings, it is a place that encourages you to be silent and contemplative, whether you are religious or not.

When I'm here I'm inevitably reminded of how far removed St Francis's essential message of simple goodness and morality is from the astonishing mysteries and obvious untruths preached by celibate old men in outrageous robes of gold and scarlet amid clouds of incense. Such suspension of belief – they'd call it Faith – is a conscious manipulation of other minds to the power, glory and riches of the priests themselves. That might have worked in the days when so many never moved more than ten miles from where they were born, and when few read or wrote – but in the 21st century?

If I find myself becoming over-intoxicated by the glorious music or the sensational art and architecture that Christianity has inspired, I check myself by thinking of the stag's penis and the reality of the Shroud of Turin. Providing you can distance yourself from belief in things you know simply can't be true, the Church's legacy of inspirational beauty in objects and sound more than makes up for the nonsense of the world's most enduring PR spin.

I come to Le Celle because it is so beautiful and quiet. So do young men who are contemplating priesthood, and so do troubled priests who wish to spend time in solitary prayer. Padre Orlando, a young priest from Trento, told me more about the history of the place one bright summer afternoon. I commented upon the zucchini and beans he was picking in one of the monastery's abundant and well-tended vegetable gardens and he used the opportunity to take a break. He asked me whether I knew about Brother Elias of Cortona and, when I said I did, he told me stories that are missed out of official guide books.

'Franciscans believe that four months before St Francis died in Assisi he dictated his will here, possibly to Elias. Following the saint's death, Brother Elias came and lived here for a while and carried out a number of improvements. I am staying in one of the eight small rooms he built, each just large enough for a bed, a table and a chair.

'After Brother Elias died in Cortona in 1253, the Franciscan Order fell foul of a complicated series of internal divisions. As a consequence the hermitage was occupied by a non-Franciscan community for over a hundred years, but they were eventually excommunicated and left.

'For the next 200 years this place lay abandoned and then, in 1537, the newly founded Capuchins, or Third Order of Franciscans, established their monastery here. What you see today is largely what they constructed and this Order still provides a place for people like me who want to get away for a period of solitary prayer. They also offer lodgings to those contemplating a vocational life and who are willing to take part in the community's activities as a way of confirming their calling.'

Padre Orlando proved to be a talkative soul and very unlike your average priest, not least because of the trainers he wore on his feet and the large watch held to his wrist by a bright red strap. He wanted to know what I did, how I came to be at Le Celle, and about my previous life in London. I had the distinct feeling that he was thinking of leaving the priesthood and wanted to experience life outside Italy and away from the Catholic Church.

I plucked up courage and asked him how he saw the role of religion in modern society. His smiling face turned solemn. 'Sometimes I wonder whether religion has lost its battle with science in the modern world. It seems new inventions and discoveries in science are proving more and more religious thoughts wrong. Also, in this fast-moving world, I see far too many people ending up by having no time for themselves, so how will they ever find time for God?'

We said our goodbyes and I gave him my details and invited him to visit us next time he was in Cortona. I held out the carrot of St Francis having walked across our land. He replied with a wink, 'Don't believe that everything a Catholic tells you is true.'

NINE

Anything for a Party

IN CELEBRATION OF THE FISHERMAN'S FRIEND

Italians take festivity seriously. This is the way it has been for centuries. It seems they have a special talent for bringing communities together to celebrate a saint or a favourite food, a holiday or an historical event, and do so with an extraordinary amount of passion and vitality.

Living in the Tuscan countryside, I have come to appreciate simple, local food festivals where the focus is invariably an impressive cooking area where meat and vegetables are grilled over wood. But, as someone who was raised on the Full English and fish and chips, I do sometimes hanker after a fry-up. Thus it was only natural that I should accept an invitation from friends to experience a unique celebration centred around a massive frying pan on the Ligurian coast.

Camogli is a small and picturesque fishing village on the coastal strip east of Genoa known as the Riviera di Levante. I drove there passing Lucca and the marble mountains of Carrara, and then via the five medieval villages of the Cinque Terre on one of the most beautiful and unspoilt stretches of coast in Italy. After passing Rapallo, I took the turning to Camogli and found myself descending through dramatic stone cliffs to a tiny harbour surrounded by colourful buildings on the edge of the blue waters of the Mediterranean.

It was a sunny Saturday in May, the day before Camogli's *Sagra del Pesce*, and I hoped to see the local fishermen setting off that night to net what the sea would give up to them for the next day's fry-up. I checked into a local hotel overlooking the harbour, and was just in time for a late lunch of *corzetti*, a traditional Ligurian pasta shape modelled after an ancient eight-sided coin. The chef had made it that morning, just as he had the other regional speciality that followed, rabbit cooked with tiny Ligurian olives and pine nuts.

I walked down to the harbour area, revitalised but not overstuffed, to wander amongst brightly painted, slim houses up to eight storeys tall, all connected by steep steps, narrow alleys and tiny courtyards. Various shades of primary colours differentiated the dwellings, as they have done since Renaissance times, and many sported *trompe l'oeil,* carefully painted tricks that make you think the walls sport balconies, garlands, columns and statues, arches, shutters and windows.

A ruddy-faced fisherman unloading one of the equally colourful fishing boats told me I had got my facts wrong about the boats going out that night. 'We stopped fishing the night before the *sagra* years ago. The amount of fish we have to fry just got too much to catch in one night.'

He pointed to the far side of the harbour, 'Tomorrow, over there, we will be frying enough to feed the 5,000.' I thought of a certain scene from the Bible, and looked 'over there' to the shaded piazza in front of the 13th-century Dragonara castle and the 12th-century basilica of Santa Maria Assunta that is next to it. Both seemed to rise straight out of the water and created a dramatic divide between the harbour and a pebbly beach.

On the piazza side of the castle and church, a low-level stage was being set with a four-metre diameter frying pan with an even longer handle. This was carefully positioned over a lattice-work of gas jets attached to a platoon of gas cylinders that sat amongst an army of oil cans and bags galore of flour.

I walked past these preparations and on to the beach, where I discovered the rough and ready carcass of a large boat being packed with crates, furniture, planks and cardboard boxes. It was being constructed to look like a dragon and seemed to crouch at the water's edge.

My curiosity got the better of me and I took a seat on the sea wall next to an elderly couple. We soon got into conversation. They asked if this was my first time in Camogli and then started to educate me in the most charming way about the *sagra* in honour of San Fortunato, the patron saint of fishermen.

The couple remembered being part of the first festival in 1952, when small bonfires were lit on the beach so that the fishermen who went out to catch the fish for the next day's fry-up would always have the village in sight. Over the years, the Porto and Pinetto neighbourhoods of Camogli found themselves in competition with one another to produce more and more elaborate bonfires. The signora explained that previous designs had included a submarine, a windmill, a telephone and landmark towers, and that they had all been constructed from household bric-a-brac collected during the previous 12 months. The year I was there, the two neighbourhoods had decided to combine their efforts and construct just one bonfire – a 15m-long dragon boat. The couple told me that at midnight a flame would zip down a wire, strung from the top of the church next to the castle, into the boat and set it alight.

A lorry arrived and a dozen willing hands unloaded large sheets of red- and blue-painted hardboard. These were then nailed to the tumbled carcass of unwanted furniture to create a realistic and fully decorated sailing galleon with a high, square poop and a large, fiery dragon's head.

'A big bonfire every year is good for the community,' the signore proclaimed. His eyes glazed and he looked into the distance. 'Here on one night we can burn away the guilt of family feuds and business betrayals, of mothers not thanked enough and fathers forgotten, of love unacknowledged, of apologies not spoken.'

I asked my new acquaintances how the festival came into being and they said it was started to honour San Fortunato after a near-drowning of a local fisherman. Others claim it was started to give thanks to the saint for his protection during the Second World War. 'I can remember our fishermen once going out amongst the mines and returning safely with one of the biggest catches ever. It was this that kept us from starvation during one of the worst periods of the war. We salted and dried the fish, layered them in oil and brine, made fish pâtés and sauces. That fish was a gift from on high.'

The World's Largest Fry-Up

Italy is one of the most stable house markets in Europe with what estate agents call a 'strong' domestic demand for second homes, especially in the north of the country and in coastal resorts. Many properties have been inherited from relatives and are used only for holidays and at weekends by a myriad of relations. In Liguria about a third of all properties are estimated to be second homes and 80 per cent of these are owned by Italians.

Andrea and Marinella have a second home on the sixth floor of an imposing 19th-century building opposite the best *pasticceria e focacceria* in Camogli. Before going up to their flat, I joined the orderly queue outside the pastry and bread shop and, when it was my turn, copied what the person next to me was buying – slices of warm focaccia covered with slivers of onion and stuffed with soft local cheese. I also asked them to fill a large cake box with *camogliesi,* the local speciality of choux pastry balls filled with a creamy custard mix flavoured with rum.

My hosts rewarded me with a glass of the local Cinque Terre dry white wine and a stunning view of the harbour. The completed dragon-boat bonfire was still on the seashore and the sun was going down over the sea. When the sound of a marching band started to waft through the open windows, Andrea said it was time to take to the streets.

In a country with more than 10,000 saints, penitential processions are at the heart of nearly every Italian *festa*. 'They are both Catholic and pagan. I like to think of them as guilt, penitence and exuberance all melding together,' said Marinella as we went down the stairs.

The statue of San Fortunato had left the church overlooking the harbour and was on its journey through the streets, so that local people could show their gratitude for the saint's protection. We joined the crowd outside the bakery and watched as eight men dressed in white monks' habits staggered up the hill carrying a highly decorated wooden platform upon which a life-size statue of the saint was surrounded by dozens of tall candles. Behind them came more men in white and hundreds of black-dressed women fondling rosaries. The town's band played solemn music to complete the official procession but sometimes the musicians upped the tempo to a cheerful tune, much to the delight of everyone, especially the children following the band.

I asked Marinella if she knew the story of San Fortunato. 'There are many saints with this name. Ours is said to have come from Rome. They say that he devoted his life to helping the sick and poor and was martyred in 400. For some reason his bones ended up under the altar of the Convento di San Fortunato in Montefalco in Umbria quite near where you live.'

I said that I thought that St Peter was the patron saint of fishermen. 'Yes, so did I until we bought our flat here and that was when I realised that communities have always appropriated their saints to look after their local needs. Anyway, the Catholic Church has always been happy to go along with local legends when it suits them.'

We returned to the apartment for a ring-side view of the fireworks that had been positioned to go off near the water's edge and around the castle and the basilica. While we were on the streets, the baker from the *pasticceria* and his large and jolly wife had let themselves in and filled the living room with food.

I showed a special interest in a salad of a variety of cooked fishes, including gurnard, lobster and langoustine arranged in layers with green beans, cauliflower, artichokes, celery, potato, salsify, hard-boiled eggs, olives and mushrooms, each of which was dressed with a green sauce that tasted like a cross between *salsa verde* and mayonnaise. Their eyes lit up and the baker's wife explained, 'That is *cappon magro,* a local speciality,' and pointing to another dish said, 'This is another Ligurian treat, *pansotti con tocco de noxe,* triangles of herb-filled pasta with a walnut sauce. In the pot on the stove in the kitchen is our special *buridda,* a stew made with the best local fish.'

There were also dishes of fresh anchovies, stuffed specialities including mussels, breasts of veal and every type of vegetable plus the baker's pride and joy, his *farinata* chickpea flour crepes and his focaccia, in this case a particularly light, soft flat bread enriched with olive oil and garnished with fennel seeds. Joining these two, was his *sardenaira* tart, a speciality similar to a pizza but with the tomatoes and onions cooked before putting them on the bread base, as opposed to a pizza where the topping is left uncooked before going into the oven. The sauce was particularly tasty being made from locally caught sardines, capers, garlic, Ligurian black olives and oregano.

We all ate far more than we should and, as midnight approached, a canvas of colours, starbursts and cascades was splashed on to the black sky accompanied by a cacophony of whistles, hums, crackles and bangs. The best were silver bouquets that rose noisily, but then fell silently into the sea. Finally the clock on the basilica chimed 12 times, heralding the start of Sunday. The crowd on the beach and promenade cheered and a flame shot down from the top of the church and set the elaborate bonfire alight. What a way to welcome the fry-up that would come tomorrow.

Next morning I walked along the beach past the smouldering ashes of the burnt-out dragon boat and joined the crowd outside the basilica. Here we waited patiently for the priest and his attendants to appear. At last they filed out onto the steps, and proceeded reverently to the boxes of fish on the quayside to bless them before they ended up in the giant frying pan and the mouths of thousands.

Thirty or so helpers dusted the blessed fish with flour and then gave them to the team of fryers, who put them into 28 oversized fish-fryer's baskets that were then placed in the bubbling oil of the frying pan to cook for a short while. As each basket of fish became ready to eat, nifty hands made light work of taking them out of the oil, giving them a serious shake, and tipping the golden fish into large plastic trays lined with paper that soaked up any remaining cooking oil.

Two orderly queues formed either side of the frying pan and within minutes small takeaway containers of hot fish sprinkled with salt were being served at breakneck speed by the jolly posse of helpers in red t-shirts. Food in hand, I sat on the harbour's edge and enjoyed the freshest anchovies, sardines and *pesce azzurro*, a local deep-sea blue fish specialty.

Queuing is not something the Italians are good at but, as the sun broke through on a glorious late spring day, no-one on the quayside shoved or got impatient waiting for their free fish. The Carabinieri saw that their law-and-order responsibilities were redundant and tucked in with the rest of us. Serving went on well into the afternoon, filling the air around the harbour with the mouth-watering aromas of fried fish travelling up through the hollow handle of the frying pan, a cunning invention which had been designed to act as a chimney.

I know from my own unsavoury past, as someone who once tried to set the record for creating the world's largest steak and kidney pie, that cooking on a big scale can be a hit-and-miss affair. The complexities of engineering the equipment and the logistics and timings involved are considerable. Health and safety regulations alone can easily put a damper on the proceedings. But this being Italy, I saw no obvious concern amongst the thousands of appreciative fish eaters crowding around an open pan filled with 700 litres of boiling oil.

THE INTRIGUES OF THE LOCAL PALIO

Festivals tend to fall into four groups. There's the type of country festival called *sagra* which celebrates the fertility of nature, like the fish one in Camogli; and religious festivals which celebrate such divine blessings as saints' feast days that take place in most towns and villages. Then there are also political festivals and civic festivals that glorify a city's prosperity.

Perhaps most famous of these civic festivals is Siena's *Corsa del Palio* where ten *contrade*, administrative wards from the three districts of the city, are selected to compete in an extraordinary horse race that was first run in 1310. Every July, and then again in August, 30,000 people crowd into the main *campo* to watch the three-lap spectacular which prompts intense rivalry between the *contrade* and, as a consequence, creates an extraordinary atmosphere throughout the city.

We have a local equivalent on a less-grand scale, the *Palio dei Rioni,* which is staged in nearby Castiglion Fiorentino on the third Sunday of June. This is a real eye-opener into how Tuscans are masters at stretching just 90 seconds of action into a celebration that lasts all weekend.

Castiglion Fiorentino is one of those neat, small towns where nothing much seems to happen for most of the year. The fact that it stages such an infectious and exhilarating event not only reflects how deep neighbourhood and civic pride and rivalries go, but also how Italians love a spectacle and are enthusiastic about keeping ancient traditions alive.

Local historian Alessio Gasparri showed me documents in the town's official archives that refer to a palio taking place here in celebration of the Madonna delle Grazie del Rivaio in 1864. 'An annual celebration of the town's own Madonna had been going on for centuries. A palio was apparently staged on various occasions from the 1930s until before the war, and then was resurrected in 1977 as a way of honouring our lady,' he explained.

The flags of the three *rioni*, neighbourhoods, that compete against one another in this less-than-gentlemanly horse race start appearing weeks before the event. Whichever road you take into Castiglion Fiorentino, and long before you reach the hilltop community, they flutter majestically in support and anticipation from gateposts and bedroom windows. During the final days before the palio, and especially over the weekend when the race takes place, there are processions, much flag waving and throwing, rehearsals, veterinary checks and church blessings for the horses and their riders.

Over the years this palio took place in many locations in and around the town until eventually it found the perfect home in the circular Piazza Garibaldi, close to an ancient entrance into the walled old town. Some 4,000 people watch the race standing shoulder to shoulder in the centre of the piazza. Their shirts and banners create a brilliant backdrop of the colours of their favoured *rione* – green, orange, white, blue, red and yellow.

Alessio managed to get us into the centre of things, sitting on a wooden bench overlooking the start line. This proved to be uncomfortably close to the horses and the riders, but it did enable me to see and hear many of the intrigues and to witness the skulduggeries that characterise this event. Palio events are run all over Italy and are said to be the world's most bent horse races.

I asked Alessio if this was true. 'They grew out of attempts by town and city councils in the Middle Ages to subdue civic riots which occurred each year during carnival time. Their solution was to organise competitions between rival *rioni* and *contrade,* which included everything from bloody primeval ball games, like your rugby, to jousts on horseback and to chasing and fighting bulls. Unfortunately, most of these left an alarming number of people dead on the streets. The palio is the sole survivor from these times because it was the gentlest competition of them all. Not that an undercurrent of violence doesn't run through many of today's palio races . . .'

The word *palio* refers to the embroidered banner offered as a prize to the winning neighbourhood and the jockeys are called *fantini.* Most are professional or semi-professional palio riders, usually Sardinian, that have been hired by each neighbourhood. The horses are half breeds trained for the demands of the courses and to stand the strain of the excitement.

I am not a racing man but it seemed that the animals on the track at Castiglion Fiorentino, along with those held in a reserve stable, were all fit, lean and mean athletes, as keen to race and win as their riders. The jockeys were just mean. Universally dark and swarthy, without the hint of a smile and certainly not the sort one would choose to insult or upset.

We took our seats 30 minutes before the race, fortified with a bottle of water, a plastic cup brimming with beer, and a sandwich filled with *porchetta*, roast stuffed pork, all purchased from an oversized catering truck doing a roaring trade nearby.

First, a large tractor raked the ten-metre-wide dirt and sand track and then watered it. The driver, cigarette in mouth, seemed pleased to be the centre of attention, waving to friends with both hands thus allowing his hefty charge to veer perilously close to the crowd packing the barriers.

Next came the officials, all of them immaculately turned out in summer suits, collars and ties and led by a handsome George Clooney look-alike who turned out to be the starter. The group stepped up to the starter's platform and proceeded to direct the track staff about the location of two ropes that would be stretched across the track to form a pen in which the horses would line up.

To the sound of an expectedly off-tune town band, the runners and their evil-looking riders entered the track a few minutes after seven o'clock in the early evening. Each of the three *rioni* had two horses running. The jockeys rode bareback and were dressed in bright silk shirts and riding hats decorated in the colours of the competing neighbourhoods. Cheers, shouts and many a ribald comment drowned out the music as supporters made it obvious who they were supporting. Some shouted for Rione di Porta Romana, in red and yellow with a Roman wolf suckling twins as their coat of arms. Terziere di Porta Fiorentina sported green and orange with a Florentine lily motive. Rione Cassero were in white and blue with a logo depicting the town's tallest tower, but were considered newcomers as they first competed only in 1977.

After a few turns around the track, the horses gathered in front of the starter's rostrum where the jockeys were issued with what proved to be potent weapons – their riding whips. No one is neutral come palio time, but local rivalries really become physical once the crops are issued. These, Alessio whispered to me with a smirk on his face, are traditionally made from calf phalluses.

Well before the two ropes had been stretched into place and before any indication that the horses should line up for the start, the *fantini* pushed, shoved, punched and used their whips to strike their rivals. One Porta Fiorentina rider seemed to come in for more than his fair share of attacks. He was unseated three times and pleaded with the officials to intervene, all to no avail. Most frightening of all was a Cassero rider who took against a spectator close to me and reached over the barrier to give him a couple of stinging slaps with his whip. I was beginning to wish we were sitting further away from the start line.

Alessio noticed my worried look and tried to reassure me by explaining the rules and regulations or, as it turned out, lack of them. 'Each *rione* has three horses and two are selected in a type of lottery to run the race. It's the horse that wins, not the jockey, even if the horse comes in rider-less. The jockeys are not allowed to seize the reins of an opponent but everything else goes, as you will see. And, of course, bribing opposing jockeys, making an alliance with another *rione* and ambushing jockeys before the race is quite common.'

I was bemused but, to be fair, I had not seen any obvious or surreptitious signs of betting. 'It is not a race for money and supposedly there are no illegal side-bets. But I know baskets of euros ride on the outcome of the Siena palio and so I bet the same goes on here', Alessio told me.

The order in which the horses line up is predetermined by ballot and getting them in place so they all start together takes forever. In the process the animals get more and more agitated, and kick out and rear up as their riders try to whip them into position whilst taking every opportunity to taunt other riders and horses.

After more than ten minutes, the rope in front of the horses dropped only to be followed by a loud cannon shot. It had been a false start. There were two more of these over the next half an hour and more pushing, punching and whippings. Then eventually they were off. The pace was fast and the shoving continued, but it seemed to me that the horses were in control and were enjoying racing at full pelt against one another, enjoying the ancient herd instinct that had never faded.

Each lap takes only 20 seconds. On the first, one of the Porta Fiorentina riders was pulled off his mount and after four laps the two Cassero horses came in first and second. The Cassero supporters went wild and hundreds of blue-and-white-clad fans grabbed the palio banner from an official getting ready to make the formal presentation. The losing horses and their defeated jockeys made for safe cover in an out-of-sight paddock area, and the red and yellow, green and orange supporters evaporated. The official starter made a dash for the exit under the protection of the Carabinieri, just in case the losing *rioni* decided to protest about his handling of the race. The celebrations in the Cassero neighbourhood would continue well into the next day.

I said goodbye to Alessio and made for the car park, seeing a group of young female fans wrapped in Cassero flags being ogled and quietly threatened by a crowd of untidily dressed middle-aged men. Then I saw the vocal spectator who had been whipped by one of the jockeys. I pointed out the stand-off and also asked him if he was alright. He replied with a wry smile and the age-old retort *'carnevale, quando ogni scherzo vale',* during carnival, anything goes.

The Garage Banquet

Ferragosto is a celebration that may have originally been allied to the middle of summer and the end of hard labour in the fields. Today it's a national holiday on 15th August each year, celebrating the day of the Assumption of the Virgin Mary, when Mary was transported directly to heaven to be with her son, Jesus. For many people it means the start of an extended break or the commencement of their main summer holiday.

Traditionally, Ferragosto is a day when families get together to create their own festa with a large and lengthy lunch at its heart. During the preceding days sales of meat and poultry go through the roof, and here in Tuscany its famous Chianina beef becomes a must to serve on the big day.

Cortona's lofty position overlooks the Val di Chiana, where the white Chianina cattle live a charmed life. So it's not surprising that the town is host to a two-day Ferragosto celebration of these animals' most prized asset cut – their glorious T-bone steaks which are cooked over a wood fire, *alla Fiorentina*.

The first time I went to this long-established event, I decided to get in shape by taking an early morning walk along the old Roman road that runs near the crest of the hill above our house. The plan was that I would skip lunch and dine out with the thousands that attend the steak festa. A chance invitation from the ever-generous Carrai family changed all that.

The path down from the ridge takes me through my nearest hamlet and by their houses. As I passed I was greeted by the grandchildren, all keen to show me the signs they had painted for their festa lunch. One said 'parking', making it clear this wasn't going to be a small affair.

Scrumptious smells were coming from Maura's kitchen. She came to the door and beckoned me in to inspect the large duck and an even bigger goose about to join one another in the oven. 'Please join us for lunch, we have so much food,' she pleaded. 'It is family and a few friends, nothing grand, only 21 of us.' Her daughter-in-law Cinzia joined us, adding, 'Marcello is cooking some great steaks, too.'

Val and I returned at one o'clock as drinks were being served unceremoniously behind their garage, a location with spectacular views of the surrounding hillsides. Here a few old bricks supported a grill upon which half-a-dozen large steaks and dozens of sausages were being cooked over a mound of white embers.

Chilled, softly sparkling prosecco from the Veneto was poured, and plates of crumbling pieces of three-year-old goats' milk cheese were handed round by the youngsters. The cheese had been brought back from Sardinia by Marcello and was curiously similar to Parmesan, but sweeter.

The summons to lunch took us into the garage where one table was reserved for six children, and one very long table with benches was set for the adults. There would have been much more space out in the garden, but in the heat of summer few self-respecting Italians would be seen dead eating outside and the garage was the only covered space that could accommodate such a big party.

I now thoroughly recommend eating in a garage as long as it is clean, painted white, and has large doors that are fully open and act as a picture window to marvellous scenery bathed in sunshine. I was not so sure about the plastic cups and plates and paper napkins but, in their way, they did seem to suit the functional venue. The sole picture hanging in the garage was an ancient stained photograph of Tonio Carrai's *nonno,* his grandfather, who seemed to beam proudly over the scene before him, as course followed course. If the surroundings and crockery were not grand, the food certainly was . . .

The antipasti of *crostini,* one with a tomato topping, another thick with freshly made chicken liver pâté, were served with platters of roughly cut Tuscan prosciutto, fennel-flavoured Tuscan salami, chorizo-like salami from Naples and delicious *cantalupo* melon grown by one of the relations. Then followed wide ribbons of pasta with a *sugo,* sauce, made from the livers of the duck and goose I had seen earlier.

If that, and the help-yourself chunks of unsalted bread, flagons of red wine and water, wasn't quite enough, next came the first meat course. Two types of sausages, one pork and the other wild boar made by a farmer friend, were offered together with *fagiolini di sant'anna,* a home-grown Tuscan variety of thin, slightly bitter green beans. These had been dressed with a small quantity of rich, warm, homemade tomato sauce.

Behind me the children were all tucking in and demonstrating perfect table manners as they talked without shouting, nineteen to the dozen and without ever indicating they wanted to be part of the adults' table or its conversations.

With comments that confirmed all that had gone before were mere appetisers, loud cheers greeted the arrival of the main meat course. There were piled up dishes galore of roughly jointed duck and goose, of rare, slightly charred Chianina steaks and of succulent pork ribs. A bowl of green salad leaves and a bowl of chopped tomatoes, both of which were dressed with a little peppery Tuscan olive oil, were courtesy of Cinzia's parents and their vegetable garden.

By this time the acoustics in the garage were fighting a losing battle against the multitude of conversations going on, many moaning about the government and Italian bureaucracy but most being about food. Yet all the way through lunch and whatever the noise level, there was the disconcerting sound of what I imagined to be water torture. Where was the drip-drip coming from? What could it indicate?

As plastic plates full of bones and scraps that would delight a hundred dogs were cleared, a sink with a dripping tap became the focus of the next course. It was in a dark corner of the garage and contained a green-skinned *cocomero,* watermelon, so large that it took two people to lift it. Dripping cold water from the tap had been keeping it perfectly cool, as directed by Cinzia's parents who had grown it.

Cocomero is the summer fruit in Italy and the green-striped variety is the most popular because of its full flavour. Italian children love watermelon and the enjoyment carries on right into old age, clearly illustrated by both the oldest and youngest at the lunch, a boy of two and a grandfather of 83, taking equal refreshment from thick slices of the fresh, cool fruit in the same messy way.

That was it, I thought. But, oh no, next there were grapes and green plums, again grown by Cinzia's parents. These were followed by three types of homemade *dolce,* dessert: a rich chocolate cake, a jam tart, and a melt-in-your-mouth almond and cream sponge cake. As these were put before us, new plastic beakers were passed around and we were encouraged to help ourselves to the best grappa money can buy, or a slug or two from an unlabelled bottle of vin santo. Not to fill your own beaker meant doing battle with the person opposite or next to you trying to make sure it was always full. The many talents of Cinzia's parents again got the most praise. The intense, aromatic, ten-year-old vin santo dessert wine had been made by her father from grapes he had grown, dried before vinification, and then aged the Tuscan way in small *caratelli* barrels.

It took some doing to get up from my seat, but I managed to join the clumps of men propping one another up while carefully holding half-empty spirit bottles. The short stagger to the shade of the nearest walnut tree was a relatively painless exercise and bountifully rewarded. Here Tuscan cigars were produced and cut in half to share, along with a common wish that every day should be like Ferragosto.

We left with gifts of boxes containing the three *dolci* and a large dish of one of the pasta dishes to heat up and eat the next day. A siesta beckoned before I turned my attention to food once again, and those steaks promised in Cortona that night. Surely they would never be as good as those served at lunchtime?

CHIANINA CUCINA

Back home on Casa Amari's terrace, chin on chest and the still of the early-evening air resounding to my occasional snore, I was woken by the ringing of the old brass bell that hangs on our gates. My English jeweller friend Jacob, who has a house in nearby Teverina, had unexpectedly turned up wanting to find out more about my efforts to keep the wild boar from turning my garden into a badly ploughed field.

I think I was able to give him some useful information about electric fencing from my lethargic and overstuffed state. I couldn't avoid telling him about lunch and, seeing his attention was held by this talk of food, then chanced my luck by asking whether he would like to chauffeur me into Cortona for a steak supper? Jacob is a perceptive and kind soul. He saw I was much in need of manly support, and perhaps even of physical assistance, to make it to my next Ferragosto meal.

Until tractors became commonplace just 50 years ago, white Chianina cattle were the most common sight in Tuscan fields and roads. They grazed in the fields, pulled the ploughs and dragged heavy loads on sleds. The Chianina breed is one of the purest and most ancient in the world, so-called because it originated in the Val di Chiana. Chianina were known in Roman times and revered for their strength and their beauty, and thus the snow-white cattle that took part in sacrificial processions in Rome were probably Chianini. Today they are particularly found in our local province of Arezzo; in the Tuscan provinces of Livorno, Pisa and Siena; and around Perugia in Umbria.

Chianina cattle are easily recognisable by their porcelain-white to steel-grey, short-haired coat covering black pigmented skin, their black nose, eyes, tail and hooves, their lack of neck and their light and elegant short-horned heads that have a hump behind them. Their long cylindrical body has a wide and well-rounded rump and loins, and the limbs are longer than those of other breeds. They also have the distinction of being the largest bovines on earth. The world record is held by a celebrated beast called 'Donetto', a Chianina bull weighing in at an impressive 1,750kg. Nothing beats the tender, marbled meat of these exceptional animals, especially that prime cut *bistecca alla Fiorentina,* what we call a T-bone.

When this large breed was a working animal it was surprisingly agile and muscular with relatively long legs, and much valued because it was so docile, gentle and good tempered. Today's breeders maintain these characteristics, including size, but have improved its rate of growth.

Sadly the majestic nature of the Chianina breed was missing from Cortona's Bistecca Festa. There was not even a display board or leaflet about them. Perhaps this is because the volume of steaks served at this festa means that the meat is not exclusively from Chianina cattle, if any of it is.

Cooking meat in the open in large quantities is not an aesthetic activity. The distinctive acrid smell of grilling flesh was everywhere, as we battled with heavy traffic, with parking, and then with elbowing our way through the crowds to reach the clouds of smoke in the Partere, Cortona's shady public gardens. Here in a large fenced-off area was a barbecue the size of six king-sized beds put together. The grills were supported on a purpose-built brick construction which contained the burning charcoal, and a hose was used to dampen down any flare-ups. One man did nothing but add charcoal, while eight others turned the steaks with pitch forks.

T-bone steaks the size of a large dinner plate and at least as thick as a good book were what everyone had come for. And they certainly looked good when they were cooked. What was off-putting was the soulless and bloody nature of getting the steaks onto the grill. Refrigerated trucks stacked high with boxes of meat formed the backdrop to the grilling area. In front of them a fat, red-faced butcher wearing a blooded apron wielded a cleaver to trim the raw meat, which he then threw haphazardly onto the grill, so that a hundred or so steaks were cooking at any one time.

The park upwind of the barbecue area was crammed with white plastic tables and chairs providing a practical if style-free setting in which to dine. Each table seated eight, but first you had to buy a meal ticket and then queue for up to an hour to collect your steak. The deal wasn't a bad one, given the size of the steaks. For 25 euros you got a large, orange plastic plate that precariously supported your steak, the proper cutlery to enjoy it with, plus plastic dishes containing a choice of beans or tomatoes, some bread and a peach for dessert. Once you were seated, teenagers from the town served a half bottle of red wine and mineral water to each diner.

For many families and friends it was obviously a real treat and the focus of their Ferragosto celebrations. At least 4,000 steaks are served at the festa, but neither Jacob nor I were that keen on sampling such meaty mass catering. I had certainly eaten enough for one day and, anyway, what could be better than my lunch-in-a-garage with the Carrai tribe?

We waved goodbye to the men with the pitch forks and set off home agreeing we wanted something light and perhaps vegetarian for supper, hoping that no-one on the streets of Cortona heard us.

TEN

The Italian Way of Justice

Revenge and Suicide

In the 1960s and 1970s the ancient *mezzadria* system of share cropping was coming to an end in Tuscany and farm properties were being put up for sale cheap or being abandoned. A few adventurous foreigners and young people from Italy's big cities arrived in the Cortona area in search of a simpler life by taking advantage of the changes, believing they could largely live off the land as men and women had done for countless centuries.

Three of these newcomers were the Attwoods – Martin, brother John and sister Jane. They had spent their childhood in Kenya, gone on to England and, after the death of their mother there, decided to try farming on the Tuscan hillside that I can see from my terrace. A large house was included and that is still owned by John.

Their friends and neighbours were either elderly *mezzadria* farmers or other free spirits who had recently rented or bought houses locally. These included our painter and sculptor friends, Joe and Jos Tilson, and such luminaries as the feminist writer Germaine Greer and the campaigning journalist John Pilger.

By the early 80s the Attwoods had discovered how to scratch a living from their farming efforts. They also ventured into making and selling wood-burning stoves with some degree of success. By the time Val and I settled in the area, Jane was in the big house keeping horses; John had married a German girl and was working as a model maker in Munich; while Martin, by then married and divorced, was living in straitened circumstances in the smaller house on the farm.

When Jos Tilson first suggested I buy Martin's house, she told me that he needed the money because of 'a bit of local, legal difficulty' and she also warned me that he was 'very theatrical'. I had just read a book Martin had written in 1998 about his life in the Cortona area. This hinted at his experiences as a teacher here, but no mention was made of how this had led to forays into the dark underbelly of student life in nearby Perugia, or the real reason he had to sell his only asset in the world. My negotiations with Martin sadly faltered, but eventually he did sell the house and left.

Over the years I occasionally saw his lean frame, darting eyes and tousled hair when we passed on the pavements of the Via Nazionale in Cortona. Neighbours whispered that he was living hand-to-mouth in Orvieto, an hour south of us, with a sword of Damocles hanging over his head. Here is what I subsequently discovered about his predicament.

As a teacher, Martin came into contact with many young women living away from home in a foreign country for the first time. He was a friend to many and became a major figure in the lives of others who were lost and lonely. One of these was Astrid, a Californian who became heavily involved with the drug scene in Perugia.

Perugia is in Umbria, the region with the highest rate of drug-related deaths in Europe. Out of a population of 166,000 inhabitants, 40,000 are students of two crowded universities, one of which is exclusively for foreign students. The city's drug-related death rate is three times the national average and it has the most drug users per capita in Italy. Organised crime and Mafia groups are well entrenched and immigrants, especially from North Africa and Near-East countries, form a sizeable demographic.

I've heard Perugia described as Italy's 'Disneyland of drugs' and it seems well deserved. Many of the drug pushers arrive as fake students and are difficult to distinguish from the real ones. Heroin is the most common drug used and after this come cocaine, marijuana and hashish. Methamphetamine, ecstasy and other synthetic drugs are also widely available. Drugs are so universal that whenever we visit the galleries on Perugia's main *corso* it's nothing to see drug deals happening on the steps of the cathedral.

At one point during Martin and Astrid's relationship, she came under the influence of a heroin addict in Perugia and was spending extended periods of time at his house. Martin heard stories about how the addict had drugged, beaten and raped Astrid and took it upon himself to rescue her, enlisting the help of Pete, an ex-British Army friend who had done time in British jails. Those who were there the night the plot was hatched, say Martin was warned that his friend was 'a potential killer' and carried a Stanley knife as his weapon of choice.

As the two of them drove to Perugia it was decided that Martin would stay in the car ready to make a fast getaway, while Pete went inside and persuaded Astrid to leave with him. In less than ten minutes, Pete had made his mark by slashing the face and back of the man who was Astrid's alleged captor. She rushed to the car followed by Pete, and with Martin at the wheel they made a hasty getaway leaving behind a living but disfigured man.

Within days Martin and Pete were being questioned by the police, who told them Astrid's captor, Kazim, was a registered political refugee and also known to them as a heroin addict and dealer. The police seemed to accept Martin's account of why and what had happened, and told him that that they might prosecute Kazim for what he had done to Astrid. However, their preference was to brush the matter under the carpet if both sides refrained from accusing one another and from further retaliation – another name for revenge, of course.

A year later, Pete had disappeared off the face of the earth, but Martin was served with a summons citing the two of them for physically assaulting Kazim and causing him serious and permanent damage. When the case came to court, Kazim told the judge that Martin was beside Pete in the house when Pete took the knife to him and gave the instruction 'kill him'. In the event, Martin and the absent Pete were given one-year suspended sentences, and Martin was ordered to pay Kazim damages and his legal expenses.

Martin appealed, sold his house on the family farm, moved to Orvieto in Umbria, and eventually bought another property. The appeals progress dragged on for nearly five years and Martin lived in constant fear of reparations by Kazim, his family and others involved in the drug scene in Perugia. When the court rejected Martin's appeal, Kazim began a civil action against him. The courts then put a 50,000 euro injunction on Martin's home and he had to sell up once again. He was now virtually out of funds and took to living in a camper van that he drove around Italy, France and Spain.

Martin Attwood returned to Orvieto in 2009 having completed his second book. It is called *Hidden Debts* and is not an easy read. At best it is the ramblings of a tortured mind and tells the story of his slow path to ruin in characteristically theatrical terms.

Revenge and suicide can both be an impulsive and irrational act. On a sunny day in August 2009, Martin took his life by throwing himself off the ancient walls of Orvieto. The news of his death deeply saddened all those who knew him and, because he was such a complex man, no-one will ever really know why he chose to jump. The only universal agreement is that Italy's overloaded and extremely slow legal system can't have eased his state of mind. Kazim could no longer expect to win anything from him and I suppose that is a kind of revenge, too.

It is a sad truth that the majority of Italians don't fully trust their country's legal system. Coerced confessions, claims dreamt up by prosecutors that are then presented as evidence, and forensic tests that have taken place solely in the labs of the state police are accepted as commonplace. Newspapers regularly blame blood crimes on suspects belonging to 'dangerous minorities', which means immigrants, not only perverting the course of justice but inciting racism.

The major problem is that Italian justice rarely delivers conclusive, door-slamming certainty. Instead the judicial door is left wide open to take your case to the next level, first to appeal and then to the *Corte Suprema di Cassazione,* the Supreme Court of Cassation. Italy's top appeal court reviews about 80,000 cases a year. In the US, a country with five times the population, its Supreme Court reviews about 100 cases a year. France has a population similar to Italy and has 54,000 lawyers, but just 25 specialise in Supreme Court cases. In comparison, Italy has 240,000 lawyers of whom 40,000 are focused upon Supreme Court submissions and representation. It's a way of life for the lawyers, but pity the ordinary citizen who gets drawn into their chaotic, Byzantine legal system which is more likely to reduce them to despair than solve their problem. All grist to the financial mills of lawyers, of course, in a country where nearly three million cases were brought in 2011 alone.

The average time to settle a civil case in Italy is over seven years; a criminal case can take nearly five. And except in the most serious criminal cases, those found guilty will not be jailed until they have exhausted the appeals process – a nicety played to the extreme by Silvio Berlusconi over many years and his thousands of court hearings.

The pain felt by families who have suffered as a result of the slowness of the law runs deep in Italian society but it is not forgotten. Vendettas are not solely the preserve of the Mafia.

Long Ago But Not Forgotten

The day Martin Attwood was buried in Cortona, a judge in Munich passed sentence on 90-year-old Josef Scheungraber, a former Nazi soldier, for an act of revenge that he had committed more than six decades ago in a hamlet near our house. Amongst those in the courtroom, were Italian Nazi hunters and some of the Italian relatives of those who had died on Scheungraber's instructions. They were there for justice but were also unquestionably hoping for revenge.

With the exception of a few military tribunals in the immediate post-war period, Italy had little interest in prosecuting Nazi and Fascist crimes, which meant many wounds were never salved and thus never healed. In the early 1950s, when memories were still fresh and many of the culprits would easily have been apprehended, most files were closed. Then, at the start of the 21st century, cases started to come to court, the result of years of discreet and painstaking work by Italians who knew justice had not been done. Many of these were spurred on by the encouragement of Simon Wiesenthal, the controversial Nazi hunter, who died in 2005. Today, Italy and the United States are the two most successful countries in bringing former Nazi war criminals to justice, or managing to convict them in absentia.

As a 25-year-old Wehrmacht lieutenant, Josef Scheungraber ordered 11 civilians in the hamlet of Falzano to be massacred in retaliation for an attack by Italian partisans from nearby Poggioni that killed two German soldiers.

During the months before the Allies liberated our area in July 1944, the most active local partisans were the Poggioni group led by a local hero, Bruno Valli from Cortona. The Poggioni partisans took their name from the hamlet of the same name, where Bruno Valli's mother lived. On 27th June 1944, the location of the Poggioni partisans' headquarters became known to the Germans.

Scheungraber mounted a major attack, deploying almost a full company of between 100 to 150 troops to descend on the hamlet. Lookouts spotted them coming and the partisans withdrew to high ground and escaped.

Scheungraber was furious. He felt that he could not leave the area without inflicting some revenge for the dead Germans on the local population. His soldiers left Poggioni and set out for the nearby hamlet of Falzano, killing a 74-year-old woman and three men on the way. When they arrived in Falzano they blew up its church, four houses and a farm. Then they rounded up 11 local men, imprisoned them in a barn and blew that up. Miraculously one of the 11, then a 15-year-old boy, survived. At the age of 80, Gino Massetti told his first-hand account of the massacre at the trial.

The local population was so shocked by the killings that it insisted the partisans suspend their activities for a few days and hide their weapons. A relative of one of those who died told me that many felt the partisans were partially, if not totally, responsible for the murders.

A poignant reminder of the Falzano massacre still exists in the hamlet. It takes the form of a roughly carved stone cross on top of a pile of masonry retrieved from the burnt-out barn. This simple memorial stands on a small green surrounded by five cypresses and marks the spot where the barn, with the innocents inside, was blown up and burnt down. The plaque at the foot of the cross lists the names of those that died, and makes it clear what is thought about the perpetrators: 'In memory of the victims of the Germans' barbarism, who fell on 27 June 1944.'

The Falzano massacre was one of the worst crimes to take place in Tuscany during the German occupation. At Scheungraber's trial, the judge said in his summing up: 'This was about revenge … this man was the only officer present … he was not someone who allowed what he thought was an important matter to be taken out of his hands.'

Until his trial Scheungraber had lived a quiet, unassuming life in his home town of Ottobrunn near Munich, where he ran a furniture shop and sat on the town council. Ninety-year-old Scheungraber, dressed in a typical Bavarian jacket and looking in excellent health, was found guilty of ordering the killings and jailed for life. The trial had lasted 11 months and was one of the last Nazi war-crime trials to take place in Germany. Some relatives of the massacred travelled there to hear the verdict. Angiola Lescai is the granddaughter of one of the victims and said the verdict was an important and just outcome and 'a gesture of reconciliation to all those other victims who never had their day of revenge'.

A few days after the verdict Val and I walked down our valley to Falzano. The hills either side of the hamlet were luscious and green. The few houses we passed had been nicely restored. When we reached the plain, we crossed a small dried-up river that was once at the heart of the hamlet. Now, apart from a few recently felled trees, the place seemed devoid of any signs of human life. We approached the simple stone memorial that stands alone at a crossroads where the sign points to Poggioni, whence the German troops had come.

The June 1944 massacre has not been forgotten. A small potted plant, a common kalanchoe from a supermarket, had recently been placed on the memorial, together with a card from a descendant of one of the victims. As the bees and butterflies buzzed around us on a beautiful, cloudless day, we could not stop ourselves questioning the nature of revenge.

A week later we found ourselves quizzed about the Italian legal system by British friends who had invited us to dinner at their holiday villa near Perugia. It was the summer of 2009 and they were avid followers of the stories of the murder there of British student Meredith Kercher.

Guilty Until Proven Innocent

The now infamous Meredith Kircher murder case began on 1st November 2007 when two police officers were despatched to return the young woman's stolen mobile phone, which had been found in a garden near her apartment in Perugia. It was a routine call but they were confronted with *'una scena di orrore e caos'*, a scene of horror and chaos. The door was open, a window was smashed, and there were bloodstains in the bathroom. Behind a locked bedroom door, lying in a pool of blood, was the body of the 21-year-old Leeds University student, her windpipe crushed and her throat slashed.

The discussions with our British friends made me realise that the Kercher case was painting a picture of Italy's legal woes abroad like no other had done in recent years. Rudy Guede, a drifter from the Ivory Coast, had already been convicted of the murder, and the case against him had been based upon solid forensic clues found at the crime scene. His bloody handprint was on a pillow, his DNA was on the victim's genitals, and his faeces in the toilet. Three weeks after the murder, he surrendered after being tracked down to the German city of Mainz where he had fled.

The prosecution alleged that Guede had participated in an orgy with two other students, Amanda Knox and Raffaele Sollecito, which had resulted in Kercher's murder, but no supporting evidence was introduced about their involvement. Guede's defence opted for a so-called 'fast-track' trial, something introduced in an attempt to accelerate the sluggish pace of Italian justice. Thus it was that he was found guilty in October 2008 and sentenced to 30 years' imprisonment

In 2009 Kercher's flatmate, Amanda Knox from Seattle, and her Italian boyfriend, Raffaele Sollecito, were tried for complicity in the same murder. Knox and Sollecito were put on trial but, given the huge amount of media and web-based reporting on the case, it seemed as if the media rather than the facts were shaping the outcome of the two trials.

Over the next three years I spent an unhealthy amount of time seeking local insights into the way the case was being run and the likely outcome. Like many people, I had become fascinated by the way the police had conducted themselves and what seemed to me, as someone vaguely familiar with British law, the bizarre legal process that was in progress.

The trials of Knox and Sollecito began in January 2009 in front of a jury of six Umbrian citizens and two judges. However, it seemed that the law had made up its mind about whether the two were guilty – or not – well before the case came to court. I say this because there is no functioning equivalent law of contempt in Italy, as there is in Britain and America, which prevents upcoming trials being discussed publicly. And here I must introduce you to Perugia's Public Prosecutor, Giuliano Mignini.

Within a few days of the murder, he leaked a story to a few selected Italian journalists saying the case was solved. He claimed that Meredith Kercher had been 'done to death' by Knox, Sollecito and a local African bar owner, Patrick Lumumba, at the culmination of a sex orgy in which Kercher had refused to participate. These were personal views, but in Italy there was nothing anyone could have done to stop him voicing them and clearly he saw no conflicts with his role as Public Prosecutor.

Word spread like wild fire around the world and established the common perception that Knox was not an innocent young student but a murderous, sex-mad femme fatale. However, Lumumba had an excellent alibi for the night of the murder and it turned out that Mignini's views were based upon a so-called confession by Knox that came after an all-night session at a police station where she says she was abused and slapped around the head. Once the accusation against Lumumba was found to be untrue, what else of this 'confession' could be believed? Might not Mignini have apologised? Instead, his position became more entrenched.

Silvio Pinelli, a friend who is a lawyer in Arezzo, explained to me the role of public prosecutors in Italy. 'They have a great deal of discretion and many of us in the legal profession believe that this is unhealthy. It is also not uncommon for them to make baseless accusations before anything ever gets to court.'

I voiced my opinion that once Patrick Lumumba had been discounted as a suspect, it seemed as though Guede, already convicted for the murder and in prison, was simply plugged into the prosecution's case as Knox's and Sollecito's accomplice. Silvio agreed and pointed out that 'there is common belief that in Italy you are guilty until you prove yourself innocent and what happened here seems to confirm that.'

As the case progressed, it was obvious that there were no fingerprints and no DNA samples of either Knox or Sollecito at the crime scene; only a hotly contested DNA sample recovered from Sollecito that was collected 45 days after the murder. Also, that neither Knox nor Sollecito were friends of Guede. In other words, there weren't any hard facts presented by Mignini that proved beyond doubt that they were at the house the night Kercher was murdered.

I discussed motive with Silvio. 'Of course motive has to be an important consideration in deciding the outcome of a murder trial,' he agreed. 'And it does seem in this case that nothing plausible has been presented.'

The fact that Amanda Knox often changed her story didn't help her case, nor did the claims by a handful of local people that they had seen her and Guede together the night before the murder, then buying bleach the day after. But these, and other incidents and speculations, did not translate into factual, sustainable evidence. Even so, on 4th December 2009 Knox and Sollecito were found guilty of murder, sexual violence and other charges. Knox was sentenced to 26 years in prison, while Sollecito received 25 years. Prosecutors had sought life terms for both of them.

The next day an article in the Italian daily newspaper *La Repubblica* viewed the verdict as 'a most surprising judgement' – an anodyne way of saying the judge and jury might have got it wrong. The British and US press were in no doubt that justice had not been done. One ran a large photograph of the sign 'The Law is Equal for All' that hangs on the wall of the Perugia courtroom and captioned it 'Shame on Italy'.

From the day Amanda Knox was arrested, she was supported by the type of vigorous, justice-seeking campaign that Americans do so well. Possibly this worked against her because in Italy, as in many other countries, America is a symbol of decadence. This, and factors such as the powerful influence that America exerted on Italian politics after the Second World War, creates an unstable mixture of admiration and resentment for the US in the minds of many Italians. Not surprisingly, both Knox and Sollecito said they would launch appeals.

Salvare la faccia, saving face, is very important in Italy. It seems to me that this had been uppermost in the minds of the Perugia judges, Giancarlo Massei and his colleague Beatrice Cristiani, when three months after the trial they published a 427-page document explaining why they had persuaded the jurors to come to the decision they did. They claimed the case was 'without holes and inconsistencies' and that 'it was murder without planning and the culprits had no ill feeling to Meredith'. They also said the evidence presented by Public Prosecutor Mignini led to the convictions as 'a necessary and strictly consequential outcome'.

After nearly two years in jail it was announced that the appeals of Knox and Sollecito would be heard at the end of November 2010. Immediately they were in the Appeals Court, the judge granted a review of the forensic evidence used to convict them. This took the form of an independent report on the disputed evidence, in particular of the DNA from both of them supposedly found on a knife, and Solliceto's DNA on the clasp of Meredith Kercher's bra.

After months of expert submissions the court concluded that the DNA evidence may have been contaminated. The prosecution responded by asking for further tests; a request which the judge rejected. Nine months after their appeal began, and after spending more than 1,000 days in prison, Knox and Sollecito heard their lawyers begin their summing up on 23rd September 2011.

Knox's lawyer highlighted numerous errors that had been made during the police investigation, and also pointed out that his client's civil rights had been breached by police and prosecutors during questioning. He also stressed the crucial importance of the independent report into the DNA evidence ordered by the Appeals Court judge, underlining this by saying 'the truth never lies'. Amongst the submissions made by Sollecito's lawyers was a claim that the trace of his DNA, found on the murdered student's bra strap more than six weeks after the discovery of the body, could have been planted. Giuliano Mignini hadn't moved an inch. He stressed that an 'obsessive' media campaign to free Knox had distracted jurors and that no-one should be misled by Knox's appearance. 'Every one of us has a dark side and it would be superficial to think that just because someone looks innocent that they are not capable of killing,' he said.

In an emotive final address he insisted that in 2007 Knox and Raffaele Sollecito had joined Rudy Guede in trying to cajole Meredith Kercher into a drug-fuelled sex game. When Kercher resisted, Mignini said, she was stabbed to death.

On the evening of 3rd October 2011, Amanda Knox and Sollecito were acquitted of Meredith Kercher's murder. Outside the court several hundred mainly young people chanted 'Vergogna, Vergogna' – Disgrace, Disgrace' in protest at the acquittal.

Locally, I found many of my friends resentful about the way the American media had denigrated the Italian justice system from the day Knox was first arrested. They bristled at being judged by the land of O.J. Simpson – a country that still dishes out the death penalty in some states. At that time many still felt that Knox and Sollecito were guilty.

My friend Silvio Pinelli defended the legal profession and the Italian system of justice, pointing out that this acquittal demonstrated how the law in Italy is able to react to errors. He asked me to consider that 'whatever the result of the original sentence, it is guaranteed that the accused will be heard by another, completely independent judge.'

It seems to me this is the very least a legal system should offer, and he had nothing to say about how long it took. Furthermore, he couldn't explain why Guede wasn't called as a witness for the prosecution or the defence at either the trial or the appeal hearing.

The Not-So-Perfect Prosecutor

The role of public prosecutors in Italy is unique in Europe. Italian prosecutors are members of the judiciary, are appointed for life and, despite an ingrained Italian love of hierarchical titles, do not operate within a hierarchy. Public prosecutors must investigate crimes they are made aware of, and prosecute where there is sufficient evidence that a crime has been committed. They have no discretionary power, but may either direct investigations themselves or through the police. The police may also operate their own separate investigations.

Once initial evidence has been collected by the prosecutor and the police, a report is submitted to a judge who decides if there is enough evidence to charge the indicted person, or whether the case should be dismissed. If the judge rules that there is sufficient evidence, the prosecutor must bring the case to trial. At trial, Italian prosecutors operate in an adversarial system similar to that which is used to try common law cases in Italy.

Some extraordinary claims and comments were made in the original trial and when the Kercher case came to appeal Giuliano Mignini, the balding, avuncular Public Prosecutor, was especially vocal. The Perugia-born father of four ran the investigation from the moment he arrived at the murder scene on 2nd November 2007 to confer with local police and forensic investigators who had come from Rome. His supporters say his conclusions about Knox and Raffaele Sollecito were validated by a variety of pre-trial, trial and appeal judges, not least Italy's Supreme Court which ruled at the time it confirmed Rudy Guede's sentence that he did not murder Kercher alone.

Mignini's detractors, especially those in the US, claim his investigation was 'a railroad job from hell', pointing to his questioning of Knox for hours without a lawyer, his coaxing her into naming innocent Patrick Lumumba as the likely murderer, and to his suggestion that Knox and Sollecito 'were inspired by the occult when they slayed Meredith Kercher'. Criticisms came as no surprise to Mignini, who has strongly believed for years that opponents have been secretly plotting his downfall.

Just before the final summing up began in the appeal, Mignini informally discussed his handling of an older case, the one surrounding the 'Monster of Florence' serial killer, with a group of lawyers including my *avvocato* friend Silvio Pinelli. He told them his investigation of the 1985 death of Francesco Narducci, who was a Freemason, had been mysteriously blocked. 'I have felt under attack ever since I investigated Narducci,' he declared. 'It all started there.' The 16-month sentence he received for abuse of office in 2010, after he ordered unauthorised wiretaps during the Monster investigation, was a trumped-up charge that fitted the pattern of persecution, he argued. Mignini has also claimed that Douglas Preston, the US novelist who challenged Mignini's theories about the Monster of Florence, had masterminded a US press campaign against him over his handling of the Knox case. 'It's all Preston,' he claimed, meaning of course that if it wasn't the Freemasons, it was someone else out to get him.

Mignini introduced yet another conspiracy theory into his summing up at Knox's and Sollecito's appeal. He claimed that, 'Our judicial system has been subjected to a systematic denigration by a well-organised operation of a journalistic and political nature.' But even in the war of words that always goes on in courtrooms, I was shocked to hear that he accused Amanda Knox and her lawyers of 'using Nazi tactics to achieve their aims'. Can you imagine a British judge allowing that, or a prosecutor who would dare say such a thing?

Like Knox and Sollecito, the possibly paranoid prosecutor Mignini took his 16-month suspended prison sentence to appeal but, unlike them, he was able to continue living and working normally. In November 2011 the Appeals Court in Florence overturned his conviction and referred the case to the prosecutor in Turin to decide whether to re-file charges. To this day, he still hasn't been removed from office and seems to have spent a good amount of time filing defamation claims, including ones to Knox's parents, Sollecito and, of course, the media.

WILL WE EVER KNOW THE TRUTH?

After being released from prison in October 2011, Knox returned to her family in Seattle; Solliceto to his father and stepmother at their home in Puglia in the south-east of Italy. But this being Italy, their troubles did not finish when they left the court.

Just over four months later, the Perugia prosecutors claimed that important DNA evidence had been disregarded and asked Italy's highest Appeals Court to reinstate the murder convictions for Knox and Sollecito. After a further 13 months of delays and deliberations, it pronounced that both acquittals should be overturned and ordered a re-trial in Florence.

The Court of Cassation sharply criticised the Appeals Court for the acquittals, saying it had ignored some of the evidence and had not properly considered other evidence. The appeal judges were also criticised for not taking into account the fact that Knox had originally accused local bar owner Patrick Lumumba, who was later proved to be innocent, as well as the sentence that was passed against Rudy Guede, saying he had not acted alone.

On 26th March 2013 the media was told that the decision to hold a re-trial did not suggest that the two were guilty, rather that 'it may have been possible that the Appeals Court did not apply the law correctly'. In other words, the Florence hearing was a re-run of the appeals process; thus technically not a new trial but a continuation of the original one.

After a week of preliminary hearings, the proceedings started in earnest on 6 November 2013. The Italian legal system had no power to summon Knox to the hearing and there was no way she planned to set foot on Italian soil again. Instead, she sent a five-page e-mail to the court insisting on her complete innocence and expressing her fear that the 'vehemence of the prosecution' would 'blind' the court. Her legal team claimed that she had, in effect, already been tried and then cleared before this re-trial and stated that the concept of double jeopardy, one of the oldest legal theories in Western civilisation, applied. Sollecito, who attended the new trial, said it made 'no real sense' for him to have committed 'such an atrocious act'.

On the morning of Thursday 30 January 2013 Knox's lawyer, Carlo Dalla Vedova, summed up and told the court her innonence was 'rock-solid and it allows us to await the verdict with serenity'. The two judges and six jurors then retired to consider their verdict.

After nearly 12 hours of deliberations the presiding judge, Alessandro Nencini, reinstated the verdicts first handed down in 2009 but overturned in 2011, when the pair were freed after four years in jail. The packed and silent Florence courtroom heard him sentence Knox to 28 years and 6 months in jail – more than the original sentence – while Sollecito was sentenced to 25 years.

He also ordered that the passport of Raffaele Sollecito should be revoked but made no requests for limits on Knox's movements, saying she was 'justifiably abroad'. Furthermore, Nencini instructed that the pair pay damages to the family of Meredith Kercher, whose brother Lyle and sister Stephanie were present when the verdict was read out.

On a wet night in Florence the world's media scrambled to secure interviews with the lawyers. Luca Maori, Sollecito's counsel, said his client was 'struck dumb' after hearing the verdict and looked 'annihilated'.

Knox immediately issued a statement condemning what she described as 'an overzealous and intransigent prosecution, prejudiced and narrow-minded investigation, unwillingness to admit mistakes, reliance on unreliable testimony and evidence, character assassination, inconsistent and unfounded accusatory theory, and counterproductive and coercive interrogation techniques that produce false confessions and inaccurate statements.' She said that she was 'frightened' and 'saddened by this unjust verdict' adding, 'having been found innocent before, I expected better from the Italian justice system. The evidence and accusatory theory do not justify a verdict of guilty beyond reasonable doubt. My family and I have suffered greatly from this wrongful persecution.'

But that was not the end of it. Lawyers for both Knox and Sollecito vowed immediately to take the case back to the Court of Cassation. It could either uphold the verdict and make the convictions definitive, in which case Italy could request Knox's extradition and Sollecito would be facing a return to jail, or even send the case back for yet another appeal.

Coming from a country where we have a system where guilty verdicts are only handed down when the charge has been 'proven beyond reasonable doubt', I am appalled at the way this case has been handled. From the moment the murder was discovered, injustice was committed by a small group of individuals that abused their power to protect their own better interests. The case was solved in record time, long before any evidence had been collected. When the actual truth came to light and Rudy Guede was arrested, the initial mistake could have been corrected but fragile reputations were on the line, especially those of the lead investigator Edgardo Giobbi and lead prosecutor Giuliano Mignini. Careers would be made on this case and personal interest outweighed the truth.

I don't honestly think that all of Perugia's police force was part of a big conspiracy against Knox and Sollecito. The investigators believed they were doing the right thing because they were told by the higher ups that Knox and Sollecito were guilty. Believing that they were guilty allowed them to justify 'bending' the rules to bring the desired results. Mignini quickly took charge and told the police what to look for. He told them what evidence to analyse and what evidence to disregard. This was an awful lot of power to hand over to a man with his record.

It cannot be right that Knox and Sollecito sat in prison for a year before they were even charged with a crime. As it was in their case, this waiting period is not considered time served if you are eventually convicted. The simple act of being arrested has a high presumption of guilt attached. This reasoning leads to a very high success rate in the initial ruling of guilt. This also explains the high rate of acquittals during the appeals process (50 per cent are adjusted or overturned on appeal). Their trial took another year to conclude, with all those involved meeting only two days a week and taking the summer off.

Having been a juror in the UK, I am amazed that the Perugia jury wasn't sequestered. The jurors associated with the lawyers when they went to lunch at restaurants during the trial. During court recesses, they mixed with the legal teams and journalists in the local bars. Jurors were allowed to discuss the case and follow all of the press coverage.

It seems that in Italy inquiries are conducted without any reliable methods, and independent observers do not have access to the police's work.

Until this case, I thought all judges had training in order to be able to evaluate forensic evidence. Then I discovered that in Italy the judiciary seem to accept everything without questioning, as long as it comes from the institutional laboratory.

Italian civil rights groups are intense in their criticism of what they view as kangaroo courts. No system of law is perfect but, like many Italians, I only see a court system that is unreliable and compromised, especially when it comes to serious crimes such as murder. In these cases, there are two professional judges and six so-called 'lay judges' who are citizens of the town and are chosen at random. They are not under oath and are not questioned by the prosecution or the defence before they are elected. The two professional judges guide the jury as it sorts through the facts of the case. One of the professional judges acts as the lead judge and runs the court proceedings. The judge that runs the trial in court is also a member of the jury. The ruling only needs to be a simple majority. You can be sentenced to life in prison on a 5-3 vote. To be judged by Italian judges and an Italian jury is a very hit-and-miss affair.

Books and films have already been published on the Kercher case and many more will surely follow. Films have been aired and others are being planned and are in production. Whatever they claim, it seems so wrong that Meredith Kercher was virtually forgotten during the seven years when the case was being tried and re-tried. Even after the guilty verdict was handed down in Florence, I couldn't help feeling that the Kercher family were no closer to knowing how and why she was murdered. Their hope until then, according to Francesco Maresca, the family's lawyer, was that this further trial would 'review the definitive and final truth of Meredith's murder'. But, as her brother said after the guilty verdict was reinstated, it was 'the best we could have hoped for'.

If the law is correct, and if Knox and Sollecito are truly innocent, themselves at very least victims of judicial crime and prejudice, this makes the Kerchers' situation even worse. Is it true that someone else was involved with their daughter's death and that they remain free? As the family continues to nurse their pain, they can do little more than hope that the truth will eventually emerge.

If someone else is as guilty as the imprisoned Guede, I hope they think daily of what happened to the Nazi soldier Scheungraber so many decades after his crime was committed. Justice is indeed better served cold, and it tastes no less sweet for being decades late. If the Italian legal system can't deliver the certainty their daughter deserves, it might comfort the Kerchers to remember it wasn't Italy that finally sent Josef Scheungraber to prison.

ELEVEN

Formaggio e Vino

Lessons in Pecorino Production

Her smile and suntan were as spectacular as her ample figure. Red-framed spectacles made sure you noticed her sparkling eyes, and these were complemented by her expensive, straw-coloured hair and perfect tan.

Her domain was the longest, cleanest truck I have ever seen, and the most ingenious. To set up shop all she had to do was place a key in a panel near the back wheels, pull a couple of knobs, and the whole of one side lifted up to form a canopy over a cheese-lover's paradise.

Monique Orlando's truck is food theatre. She stood beside her handsome son and looked down on me as though over footlights, but actually over a glass-fronted counter containing a cast of a dozen or more different ewes' milk cheeses. The fact that the cheeses are at eye-level, and that I must look up to talk to the signora like a schoolboy before a school mistress, always makes it a curiously more rewarding shopping experience than usual. Or perhaps this is just because I cannot live without our local pecorino cheeses and that she sells the best of them?

Long before Monique set me off discovering the delights of pecorino Toscana, I was introduced to the world of the *caseificio,* the dairy, in Sardinia. There, on an island populated by three million sheep and half that number of people, I was lucky enough to spend time with the Podda family, legendary cheese makers introduced to me by friends from Piedmont.

For generations the Poddas have been making pecorino and Fiore Sardo cheeses in the wild and remote landscape near Orgosolo in the centre of Sardinia. Livestock farming is still the main source of income on the island, and sheep or goat herding one of the main occupations. Wherever you go in the countryside, it isn't long before you hear the distinctly musical sound of sheep bells. The flocks are huge, the sheep much larger than our local Tuscan breeds, and the shepherds who accompany them will often be dressed in the same types of sheepskins and stocking caps their ancestors wore.

Giovanni Podda claims that it is the wild sage and rosemary in his sheep's diet that helps him make the best pecorino on the island. After spending time with him, I concluded it was also because he farms in the place of his birth, where old customs and traditions still matter and where monetary success is not the family's main motivator. His brother Pinuccio showed me the bulky tepee, called a *pinnetu,* which was his father's winter home while he watched over his flocks in the mountains. The base was made of stone; the roof from juniper branches which allowed smoke from the fire inside to escape while still imprisoning enough heat to keep him safe and warm.

The Podda family start making cheese after Christmas each year and continue for the next six months. Giovanni had told me that 'the milk is at its best in spring', and I could see the season's bright flowers in the valley when I visited.

Their dairying complex is a cluster of rustic buildings on one side of a beautiful valley dotted with pine trees and ilexes. Inside the biggest building all was *tutto biologico,* with spotlessly clean, stainless steel equipment and work surfaces, white-tiled walls and non-slip floors. It was very EEU compliant, yet I slowly realised the cheeses made here still needed the sure touch of the artisan.

I watched as rennet, made from the stomach of a young lamb, was carefully mixed into a large copper-lined vat of sheep's milk heated to 38 degrees centigrade. As the milk coagulated, thin whey formed which Pinuccio carefully skimmed off the top. 'Now it's your turn,' he said.

He showed me how to press the soft curdled milk through sieves to get rid of any remaining whey, and then to put this gently into circular, straight-sided, lightweight plastic moulds to shape the cheeses before they were washed in brine. The whole process was still very natural and thus felt amazingly therapeutic, but I appreciated that Pinuccio's skilled hands and experience knew far better than mine what was the exact pressure or the exact amount of curd to put into the sieves; and that these would vary from day to day, month to month, as the quality of his ewes' milk changed in line with the animals' diet.

Most of the buildings at the dairy were still and silent: safe, cool homes to hundreds of cylindrical cheeses of different sizes being aged. The smells were intriguing and the aromas made me ravenously hungry in spite of the dispiriting stainless steel. I was surrounded by the work of artists, of artisans, and was sharing experiences of sight and smell that would be recognised by Leonardo da Vinci and all the millions of Tuscans before and after him.

Anxious to try pecorino Sardo in all its various forms, I went with the brothers to Orgosolo, Sardinia's most notorious town, a byword for banditry and violence that once blighted the centre of the island, and now famous for its hundreds of graffiti-style protest murals. This is where the family have a shop with a cave at the back where they store their cheeses. Here there were fresh, two-week and eight-week-old pecorinos and one that had been aged for about three months. The youngest cheeses, soft and whitish, had a comparatively mild yet still robust flavour, and the older became richer in colour as they aged, developing a firmer texture and a saltier, more concentrated flavour.

My favourite was Fiore Sardo, the flower of Sardinia, a cheese in existence before the Romans conquered the island in 238 BC. This cheese has a typical wheel shape with curved sides, is about 15cm high and comes in sizes weighing from 1.5 to 5kg. Unlike the examples I saw ageing at the *caseificio,* these are dried in caves where a fire burns so that the cheese acquires a slightly smoked taste that perfectly balances its essential piquancy and further enhances the flavour of its nutty and creamy finish. At three and half months old Fiore Sardo is at its peak as a table cheese. An older version, aged a minimum of six months, is meant for cooking and grating. It's the ideal partner to Parmesan in making a great pesto, but if there's any in the house I'll nibble and eat it just by itself.

So, who makes the best pecorino – the Sardinians or the Tuscans? Pecorino lovers invariably agree to disagree on this subject, but there's no doubt that the current generation of Tuscan cheese makers owe much to the island in the middle of the Mediterranean.

In the 1960s Sardinian farms were being sold off as the *mezzadria* system ended and rural families gave up working the land in favour of employment in towns and cities. There was mass migration from Sardinia, and many shepherd families headed for the easier climate and opportunities of Tuscany. Today, Sardinians make up an estimated ten per cent of farming families in Siena province, our main local producers of pecorino cheese.

In Cortona market I told Monique Orlando about my cheese-making excursion to the Podda family. She confirmed that the local farms where she buys her cheese are peppered with Sardinians, even though they make Tuscan-style cheeses. She didn't mind this at all. 'I like the men who run them,' she said with a wicked smile that she sheltered from her son's sight. 'They are often *provocanti,* flirtatious, even though they appear a little reserved at first.'

Monique is a Tuscan through and through and a champion of local *formaggio* producers. Naturally, she says Tuscan pecorino is best and, in spite of any personal interests she might have developed, she doesn't mind insulting Sardinians and their cheeses. She leaned over the counter as far as her chest permitted: 'Only in Sardinia would they serve pecorino riddled with writhing maggots that try to jump into your eyeballs as you eat it.'

I knew she meant casu marzu, a soft, liquefying and pungent blue cheese, rather like badly over-ripened Stilton and with live maggots as an essential ingredient. The sale of the monstrosity has been banned, but some Sicilian families still make this rarefied pecorino for special occasions. Monique sensed that if ever I met casu marzu I would try it, and she warned me that the maggots had to be alive and wriggling when you put them and the cheese into your mouth. She leaned even closer to my ear: 'They say if you eat it when the maggots inside are dead you will surely die.'

Spoilt for Choice

Italy is home to more than 500 different cheeses, most of them made in the north of the country. Of these Parmigiano-Reggiano, Grana Padano, Bel Paese, mozzarella, mascarpone, creamy blue gorgonzola, dolcelatte and pecorino made with ewes' milk are the most famous. All of Italy's cheeses and cheese producers are defined by the milk they use, which can be cow, ewe, goat or buffalo milk, or a mixture of two or more of these. The cheese they make will then be soft and ready to eat once it is made; or semi-soft to be enjoyed within two months; semi-hard which is ready within six months; and hard which has aged for six months and up to several years. Some producers make cheeses that are both eaten young or matured until they are semi-soft or semi-hard. A lesser classification divides all cheeses as being for the table or for grating and cooking. We rarely use soft and semi-soft cheeses for cooking, but love the more complex flavours you get from a crumbly flaky piece of an older cheese supposedly only for cooking but classically enjoyed with fresh fruit or with red wine, of course.

Two of the best-known pecorino styles are Romano, which is aged for grating, and Siciliano which can be eaten the day after it is made but is also aged for up to four months, when it becomes a grating cheese. Then there are the worlds of pecorino Sardo and pecorino Toscana, both of which yield cheeses of all ages and textures.

At home, we are besotted by two-week-old Toscana. The body is still soft and supple and the flavour has subtle, nutty, oak-leaf overtones. We discovered it when I noticed a discreet roadside sign with a stylish graphic of a sheep on it pointing the way to the Cugusi family's caseificio. Their unassuming farmhouse and outbuildings sit on a hillside with a stunning view of Montepulciano and the huge church of Tempo di San Biagio, the High Renaissance masterpiece by Antonio da Sangallo the Elder, below it.

It was late afternoon when I first arrived at the farm. Scrub oak trees and an old, raised circular well were casting long shadows across the newly mown lawn in front of the main building. I made my way through a faded, striped curtain that protected an open doorway, and into a cool, darkened anteroom off the cheese-making area. This, like the Podda's dairy in Sardinia, was all stainless steel, white tiles and *tutto biologico*. A modern-day dairy maid, dressed in a dazzling white coat, white gumboots and a white hairnet, greeted me. I didn't need much encouragement to take up her offer of a tutored tasting of the different ages and types of Tuscan pecorino they made.

My Sardinian experience had taught me enough to know that Tuscan cheeses were made very much the same way. The ewes' milk was heated to 35 and 38 degrees centigrade and then curdled with rennet for about 20 minutes. The curds were then turned out into a trough, scooped into moulds, and pressed lightly to drive out more of the whey which would, in turn, be boiled up to give ricotta from the remaining protein. In some Tuscan dairies, the very fresh pressed cheeses are sometimes steamed to help drive out more of the whey. Here all the cheeses are salted or soaked in brine for between 8 to 12 hours per kilo, which firms them up further and creates an outer skin. Then they are aged in cool, dark rooms for a minimum of 20 days if they are to be sold fresh, or for at least four months if they are to be sold aged when they become pecorino stagionato.

The flavour of aged Tuscan pecorino is strong and sharp, and when crumbled over food it's akin to Parmesan but creamier and perhaps more complex, though not as sharp and salty as an aged pecorino Romano. There's a good reason for this difference. Historically, most of the Tuscan version was always meant to be eaten fresh rather than aged and as a snack or, in later centuries, in sandwiches. The Romano version was produced to be aged and used for grating and cooking, like a condiment, and was carried by Roman legions precisely for that. Although still made in Rome's province of Lazio, many cheese makers left this area after prohibitive local regulations in the 1880s and went, you've guessed it, to Sardinia and there they make pecorino Romano rather than pecorino Sardo. So the pecorino makers who came to Tuscany from Sardinia might well be descendants of Lazio who had migrated to Sardinia . . .

Over the next half hour, I also sampled pecorino of different ages and versions that had acquired, or had been made with, an added flavour. Three were very distinctive – the black pepper, the chilli and the black truffle flavoured cheeses. The most delicious was a style rolled in ash, another that had been aged underground, and one wrapped and aged in walnut leaves, pecorino con foglie di noce. Last of all, I sampled the much rarer blue cheese, pecorino erborinato, and a version macerated in the mash of moist vine stems, grape skin and pips left after grapes are pressed for wine. Both were good but not entirely to my taste.

Good cheese is not cheap and I easily spent 60 euros on a selection of different types of pecorino and a pot of ricotta. As I said goodbye to my dairy-maid tutor, she continued lecturing me; impressing on me that the breed of sheep and its diet greatly affect the taste of pecorino. 'Ewes' milk is not prone to TB bacillus or other human-threatening diseases. That is why we can use it raw, so we can create a cheese with milk that is a true reflection of the season and what the sheep have eaten.' It's worth adding here that although a few pecorino cheeses can have a farmy tang to them, none ever has the throat-catching he-goat taste that goats' milk cheeses often possess.

It is easy to get obsessive about Tuscan pecorino when you live here. I have even met what can only be described as pecorino nutters, obsessives who want to know exactly when a cheese was made, and then check to locate where the sheep were feeding and on what at that time of the year. One of them told me, 'Once I know these things I can eat the same cheese from the same maker but get different tastes and flavours as the year progresses.' Well, yes, I thought but walked away wondering if life was too short for such passions. And then I discovered marzolino.

The name comes from *marzo,* the Italian name for March. It is made only in that month, when ewes' milk is arguably at its best as they graze on the luscious new herbs and grasses that burgeon in spring. It is much loved by pecorino fanatics, who buy some to eat fresh and a further supply to age at home when the cheese becomes hard and slightly piquant.

In pursuit of *la bella figura,* many younger Italians are becoming far more aware of the sugar and fat content of foods than their parents. Gina is 36 and our slim and attractive local dentist. As always, when we visit her the conversation turns to food, her favourite subject. I am not sure how the subject of cheese and diet came up, but I am indebted to her for making me aware that the fat content of cheese is not necessarily what you think it is.

She explained the conundrum as follows. 'If, say, a cheese is labelled as having a 55 per cent fat content, this does not mean that 55 per cent of what you see or eat is fat. That percentage is of the dry matter in the cheese.' She went on to give me an example. 'To work out the percentage of fat in a wet cheese, like mozzarella or Gorgonzola, you first have to get rid of all the liquid because it's what's left that you analyse. As a general rule, a piece of soft creamy cheese will almost always have a lower overall fat content, and thus calorie count, than a hard cheese and that even includes Parmesan, which is made with skimmed-milk.'

Thus to keep slim she said she chooses softer varieties, including imported French Brie or Camembert. 'Brie might have a stated 55 per cent fat content but that will be only 15 per cent of what I see and put in my mouth. Because there is so little liquid left in a Parmesan, the fat percentage you get is very close to what is on the label.'

Because it's impossible to extract the cream content from ewes' milk they have amongst the highest fat content of all cheeses, young or old, and that's just one of the myriad reasons they are so delicious. When I tried to impress Monique in her theatrical cheese truck with my new knowledge so I could compare the calorie content of her fresh and her aged cheeses, her reaction was predictably dismissive and audacious. 'If nature intended our skeletons to be visible she would have put them on the outside of our bodies. I accept there are some people who think there is a thin person waiting to get out of them, but this instinct is easily sedated with a few pieces of pecorino and a bottle of Tuscan red.'

The Secret Vineyard

At the party after our neighbours Alison and Mario were married, Giuseppe Bino introduced himself as the winemaker at Castelli Martinozzi and insisted I taste what was in the bottle he held. It was the latest vintage of the vineyard's Rosso di Montalcino. I smelt, swirled and supped and then congratulated him on the wine, one of his first for the Castelli Martinozzi label of Villa San Restituta.

A few weeks later Giuseppe sat on our terrace and told me something of the 300-year history of the Castelli family who owned Villa San Restituta: how their *mezzadria* farmers traditionally grew grapes; how they had once bred silk worms, produced olive oil, and won awards for over 100 years for their fine Castelli Martinozzi Montalcino wines. His invitation to visit him and the owners of this private estate was an honour and I accepted with much anticipation.

The Tuscan hill towns of Montepulciano and Montalcino are at the heart of two of Italy's greatest wine regions, the latter about 30km south-west of the former. The main red grape in both is a local version of Tuscany's favourite Sangiovese grape, Prugnolo Gentile in Montepulciano and Brunello in Montalcino.

Montepulciano is the loftiest and grandest of all southern Tuscan hill towns. Henry James described his reason for visiting it as 'largely just in the beauty of the name (for could any beauty be greater?)', reinforced no doubt by the fame of the local vintage and the sense of how he could quaff it on the spot.

On a perfect September day I set out with Val and two friends early in the morning for Villa San Restituta, taking the road via Montepulciano. As you get closer to the town, *cantine* with outdoor terraces offer plenty of opportunities to stop and sample the local wines but the architecture in the centre of the town always draws me on. Wonderfully ornate Renaissance palaces flank the main corso while the Piazza Grande, at the top of the town, is home to a breathtaking quartet of buildings including the unfinished brick exterior of the duomo. In here is one of the greatest of all 14th-century Sienese paintings, Taddeo di Bartolo's *Assumption,* as well as a charming painting of a ginger-haired infant Jesus by the 15th-century Sienese artist, Sano di Pietro.

My real objective that morning was to stop at Pienza for a reviving *caffe lungo* and a *cornetto,* croissant. There is no better place in the southern Tuscan landscape to dawdle than in what was conceived as a Renaissance Utopia, the jewel that is Pienza. Pope Pius II was born here and in 1458 commissioned the architect Bernardo Rossellino to fulfil a vision to make his country birthplace into an ideal city. Alas, the dream died in 1464, as did the Pope, but posterity inherited a perfectly proportioned piazza surrounded by an almost perfect papal palace, a town hall and a cathedral. We could have marvelled all morning from the Caffe la Posta, our coffee stop on the piazza, but we had wine on our minds.

The road from Pienza to Montalcino winds through the most glorious, archetypical Tuscan landscape. To the left, just before Montalcino, is the isolated hilltop chapel framed by cypresses that is so often used to illustrate articles about Tuscany and the region's most popular postcards. With rather sketchy directions to guide me to our destination, it took a few mis-directed adventures before we descended a steep hill and still almost missed the dirt track with its discreet sign to Villa San Restituta. If there is such a thing as a secret vineyard this is it.

We entered through tall, ornate gates into a private world of calm, untouched by restorers and the modern world, where order was of its own making and obviously had been for centuries. Low terracotta-roofed, grey stone barns of different sizes and shapes made three sides of a large, sloping gravelled courtyard with an ancient rainwater cistern and a large covered well at its centre. Horse chestnut trees provided shade; lemon trees in pots dated 1922 wafted citrus scents. In one corner was a small stone-built clock tower with a round, grey marble face, Roman numerals, and a single and simple brass hour hand. It was as though the concept of time was incidental to those who lived and worked here.

Dotted around the courtyard were little collections of fossilised fish and other creatures from thousands of years ago, a reminder that the land here was once covered by sea. Some were sea anemones as big as footballs. Doors in the barns were open but there was no-one around. The only sounds we could hear were insects going about their business, and birds singing whenever and wherever the fancy took them.

I ventured through a gate into another courtyard covered with tangled vines heavy with ready-to-eat young Sangiovese grapes that had the fresh, fruity flavour of strawberry and a little spiciness. Here there were domestic buildings and signs of our times – a plastic flower pot, a modern doormat in front of a curtained door. Then, from a path at the rear of the courtyard, came an open-faced woman walking with a purposeful stride. Cristina Castelli introduced herself and warmly welcomed us to her family's villa. She was shortly joined by a rather studious-looking young man, her son Federico, and then by my new friend Giuseppe, the winemaker.

Everything they told us about the estate was done in a modest, unassuming way. Everywhere they showed us was a visual revelation. The buildings along the top of the large courtyard housed the wine cellars that had been in use for centuries. Huge oak casks of Brunello wine of different vintages were maturing here before being bottled. 'It's the perfect environment,' Federico explained, 'because the temperature never alters.' We walked slowly across the cellars' packed earth and flagstone floors; talked quietly about the minimum ageing period of three years and the great vintages of recent years; mused about the weather during the few weeks remaining before the harvest.

Apologies were made for the absence of Cristina's father, Cesare, who would join us later. He had asked that we be shown his ancient stone olive press, and so we were led into another old building and a small room that was possibly once a kitchen. In one of the walls was the metal door of a *forno,* the traditional wood-burning oven, and on the floor and on many shelves a jumble of rusting coffee grinders and pots, discarded wooden cooking utensils, large black saucepans and chipped crockery. From here we went through to a large, dark room dimly lit only by a shaft of dust-filled sunlight, and nothing could have prepared us for what we saw.

The workings of the olive press were explained to us, but our concentration was not good for we were under the spell of everything else around us. As our eyes became accustomed to the gloom of the cobweb-filled space, we realised that, as well as the centuries-old olive press, this was where all those things once essential to daily life in the villa and on the farm had been abandoned by previous generations. A child's three-wheeled tricycle and a crudely made highchair, both at least 100 years old, stood forlornly by an even older wooden grape press. A large wooden birdcage with peeling white paint sat on an oak table worn down at the edges by the arms and elbows of generations of diners. Rows of iron keys of different sizes hung next to racks of dusty brown bottles. Barrels, winemakers' paddles, sleds and ploughs that farm oxen had once pulled, all manner of tables and chairs, and a large terracotta pot fired in 1797 had also found their resting place among this tangle of family heritage.

It was time to move on, said Federico, and we reluctantly adjusted our eyes to the sunlight and followed our hosts across the vine-covered courtyard, past the villa's 300-year-old family chapel where past generations are buried and through a gate in the wall that surrounds the property. Once again we were not prepared for what we would see. Here was another secret place, a private park containing a perfectly preserved section of an Etruscan road from the 7th century BC. With the sun filtering through tall cypress and umbrella pines onto moss and pine needles underfoot, we heard how this was part of a 3,000 year-old road that once ran from the Casentino mountains north of Florence to Roselle in the Maremma region of Tuscany on the coast, only a short distance from the villa. The road was stepped and picked its way through a hillside dense with ancient ilex trees with their distinct mosaic-patterned bark. This ancient type of oak once totally covered the hillside upon which Montalcino sits and was also Tuscany's most common tree.

Our mouths were getting dry in the late morning heat. It was time to taste. We followed our hosts to a nearby house via buildings that contained the stainless steel tanks used for maceration, where colour and flavour is extracted from the skins of the grapes.

Until the 1960s much of the land on the estate was worked according to the *mezzadria* system, the sharecropping arrangement which had been in use in Tuscany since the 13th century. The house in which we now found ourselves was once where Castelli Martinozzi's *fattore,* farm manager, lived and carried out his duties as the link between the *mezzadria* farmers and the Castelli family.

We assembled in the main room of the house. Cristina told us the décor and contents had been exactly left as they were some 40 years ago when the last *fattore* left and the *mezzadria* system ended on the estate. In the centre of the room was a large family dining table set with 40 wine glasses and bottles of different vintages of Castelli Martinozzi Brunello and of the estate's Rosso di Montalcino.

As Giuseppe pulled corks with great care, the door opened and into the room came an elderly yet sprightly bright-eyed gentleman in a dark suit. We were introduced to Cristina's 80-year-old father, Cesare, and were immediately charmed by his presence. Cesare is something of a legend in the wine world. In his quiet way he has helped maintain the standards amongst fellow producers that ensure Brunello maintains its ranking as one of Italy's finest wines. He took me to the window from where we could see the Mediterranean in the distance, and pointed out the location of his and his near neighbour's vineyards 400m above sea level and clustered on the crown of gentle slopes overlooking the Orcia valley. The soil there is rich in clay, sand and limey clay he told me, and their vines are an average of 40 years old with 400 plants per hectare. The location also benefits from a cool micro-climate that favours the slow ripening of the grapes, and gives the wine exceptional concentration and a rich bouquet.

Villa San Restituta is a tiny estate of 12 hectares, but is one of the oldest in the Montalcino region and produces just 400 cases of Brunello a year. Until 1970 Brunello di Montalcino was a local wine for local people produced by only a handful of estates. Today there are 200 producers, but even then their total annual production is a mere 330,000 cases and most are small growers who make 2,000 cases or less a year. By comparison, the Chianti region produces over 8 million cases a year; Bordeaux over 55 million cases.

We first tried Castelli Martinozzi's Rosso di Montalcino which is made solely from the Brunello grape, the local name for the Sangiovese Grosso grape – 'grosso' referring not to the size of the grapes but to this variety's incredible concentration of fruit and flavour. Unlike other Rosso di Montalcino wines in the area, this is not a secondary wine at Castelli Martinozzi. They don't use grapes rejected for their Brunello wines but make it from carefully selected and vinified grapes grown in separate vineyards on the property.

The wine is aged for just one year before it is released for sale, and we all agreed that it was an elegant wine with a generous colour, bouquet and taste. Giuseppe explained that it exhibited an intricate and complex balance of ripe fruit, acidity and tannin that set it apart from other Rosso di Montalcino wines. Naturally I bought a couple of cases, not least because it is about a third of the price of Brunello.

We then moved on to a number of different vintages of Castelli Martinozzi Brunello di Montalcino. These were astonishing, big, ruby-red wines that found us searching for the right words to describe what we smelt and tasted. On the nose, the fruit was rich and ripe interwoven with the scents of undergrowth, violets and musk. On the palate, we all tasted elegant fruit flavours and noted, after a prompt from Giuseppe, the perfect fruit/acid balance before savouring the intense and harmonic after-taste of each lingering mouthful. All the Brunello vintages we tried were aristocratic, exceptionally concentrated, harmonious and pleasantly austere, and I bought a case of the 2004, a five-star vintage, which I hope to keep unopened for the 15 to 20 years it might take for the wine to reach its peak. So far, so good . . .

For a century and a half, Brunello and Italy's other great red wine, Barolo from Piedmont, have been rivals competing for the title of the most-beloved Italian red wine in the world. I asked Giuseppe to try and explain in layman's terms how we should view them. 'Barolo is Italy's Burgundy, and Brunello our Bordeaux. Barolo is made from the Nebbiolo grape, one that is rather like Pinot Noir some say, and thus a very different variety from our local Sangiovese. Barolo is much too feminine for me … give me the depth, character and perfect structure of a 20-year-old Brunello from a top producer any day.'

We took our time saying grateful goodbyes, and then sped off up the hill in the direction of Montalcino counting ourselves extremely privileged to have seen one of Italy's most evocative, ancient, unspoilt and undiscovered fine wine estates.

TWELVE

Lurking in the Undergrowth

Fungi Fever

Local knowledge is everything in the mountains around Casa Amari, but when it comes to what is in the undergrowth the locals can be closed and secretive.

We get to our house by taking a rather precarious turning off a main road that is possibly the least used highway in Tuscany, even though it links Cortona with Città di Castello across the border in Umbria. The turning takes us onto a steep, unmade track that snakes through chestnut and oak woods. Having to reverse or park-up to allow the cars of one of our handful of neighbours or their occasional visitors to get by is a rarity. So, after nearly a year of living here, it was a shock to find that both our track and the main road either side of it had become car parks.

Summer was ending and for three days we had witnessed the most spectacular thunderstorms depositing serious quantities of rain onto our local hillsides and the distant Apennines. We were returning from a shopping trip in Cortona when we found the entrances to woodcutters' tracks off the main road jammed with battered Fiat Pandas, 4 x 4s, new and not-so-new family saloons, assorted vans and three-wheeled *Ape* trucks. Fungi Fever had come to our hillside.

People of all ages, shapes and sizes, entire families with children and relatives in tow, young couples, men and women in their 70s and older were taking to the woods with wicker baskets to fill with wild mushrooms. This being Italy, they had to dress correctly for the occasion. Every vehicle disgorged big boots, well-worn hats of all types and an extraordinary selection of camouflage-patterned trousers and jackets. Val and I couldn't help wondering whether fungi hunting was the Italian equivalent of going on safari.

Best of the fungi-hunting apparel were the brown cotton coats favoured by grocers in the days before there were supermarkets. These were clearly the dress of choice for gentlemen of more mature age, tightly belted with a length of sisal, finished off with dark corduroys pushed into brown wellies and topped with a battered grey trilby.

I decided to join them with a sturdy *bastone,* stick, and a bag rather than a basket. With high hopes of learning from fellow foragers, I set off on the path down to the woods below us and soon fell into step with an elderly couple who immediately reprimanded me for having a plastic bag, saying, 'the spores of anything you find must be allowed to escape and they can't from that bag'. I ran back to the house to find a basket and then caught up with them again in the woods, keen to find out where they would be looking. Their stern faces and unhelpful comment of 'go looking on your own' told me all I needed to know about getting practical help from them.

Serious fungi hunters are often loners, and woe betide the person who follows them on their forages or expects a direct answer to questions such as 'where do I look?' or 'what did you find?' Their baskets are covered with cotton cloths, as much to hide their finds from prying eyes as to keeping the fungi in good condition and yet allow their spores to escape into the atmosphere.

Undaunted I slowly consulted my near neighbours about places to go, when and what to look for. I also bought a faded brown cotton coat, a special curved knife with a brush at one end for carefully getting the dirt off fungi, and whittled myself a forked stick for this was the approved way of taking each prize from the soil.

Established woods like those in our area provide the very best places for a huge variety of species. Many varieties of fungi have a symbiotic relationship with trees and their roots, with some growing only with a particular species of tree, while others enjoy any number of different trees, or differing types of decaying wood or soil. What each has in common is a preference for damp and shady places that are also warm, ideally in humus-rich soil that is not too marshy or overgrown with thick vegetation.

I soon learned that the best time to forage was very early in the morning, especially after a thunderstorm, and always if lightning had struck the hillside. 'Fungi are sons of the Gods,' I was told on a number of occasions, 'because they are born without seeds.'

By discreetly following experienced fungi hunters, I noticed they invariably revisited certain spots that they alone appeared to know. When I later checked these out they all featured rotting wood in secret hollows and banks – sites that they knew from years of experience would produce the best specimens after a particular combination of sun, rain and temperature.

Funghi porcini (boletus edulis) are by far the most sort-after variety. In English these are ceps, the mushrooms of fairy tales, with plump, toasty-brown caps and stems that swell gently outward at the bottom. Turn one over and you discover that, like all bolete, the underside of the cap is made up of a porous, spongy substance instead of gills. If it is a true edulis there's a woody aroma you soon learn to recognise. But what if it has tiny tooth marks? Fairy feasts, rats . . . or what? Eventually a fungi-forager told me that it was rabbits and squirrels and 'that if they have nibbled a mushroom you can be assured that it is edible'. I'd been living at Casa Amari long enough to suspect the story and the storyteller. My neighbours confirmed this was a typical mountain tale, something that might be true sometimes but isn't always so.

Most people associate fungi with the autumn but they grow throughout the year in Tuscany. In our woods a wet and warmish May, and then the first sunny days of June, can bring on a bumper crop of porcini. Before then, from the autumn through winter and into spring, chanterelles can be found.

Chanterelles proved fairly elusive to my untrained hunter's eyes. When you find them they look like clumps of small apricot-coloured parasols with fine ridges that run all the way up the stem and under their caps. They have an appetising woodsy-sweet fragrance and, if cooked only briefly in butter and olive oil, have a delicate flavour and a good texture. They seem brighter tasting when cooked with a whiff of garlic and served with a sprinkle of parsley. They make the most wonderful omelettes like this, if you have enough, but for me they have an even greater attraction – they cannot be confused with any of the poisonous fungi.

Italians love all types of fungi and know a lot about them. Even so, their foraging has to be supported by specially trained officials who help identify, and if necessary discard, those found in the wild. There are probably less than a dozen deadly fungi, but plenty of others can cause digestive and respiratory problems, and the Italian incidence of poisoning by such fungi is the highest in

Europe, with over 40,000 cases a year. I consult one of the local pharmacists if I am not sure whether my foraging finds are safe to eat.

Sometimes, we hear of packs of professional fungi hunters descending on particularly productive woods. Sightings of groups who use walkie-talkies to co-ordinate their efforts are not unusual in the north of the country, but we are lucky in only having one *cercatore,* professional picker, in our area.

Gino Zancani is the most regular, early-morning visitor to our hillside. He is an elderly, small and slow-moving gentleman who always keeps his head down and never volunteers the polite *salve* with which everyone else greets one another. Signor Zancani talks to no-one when he is foraging and, according to the restaurateurs who buy from him, he can often collect 40kg of porcini on a good day. He works far fewer hours than when he was our local postman, yet it is rumoured he now pockets twice what he used to earn.

If porcini can be nice little earners, their potential for wealth creation is nothing in comparison with the money to be made from truffle hunting, especially the aristocrat of this world, the highly perfumed white truffle that's specially associated with Northern Italy.

THE TRUFFLE TRADERS

I was introduced to the secretive world of white-truffle trading and tartufo di Alba by my friend Sara. She lives in the delightful Piedmont town of Asti and early one November morning she took me to a neighbourhood near her home.

We went into a bar off a small square stuffed with expensive 4x4s and estate cars with dark-tinted windows. A dozen men of various ages, all dressed in generous, multi-pocketed all-weather coats, sat toying with their coffees. Without exception they looked as though they'd had a sleepless night. Each seemed very sensitive to each other's actions and especially to the appearance of we outsiders. Surely they weren't drug dealers, not at their age and at this time of the day? Sara spoke to a youngish, dark-skinned man with a heavy stubble from whom she had previously bought a white tartufo di Alba. His response was typical she said, 'No one has any truffles today.' So what were those smells?

I was familiar with the rich aroma of espresso emitted by the elderly Gaggia machine that permeates all Italian bars but this was spiked with something else – a powerful odour with a clear echo of garlic and a hint of ripe cheese. It smelt familiar and slightly exciting, yet totally alien and not a little forbidden.

After much animated banter between Sara, her friend and more and more of the men propping up the bar, we were eventually shown the contents of one of the deep pockets – a blue and white checked cotton bag containing just six walnut-sized truffles, each still covered with earth. I stuck my nose in. The sensation was extraordinary. Receptors I didn't know I had burst into life. My head was filled with a musky, fragrant, voluptuous aroma, as dizzying as nitrous oxide. There was none of the sweaty pungency of black truffles, or the farmyard bouquet you often get from bottles of truffle oil. These were Piedmont's famed white truffles and most of those in the bag were about 100gm in weight. I asked if I could buy one, but was told they were already promised to regular customers at 350 euros a piece.

I knew how those privileged few would enjoy them; never cooked but always sliced raw and very thinly onto a risotto of porcini perhaps, or into a warm, butter-rich brioche and eaten with a glass of chilled spumante. Before I swooned at the thought of voluptuous present and future delights, I offered a caffè corretto all round. The assembled *trifulau,* or truffle hunters, of Asti agreed to answer my questions about the inner workings of their white truffle world.

There are close to 50 varieties of truffle but only a few are edible or worth eating. In UK supermarkets largely flavourless summer truffles are passed off as winter's black truffles, and the pale-fleshed desert truffles of North Africa have as little to offer. No wonder the English don't understand the appeal and price of a true black winter truffle if they think they are getting a similar taste from the cheaper, boring summer varieties.

Because all truffles grow underground they are exceptionally difficult to find and harvest. For a while I was taken in by tales about barometric pressure and the right phases of the moon being key indicators as to when to go truffle hunting.

I believed these grizzled men's tales about mysterious rituals and secret indicators, but then a man walked in with a curious dog and I knew at once that none of these truffle gatherers relied on arcane knowledge. They each combined years of experience with secret knowledge of special places and a real feeling for, and knowledge of, truffles. Each was also a pragmatist who invariably relied on the keen sense of smell of trained dogs. Until then I had thought they used pigs, but was told they are difficult to train and are inclined to eat the truffles when they find them. Half-breed dogs are obedient and can be relied upon to give up their valuable finds in exchange for a biscuit or two.

The man with the dog looked even more tired than anyone else in the bar. In a quiet voice I asked him why. He said he and the dog had been up all night hunting truffles, adding this was when his dog's sense of smell was at its best. His mongrel looked like the result of an amorous, perhaps accidental, coupling between a terrier and a Labrador and would definitely not win prizes at Crufts. Yet, he was the friendliest of hounds, seeming not to care that his rough coat and over-sized ears did him no favours. Because white truffles are out of my financial league, I asked the dog's owner what he thought of black truffles. 'Not that bad from Norcia but not from around here,' he shrugged. 'Any I find, I give them to friends.'

Further discussions about varieties taught me that experts claim to taste the variations between white truffles found under different species of tree. For one thing they look different, so those from around an oak tree are heavy and dark, while those from the sweet chestnut are lighter. The palest and most fragrant of all are found under lime trees, but these are especially rare.

As we were leaving the café, one of the *trifulau* joined us and told us to be wary of 'foreigners selling dodgy truffles from Croatia', the only other place known to grow the white ones. Also, because we obviously liked dogs, he wanted to show us his prize hunter, resting in the back of his costly Porsche 4 x 4 after a hard night in the woods. We were not greeted by another rugged tail-wagger but by a highly strung ballet dancer, a whippet-type mongrel with long silky hair, every tendon tense, every muscle aquiver with fear or excitement. His owner confided that he had brought him to Asti to sell to another hunter for at least 5,000 euros.

At first I thought this was a ridiculous price for a dog. Then I swiftly calculated that during the white truffle season he could earn that much in a few successful mornings or nights. Where else could you make such a relatively small investment into a business and yet expect guaranteed profits so soon? I was very tempted then, and even now . . .

GROW YOUR OWN

When we wanted to buy some of the terracotta pots that are such a feature of Tuscan gardens, our gardener friend Giuseppe recommended we visit Marcello Cossiga on his smallholding set amongst sunflower fields below Cortona. He was said to make some of the best.

As ever on a shopping trip in Tuscany, time slips into irrelevance once you get into conversation with a vendor. Signor Cossiga was a craftsman potter of the old school but, as much as he loved clay and the kiln, the conversation soon turned to horticultural matters. After he helped us load our purchases into the back of the car, he insisted we see his apricot trees. They were laden with fruit, something he proudly claimed was down to his unique watering system, a Heath Robinson construction that you tripped over at every turn. It was the success of this device, he said, that had led him to make his latest purchase, half a dozen poplar saplings at the edge of the orchard that 'would produce truffles in five years' time'.

I thought he was spinning yet another tall Tuscan tale. But when he explained that you've been able to buy truffle-producing trees for some 30 years, I had to ask him to tell us more. 'Truffles develop underground as you probably know,' he said, 'and they do so in a symbiotic association with the roots of trees. When technology was developed to inoculate host trees with truffle spore, it made cultivation possible.'

Signor Cossiga had bought truffle-tree seedlings inoculated with different truffle species on differing host trees: 'I had a choice of poplar and oak seedlings. I took three of each and was told for sure that they would start producing after a few years and would continue to do so for decades.' I admired his confidence and asked about quantity and timings. 'It is something of a gamble,' he admitted. 'If I am lucky yields could be around 24 kilos per hectare in 5 to 10 years' time – or even more.'

Until we lived in Italy, I'd thought that white truffles, *tuber magnatum,* came only from Piedmont and from Istria in Croatia. But, as knowledge increases amongst the nurseries that sell these truffle trees, it is possible that yields of 100 kilos per hectare per annum could soon be possible in Tuscany. The thought is as heady as their astonishing, penetrating scent.

And then I discovered something I hardly believed true. Tuscany already had white truffles of her own and Tuscany also had her own white truffle fair in San Miniato, a hill town roughly equidistant between Florence and Pisa. It was once a crossroad on the pilgrimage route from France to Rome and today sits atop the farmland where Tuscan tobacco is grown, and I was intrigued to find there a countryside peppered with what look like severe Romanesque churches. They're actually tobacco-curing barns and I stopped at one of these temples to the evil weed about five kilometres from San Miniato, intent on finding someone who could tell me more.

The smell of burning charcoal seeped through the large barn doors as I knocked hard and knocked hard again. After a while an elderly man appeared. I apologised for intruding and explained that I was intrigued by the design of his barn. He said his was built in the early 1900s, adding 'but who designed it and why they all look like churches I have no clue'. Perhaps I looked disappointed because then my luck changed. 'Do you know,' he asked, 'that this is the last Sunday in November and is the final day of Miniato's annual white truffle market?' I was about to tell him this was really why I was here when he proudly claimed he had helped start the fair 30 years ago and would tell me why, if I had the time. I settled myself down for a long, interesting story.

'In the 1970s the area was being overrun by foreigners from Piedmont pocketing our Tuscan white truffles. They were everywhere, not just around San Miniato but in the hills around Pontedera and nearby Montopoli. This land has always been home to the best white truffles in the world, and we needed to do something to stop Tuscan truffles being passed off in Piedmont as local truffles from the Alba area. Once we were organised and ran our own white-truffle fair, things got better for us. It's true that still not many people know about us, but those who do keep us nicely in business.'

He continued talking for some time about the 'crooks' from Piedmont and their dishonourable ways, and then told me how to get the best from the dealers in the market, advice as valuable as the truffles themselves. 'You'll get the real thing up in the town,' he said, also telling me where to park, just outside the *centro storico*.

In San Miniato I followed the crowds towards the historic Prato del Duomo that crowns the town. There it was, the *Mostra Mercato Nazionale del Tartufo Bianco di San Miniato*. All the stallholders in the main tent were more open than the hunters I had met in Asti and were happy to explain truffle subtleties to me, which made more and more sense as the aroma in the closed space invaded and permeated my senses – elusive but penetrating, redolent of earth and woods and vaguely garlicky. How did my TV chef and food writer friend Glynn Christian describe them? 'A penetrating smell and overwhelming flavour, redolent of every possible perversity and prohibition and impossible to describe because it is like nothing else.'

The white truffle from this area is the *tuber magnatum pico,* a relatively large variety with an especially intense flavour. It has a thick, smooth-to-wrinkled, tan-coloured outer skin that is somewhat rough in texture. Inside it is cream or fawn with white marbling. Some of the specimens here were as much as 12cm in diameter. One weighed 500gm and I was told this would sell for 1,250 euros or more.

It had been a good year for Tuscan white truffles – not too dry, not too wet and not too damp. There were plenty and the price had eased from less burgeoning years. I chose a smaller tuber, remembering my recently collected advice to ensure that under the thin layer of dirt the truffle had neither hidden cavities nor growths that would get knocked off when I cleaned it. It had been found the previous night and retained all the strong, lingering aroma of freshness I had learned to identify. The stallholder weighed it and I paid. It was 18gm and he advised me to enjoy it quickly, because after three days it would start to lose weight and that extraordinary, libido-disturbing aroma. Of course, during those first days it could, like a black truffle, be stored in rice or amongst eggs which would then taste of truffle, too, and make the expense seem better value.

On the way back to my car I went to the market in Piazza della Republica and bought some black-truffle-speckled pecorino cheese and a few *grissini* breadsticks to sustain me on the drive back to Cortona. As I motored through the glorious Chianti countryside, I thought about what I would do with my first Tuscan white truffle. Do as others have done to you, I vowed, and promised to keep it simple.

My mouth watered as I remembered being encouraged to shave as much white truffle as I wanted onto a dish of cardoons in a light béchamel sauce. That was the first time I lunched with Carlo Ercole, the legendary Italian food producer and the man behind the famous Saclà brand of pasta sauces, at his house in Asti in Piedmont.

I carried on salivating as I recalled the veal tartare topped with white truffle shavings that Sandro and her mother had prepared for me at the Cà Vittoria restaurant in Tigliole near Asti. Then I thought back to the fresh buttered tagliatelle buried in a mountain of white truffle shavings that Val and I had shared for lunch one bitterly cold December day in Lombardy. This was in Mantua, once the home of the mighty Gonzaga family during the Renaissance, and the restaurant had a décor that mirrored the grand frescoed rooms of the Ducal Palace opposite. We feasted with every sense and once again congratulated ourselves for making the break and coming to live in Italy.

OUR LOCAL HEAVIES

As well as wild mushrooms, there's another thing that is good to eat and that also hides in the woods around Casa Amari. On most nights, as darkness starts to fall, I hear what seems to be a small army on the move, one with respiratory problems. The first time I heard the sound I took a torch, stood on the terrace, and shone it down onto the field below. The beam of light picked up the staring eyes of our local heavies, our neighbourhood gang of *cinghiali,* wild boar.

There were mum, dad, uncles and aunts and all their children – a total of 16. The moment I moved closer they hoofed it with amazing speed and agility and disappeared into the woods.

Ever since that first sighting, I have developed a love/hate relationship with the *cinghiali* that live and breed all around us. They are marvellous-looking animals but I despair at the damage they do to our land. Wild boars are the only hoofed animals known to dig burrows. Totally insensitive to my efforts to make a productive garden, our local wild boar take over when we are sleeping or are out for the evening and excavate at will, turning our lawns and borders into deep, muddy play pits. I always feel doubly insulted when I hear them squeaking, snuffling and snorting with pleasure while they do the damage.

Tuscany's wild boars have large heads, relatively short legs and compact dark-grey bodies covered with a fine fur and stiff bristles, used for toothbrushes until the 1930s. The adults we see vary in length from 120 to 180cm and are about 90cm tall. I estimate they weigh between 80 and 100kg, although boars of 150kg are not uncommon in Tuscany.

Our local adults are equipped with formidable weapons of continuously growing tusks, actually canine teeth, which make the males look extremely dangerous. Their very young offspring are soft brown in colour with longitudinal darker stripes. When they are half-grown the stripes fade and they become dark grey like the adults.

Our group is what's known hereabouts as a 'sounder'. Sounders typically contain 15 to 20 animals, but groups of over 50 have been spotted in our region. Unless it is breeding time, adult males are not part of the bunch preferring to live alone. But since wild boar breed two or three times a year, I often see them and the considerable results of their amorous actions. Birth usually occurs in a secluded area away from the sounder and a litter will typically contain 8 to 12 youngsters.

Cinghiali forage from dusk until dawn and have both day- and night-time resting periods. They eat almost anything they come across, from grass and nuts to refuse, insects, small reptiles and, if they get the chance, even young deer and the lambs of our local farmers.

Some say wild boar are naturally timid creatures and well-mannered. I am not sure about that. Apart from their destructive eating habits, they can be dangerous. Every few months we hear about someone doing serious damage to their car and/or themself by hitting one at night on our unlit country roads. I've been warned not to surprise or corner one, especially a sow with her children, since she can and will defend herself and her young with vigour. A sow's tusks are not visible, so she charges with her head up, mouth wide, and bites. If it's a male, he will lower his head, charge, and then slash upward with his tusks. Such attacks rarely cause fatalities but are always bloody and traumatic.

As with the beasts themselves, I have developed a love/hate relationship with those that hunt them. The hunting season starts on October 1st. Weekends see the most activity and this is when favourite local walks become off-limit because our hills are alive with Rambo-like men in camouflage caps and clothing, usually driving in on- or off-road convoys of small 4x4s. Many tow enclosed trailers that house their hunting dogs which they appear to regard callously as mere servants, something to be used and just as often abused. It's a side to Italian hunters we simply don't understand, but guess it has something to do with the hunters' bloodlust.

Wild boar nearly became extinct in Italy around 1900, and populations have only increased significantly since the 1970s. Thus the hunters must be licensed and the number of animals they can kill with their favoured Beretta rifles is controlled. Unfortunately, Mussolini gave them the right to cross any private property in pursuit of their prey. They are also allowed to shoot within 50 to 150m of a house and accidental shootings of non-participants are common.

After our first full year at Casa Amari, the damage the local boars were doing to our land was beyond a joke. It was time to call in our forever knowledgeable gardener friend Giuseppe. He said that to properly protect our property it would cost 'molti euro' since an L-shaped barrier would need to be set into the earth that reached a metre above ground, a metre down into the earth, and then a metre out at a right angle from the base. The cheaper option was to try an electric fence. This, I am pleased to say, seems to be working.

So, are *cinghiali* better dead than alive?

Wild boar sausages and salami are a speciality of Tuscany, and over in Chianti the best meat from the best boar is reserved for *prosciutto di cinghiale.* For this, the animal must not be too old or it will be tough, too large or it will be gamey, too small or it will absorb too much salt. Typically, boar hams are soaked for 20 days in brine, washed in wine seasoned with black pepper and garlic, and then dried in an airy space in the house to cure for two or three months.

Val and I agree the flavour of simply roasted *cinghiale* is sweet and nutty like rare-breed pork, but more intense. Neighbours say the best way to enjoy wild boar is to get hold of a boneless loin and cut this into chunks then brown it in Tuscan olive oil with bay leaves and garlic, add a glass of white wine and simmer slowly until tender, topping up with wine as needed.

Seeing a whole young wild boar being cooked for a special occasion is something that every dedicated carnivore should experience at least once. At the exceptional *agriturismo* Villa Cicchi near Ascoli Piceno in Le Marche, I witnessed how they marinated the animal for 24 hours in a chopped mixture of rosemary, wild fennel, grated lemon zest and wild garlic. It was then placed on a wire rack over a pan, and red wine was poured over the beast before it was put into a hot bread oven. The cooking juices were regularly doused over the boar during cooking, which took nearly four hours. The glistening roast was then transferred to a wooden board decorated with variegated ivy and bay leaf before being paraded round the tables to the applause of diners at a christening party.

Surprisingly, if you talk to a Tuscan who bores about boars, he will tell you that our local examples are not as good as those that come from the marshes of the Maremma part of the region. He will also say that the best way to enjoy their meat is by cooking it in a sweet and sour sauce of red wine and vinegar, caramelised sugar, pine nuts and candied orange peel – a medieval sort of dish to my mind.

So I asked my dear friend Anna Del Conte, the greatest expert on Italian food. Anna has the most wonderful collection of old Italian books and says that the most appetising recipe is *cinghiale in agrodolce,* a sweet and sour sauce originating from the borders of Tuscany and Lazio. It's a very ancient dish and not too different from the one above. Like all robust recipes, the appearance of a new ingredient is welcomed because it improves the complicated flavour. In this case, chocolate from the New World is added to such Old World favourites as prunes, pine nuts and candied peel. The boar is marinated in wine and herbs for two days, and cooked slowly in oil. Towards the end, onion, grated chocolate, prunes, pine nuts, raisins, candied citron and orange peel are added, as well as the marinade, and the dish is then served with toasted bread.

In an 1889 book the author talks about eating a boar in Sardinia cooked *a carraxiu.* A festive *carraxiu* consists of a roast where one animal, fully or partly boned, is stuffed with another and then with another, and another, and so on. I hear this is still done in parts of Sardinia, starting with a bullock and ending with a thrush – and presumably with a *cinghiale* in there somewhere.

In my experience, the wild boar from our adjoining region, Umbria, really is the tastiest in Italy. The reason is simple. Umbria's wild herb pastures, its many lakes and high mountains of chestnut and oak provide an ideal ground not only for wild boar but for truffles, those jewels of the Italian wild. Truffles are available almost year round and the wild boar of Umbria have a nose for them as keen as radar. And only in Umbria are pigs finished with flesh-perfuming truffles before the hunters and local butchers turn them into superlative salamis, sausages and hams. Truffles and truffle-flavoured wild boar meat. Such natural harmony and all on our doorstep.

THIRTEEN

Will It Ever Change?

A Very Different Type of Country

Living in the countryside is a joy, not least because we are unaware most of the time of Italy's many problems. But the moment I turn on the news or pick up a newspaper, I cannot help wondering whether the country I love will ever change profoundly. And, if so, how it may happen?

Italy is the eurozone's third biggest economy, but for years has been spending more than it earns and it has the biggest stock of public debt in the eurozone, a staggering two trillion euros, nearly 130 per cent of its annual economic output. Thus when the prospect of Greece going broke first hit the headlines, it also became clear that Italy was potentially the next country to go to the financial wall. Lenders who had treated it as an equal to such major EU countries as France and Germany suddenly demanded unsustainable lending rates, and expressed views that made Italy seem a Third-World economy.

We bought Casa Amari at the time the euro was introduced. There was much talk about change, and our Italian friends seemed to accept my view that they were living in an archaic and very different type of country from those in Northern Europe. But they insisted that 'we are about to change and become modern'. I was not sure then and am not sure now.

Eleven years later the man who was in the best possible position to instigate change, the scandal-plagued Prime Minister Silvio Berlusconi, was finally driven from office and left Italy on the edge of a financial abyss. He was replaced by something completely different, a technocrat government headed by Mario Monti, an economist and former EU commissioner. During his 15 months in power Monti may have calmed the money markets but failed to do much else, apart from making Italians poorer.

Coffee matters in Italy. It fuels its people at any time of the day as no other beverage does. In the same way that everyone used to know the price of a pint of milk in Britain, every Italian knows the cost of a single espresso in a bar. At the height of summer in 2012, the price of an espresso went up to one euro. Many said the rise was Monti's fault, while quite a few said it would never have happened if Berlusconi was still in power. 'It's the curse of the euro,' declared

Francesco Pinelli, the father of my lawyer friend Silvio. 'The dropping of the lira marked the end of our independence.'

For him, there is no question that Italy should pull out of the euro. 'It pains me to be put in a similar category to Greece and have foreigners calling Italy a risky borrower and a nation that has lost its way.' Actually, like most of the populace, he cares far less about Italy than he does about his own backyard.

Francesco and Silvio are die-hard Tuscans. They were born in Arezzo and now live in Cortona. If you were to meet them for the first time, they would say they were Tuscans not Italians, and then add that they lived in Cortona. This is not unusual because most people who live on the Italian peninsula don't immediately think of themselves as Italians. There is a more marked sense of belonging to a town or city than to a country. An 'Italian' will tell you that, 'I am a Sicilian … a Neapolitan … a Venetian … a Milanese … a Genovese … a Tuscan.' Provincialism, or *campanilismo,* loyalty to the municipal bell-tower, has always been strong.

Italy is not one state and perhaps never will be. It is not even 20 regions or over 100 provinces, but it is more than 8,000 *comuni,* or municipalities. As in the Middle Ages, essential Italy is the Italy of its communes. The government in Rome and the institutions of the European Union are seen, at best, as being remote from their needs and concerns and, at worst, the enemy.

It is easy to forget that Italy is a relatively new country. It only became a nation state in 1861. Before then it was a huge number of different kingdoms and city states. In the south was the Kingdom of Two Sicilies, ruled from Naples. Then came the Papal States and north of that the Kingdom of the House of Savoy. But within those apparent borders, prime loyalty remained fixed to the long history of much smaller fiefdoms, to city states such as Venice, Mantua or Florence, to a myriad of local dukedoms and princedoms throughout the peninsula. I reckon it is still, and this is why it took almost a century for the country to adopt a common language, which only happened after the Second World War and the growing importance of television.

I have come to value these strong traditions of regional and more localised loyalties and civic pride. You see this in the way the architectural and cultural past of old town centres is preserved. Traffic restrictions are respected, there's a notable lack of litter, everything stops for lunch, and there are many simple acts of politeness and respect for others, especially for the elderly. This heritage mind-set is also apparent in support for local businesses, the lack of chain stores, the importance placed upon local and regional food production or specialties, and support for the arts and cultural events, including public pageantry and seasonal celebrations.

Family ties also matter hugely in Italy and this makes life seem more humane and enjoyable than in other European countries. But scratch below the surface and there is a plethora of issues that need to be addressed if Italy is ever to change and become what they or we would think of as a 'normal' country.

Breaking the Rules

Sadly, corruption, organised crime and tax avoidance are also part of Italy's DNA. They rarely make a major difference to the daily life of ordinary people, but they do represent barriers to making Italy a single, manageable country.

Twenty years after the Tangentopoli corruption scandal, where more than half the members of the Italian Parliament were under indictment and 400 city and town councils were dissolved because of corruption charges, scandals continue about kickbacks given for public works' contracts.

During Berlusconi's time, breaking the rules was not only accepted but expected, and to be cunning was thought worthy of particular praise. When Mario Monti came to power he tried to change these attitudes. Despite his attempts to cut down on graft, it's believed corruption siphons off more than 60 billion euros a year from the public coffers and many of the people involved are politicians and high-profile public figures.

Just as political corruption never seems to go away, neither does organised crime. The three major organisations are the Sicilian Mafia, the Camorra and the Calabria-based 'Ndrangheta. This trio is at the centre of a web of illicit activities throughout the country and overseas. These appear to grow each year and represent a shadow economy that many experts believe is now twice the size of Italy's all-important clothing industry. Together with their well-known drug trafficking and prostitution rackets, there are signs of organised crime's involvement in large public contracts and, increasingly, in the transport and public health industries.

Along with crime and corruption, vested interests are part of the fabric of Italian society. They are in virtually every community; something that makes Italians over-dramatise the importance of their contribution and rights, especially those in the professions, commercial life or in trade unions.

'The problem is that we don't want openness in our lives,' said Giacomo Calvanese, who services our boiler. 'How do you expect ordinary Italians to respect the rules when politicians ignore the law and are themselves involved in corruption and the Mafia?' Giacomo always issues a receipt and never insists on being paid in cash. He is unusual in this respect and, although he resents paying higher taxes and seeing little in return, he believes that Italy can only be a normal country when ordinary citizens, as well as those in power, play by the rules.

As well as introducing new property ownership taxes, robust pension reforms, tighter controls on spending and cuts in government and health expenditure, Mario Monti was insistent that every citizen had to pay their taxes. In doing so, he had to contend with a deep-seated national aversion to paying any form of tax.

The adage holds that the only two certainties in life are death and taxes. In Italy attitudes are a little different. While few Italians believe they can outwit death, most are sure they can get away with cheating on their taxes. Tax evasion is almost a national sport and Berlusconi's greatest negative contribution to Italian life was to encourage this attitude, by example as well as by public stance.

Cash has always been king here when it comes to getting the best deal, but Monti banned cash transactions and promoted the new law with an advertising campaign that compared tax evaders to parasites. His prime objective was to get the huge number of self-employed people to pay up. Currently, the majority declare far less than a third of their income for taxation purposes.

We saw dramatic signs of Monti's clamp-down on tax evaders. Halfway through his term in office, packs of jack-booted *Guardia di Finanza Carabinieri* arrived in Cortona in grey buses and on powerful motorbikes. Their objective was to unearth irregularities in the tax affairs of those providing bed and break-fast or renting out their homes to tourists. They also went to local bars and restaurants to interrogate staff about pay and their tax returns.

Then we heard about luxury cars being pulled over by tax officials at exits from the A1 motorway, ten kilometres away. Their owners received a grilling in what proved to be the first stage of an investigation into their financial affairs, starting with a check on these drivers' records against their tax receipts to find out whether the owners had reported enough income to pay for their high-end cars.

Given to Sloth

Ever since the fashion for the Grand Tour began in the 17th century, the history, art and architecture of Tuscany, its natural beauty, weather, good food and wine have cast their spell over tourists. While the number of Italian visitors to the region continues to go down, reflecting the continuing slump in consumer spending which underpins Italy's deepening recession, foreign tourist numbers continue to rise.

Thus things didn't look that bad the summer before last, which was blessed by three months of virtually continuous sunshine. But when I talked to friends and neighbours I found they were worrying about sharp increases in unemployment, especially amongst young people; about the on-going squeeze of their disposable incomes; and about the impact of the government's tax-reform programmes. The main topics of conversation locally were Monti's plan to raise standard retirement age, the VAT increase and, especially, the impending massive rises in property taxes.

Soon after Monti came to power he introduced new economic measures dubbed the 'Save Italy Act'. The details were published the day after Boxing Day. 'A great way to take the pleasure out of Christmas and to put a downer on the year ahead,' said our neighbour, Paolo.

On 16 June 2012 the first instalment of a new property tax called 'IMU' *(Imposta Municipale Propria)* became due. In our case, this doubled what we had previously paid, and many of our friends faced as much as a six-fold increase.

At the same time, farmers were hit with an agricultural land tax, the first time that this type of tax had been levied in Italy. 'At least they have meat,' said our friend Cinzia, who works at the local hospital in Fratta. 'But for a lot of ordinary families it is no longer affordable. They are eating more pasta. Few have spare cash to eat out.'

Cinzia discovered that due to pension reforms she now had to delay her retirement from her job by five years. Like many other Italians, she said the sacrifices were not shared equally. 'A politician only has to be in parliament for five years and he gets the same pension as I do after labouring 45 years.' She worries constantly whether there will ever be stable jobs for her 24-year-old son and 19-year-old daughter.

The family is by far the most important social unit in Italy and in business. Small, family-run businesses dominate the country's economy. In Tuscany less than two per cent of the region's half-million companies employ more than 19 people. This could be seen as a strength, except that too many carry on the practice of *parentopoli,* hiring of relatives and friends at the expense of building a meritocracy and fostering true competitiveness.

Outwardly, family structures appear largely to be conservative and stable but, on a personal level, our friends and neighbours now express more liberal views about homosexuality, cohabitation, divorce and abortion than when we first set up home in Tuscany. Italian woman are conceiving much later in life and births outside marriage are also becoming more common, indicative perhaps of the slow loss of power of the Catholic Church. There must also be a huge defiance on edicts against contraception, because Italy has one of the lowest birth rates in the world.

Attendance at mass and other church events continues to decline and it is obvious that Catholic culture is fragmenting in the face of social change, despite the number of houses and piazzas that exhibit pictures of the Madonna and busts of Padre Pio – the priest who claimed to exhibit stigmata and who was declared a fraud by Pope John XXIII but made a saint by Pope Paul IV.

Dante, the Tuscan-born poet of the Middle Ages, observed 'the hottest places in hell are reserved for those who, in times of great moral crisis, maintain their neutrality'. And sloth does indeed appear to be the greatest underlying problem. Italians seem to excuse their sloth under the pretext of difficulty and have not had the courage to say *basta,* enough, and to face the fact that their country needs to change profoundly.

Perhaps one of the reasons for this is that they did not have the vehicle to express their views until the February 2013 elections. Then, Beppe Grillo articulated their anger at austerity, the euro and, especially, at Italian politics being rotten to the core. In response, a full quarter of the electorate massed behind him.

THE 2013 ELECTIONS

When Mario Monti first came to power, the Jesuit-educated professor of economics heard warnings from many commentators that he was leading an experiment that may not work. Anyway, he had not been voted in by the electorate but had been invited by the Italian President, Giorgio Napolitano, to lead a new but stop-gap government that would remain in office until the next scheduled general elections in 2013.

Monti's technocrat government was supported by cross-party votes, but his ministers were not politicians or members of parliament, simply experts in their fields. The problem from the start was that Monti tried to be inclusive. He didn't put his foot down enough and was naïve in his dealings with the mainstream political parties, who scuppered proposed reforms on everything from the economy to gay rights.

There were also doubts that Silvio Berlusconi would ever withdraw from the Italian political scene. My neighbour Paulo summed it up rather well at the time: 'Berlusconi's role will be what in Italy we call *il padrino,* basically the man that you don't see in power, but who in reality moves the power, behind the curtains.'

Four months before the February 2013 elections, Berlusconi claimed that he had been besieged by requests to run and guide his People of Freedom Party to victory, and declared he simply could not allow Italy to spiral into recession. The newspapers and television stations he owned reprinted his press release saying, 'The situation today is much worse than it was a year ago, when I left the government out of a sense of responsibility and a love for my country.'

His breath-taking manipulation of the facts about his resignation as Prime Minister made me doubt anyone in their right mind would ever vote for him. And then Berlusconi delivered a master class in popular electioneering that very much explained why he had been Italy's longest-serving leader since Mussolini. He spoke to the electorate in terms that mattered to them and in language they understood. 'Tax pressure is rising to intolerable levels … households are anguished about having to pay a housing levy… I promise to pay you this back if I am elected – and in cash.'

He also used the football-themed language that I remembered from when he entered politics in 1994, saying things like he would 'take the field' to save the country. To grab even more headlines, the evil genius signed the former Manchester City striker Mario Balotelli to his AC Milan side during the weeks before the election. Football always makes bigger headlines than politics, even in the newspapers he does not own, and his face appeared everywhere associated with personally bringing a huge soccer star back to Italy. It confirmed to many Italians that this was a man who really understood them.

At the beginning of January 2013, the over-tanned, then 76-year-old former cruise-ship singer hit the campaign trail, leading his right-wing alliance against Pier Luigi Bersani of the centre-left Democratic Party, and Mario Monti and his group of centrist parties. On the side-lines, as the three of them saw it, was an 'irritating distraction' in the form of Beppe Grillo's Five Star Movement (*Movimento 5 Stelle* or *M5S*) which was running its campaign out of a rented Fiat camper van.

Bushy-haired Giuseppe 'Beppe' Grillo was born 65 years ago in Genoa. He studied commercial economics, trained as an accountant, and became a comedian by chance when he improvised a monologue at an audition. He was quickly taken up by television and from then on his routines became more political. He did not pull his punches and used his considerable skills at reading company accounts, in a way few journalists and politicians can do, to name names and expose corrupt companies. He was excluded from State television in the early 1990s, something that only added to the ranting monologues that had become his specialty. Then he founded a blog that proved enormously popular with the internet-savvy generation. He developed this further with his digital-guru friend Robert Casaleggio, and it became the platform from which he launched the Five Star Movement.

M5S was founded in 2009 on the feast day of St Francis. Initially its members were supporters of Grillo's various fan clubs. They were encouraged to organise face-to-face meetings through the 'meet-up' facility on the party's web site, and to participate in internet-based forums to discuss policy. A new form of politics had been born which used the internet to consult the electorate directly, and it was this direct voice and feeling of personal participation in national politics that was about to make a big difference to Italy.

As electioneering started in earnest, I was shocked to see support rising for Silvio Berlusconi, albeit that pollsters were saying Pier Luigi Bersani's Democratic Party would win. What the predictions didn't take account of was the increasing number of undecided voters and the widespread anger at unemployment, political corruption and austerity – something that it was likely Mario Monti would continue pursuing if he was returned to power.

This time many Italians really did want something new – an end to the status quo, an end to sleaze and lack of opportunity. Surely there was a way to take the best from the left and the right? M5S offered these voters a breath of fresh air, even though most of the electorate was actually unsure what voting for Grillo might bring. But his cry of *basta* was understood at least as viscerally as Berlusconi's football images.

When voting ended at three in the afternoon of Monday 25th February, a quarter of the electorate had not bothered to vote. Of those who did, just under 30 per cent voted for the Democratic Party and a slightly smaller percentage endorsed the clownish former Prime Minister Silvio Berlusconi. And 25 per cent voted for a true comedian, Beppe Grillo, but they were not laughing with the clown, they were hoping for big changes.

THE FRIGHTENING TRUTH

Since the Second World War Italy has had more national elections and more governments than any other big European power, and only one government lasted the full five-year term. Once again history repeated itself. Yet again, elections had not produced a clear winner and the Democrats couldn't celebrate as they expected. No-one I knew admitted voting for Berlusconi, and M5S had not secured a parliamentary majority but, anyway, immediately ruled out playing a supporting role in forming a new government.

The week after the election I found myself involved in the three things guaranteed to prompt serious local debate: a bottle of red wine, Franco Benelli, and a seat next to him at the bar nearest to Casa Amari.

I had read that morning that 8.7 million people had voted in 162 *grillini*, as Grillo's new members of parliament and senators are called, most of them fresh young faces, many of them women. The one thing uniting them seemed to be inexperience. Just as intriguing was a summation in my newspaper of the party's 15-page programme of policies which called for more energy saving and renewable energy sources, more bicycle lanes, free internet access for all, the salaries of elected representatives being limited to the average national wage, a cap on the salaries of senior company executives, and the scrapping of all stock options. There would also be no funding for political parties, a two-term limit for elected officials, a wider use of cost-saving generic drugs and public spending cuts.

I asked Franco for his predictions about Grillo and his newly elected politicians. 'There will be a period of turmoil, some resignations, maybe a few reforms and then another election, but perhaps we Italians need a fantasist like him to get us to change. Grillo takes his cue from those medieval comics who bedevilled the privileged political elite. I particularly like the way Five Star supporters argue about policy on the net since it seems to mirror the way good communes have always valued working together . . . if the results of this election don't shake us out of our apathy, nothing will.'

252

Franco's comments consolidated my belief that Italy's social strength is not just based on the family but also on communal loyalties. The provincialism of its citizens is a testament to their pride and sense of responsibility. Localism, *campanilismo,* loyalty to the municipal bell tower, remains a vital ingredient in Italian life. Net-based communities ignore these boundaries but if people feel they are genuinely being heard by their *grillini,* as they would be traditionally by local officials, Italy might well be on the change to a 'normal' country, even though in a far from normal way.

Italy is a beautiful, complex and fascinating country and we think of it as *casa nostra,* our home. Its citizens are contradictory people living in a contradictory country, but the one thing that binds them is the peninsula's rich history of culture, of its world-influencing art, architecture, traditions and customs. Italy also has enormous potential but, in the near future, its fortunes are inextricably linked to the euro crisis which is far from over.

This last election proved that Italy is in political disarray and that Italians, like most European voters, are tired of austerity. For Italy, the threat of the European dream collapsing is as frightening as anything that its politicians do. There is still a long way to go before Italy becomes the modern and normal country my friends believe will come.

On the other hand, it's a stupid Italian or Italian politician who does not realise the intransigent importance of *campanilismo* and how Grillo has demonstrated its 21st century transfiguration into *webilismo.* Once every voter can be assured of speaking directly to and monitoring his national politicians in the way their forebears once dealt with local officials, the clown might not be hiding tears but be seeing Italy's true future.